A Text Book Of

PROGRAMMING IN VISUAL BASIC

For

BCA Semester - IV

As per New Revised Syllabus of Savitribai Phule Pune University

GAJANAN DESHMUKH
M.C.A.
Smt. Kashibai Navale, H.O.D. - BCA
College of Commerce
Pune

UMAKANT S. SHIRSHETTI
SENIOR LECTURER IN IT DEPT.,
SOU. VENUTAI CHAVAN POLYTECHNIC,
VADGAON (BK.),
PUNE

PROGRAMMING IN VISUAL BASIC ISBN 978-93-5164-271-8
First Edition : November 2014
© : Authors

The text of this publication, or any part thereof, should not be reproduced or transmitted in any form or stored in any computer storage system or device for distribution including photocopy, recording, taping or information retrieval system or reproduced on any disc, tape, perforated media or other information storage device etc., without the written permission of Authors with whom the rights are reserved. Breach of this condition is liable for legal action.

Every effort has been made to avoid errors or omissions in this publication. In spite of this, errors may have crept in. Any mistake, error or discrepancy so noted and shall be brought to our notice shall be taken care of in the next edition. It is notified that neither the publisher nor the authors or seller shall be responsible for any damage or loss of action to any one, of any kind, in any manner, therefrom.

Published By :
NIRALI PRAKASHAN
Abhyudaya Pragati, 1312, Shivaji Nagar,
Off J.M. Road, PUNE – 411005
Tel - (020) 25512336/37/39, Fax - (020) 25511379
Email : niralipune@pragationline.com

Printed By :
Repro Knowledgecast Limited,
Thane

DISTRIBUTION CENTRES
PUNE

Nirali Prakashan
119, Budhwar Peth, Jogeshwari Mandir Lane
Pune 411002, Maharashtra
Tel : (020) 2445 2044, 66022708, Fax : (020) 2445 1538
Email : bookorder@pragationline.com

Nirali Prakashan
S. No. 28/27, Dhyari,
Near Pari Company, Pune 411041
Tel : (022) 24690371
Email : dhyari@pragationline.com
bookorder@pragationline.com

MUMBAI
Nirali Prakashan
385, S.V.P. Road, Rasdhara Co-op. Hsg. Society Ltd.,
Girgaum, Mumbai 400004, Maharashtra
Tel : (022) 2385 6339 / 2386 9976, Fax : (022) 2386 9976
Email : niralimumbai@pragationline.com

DISTRIBUTION BRANCHES

NAGPUR
Pratibha Book Distributors
Above Maratha Mandir, Shop No. 3, First Floor,
Rani Jhanshi Square, Sitabuldi, Nagpur 440012,
Maharashtra, Tel : (0712) 254 7129

BENGALURU
Pragati Book House
House No. 1, Sanjeevappa Lane, Avenue Road Cross,
Opp. Rice Church, Bengaluru – 560002.
Tel : (080) 64513344, 64513355,
Mob : 9880582331, 9845021552
Email:bharatsavla@yahoo.com

JALGAON
Nirali Prakashan
34, V. V. Golani Market, Navi Peth, Jalgaon 425001,
Maharashtra, Tel : (0257) 222 0395
Mob : 94234 91860

KOLHAPUR
Nirali Prakashan
New Mahadvar Road,
Kedar Plaza, 1st Floor Opp. IDBI Bank
Kolhapur 416 012, Maharashtra. Mob : 9855046155

CHENNAI
Pragati Books
9/1, Montieth Road, Behind Taas Mahal, Egmore,
Chennai 600008 Tamil Nadu, Tel : (044) 6518 3535,
Mob : 94440 01782 / 98450 21552 / 98805 82331, Email : bharatsavla@yahoo.com

RETAIL OUTLETS
PUNE

Pragati Book Centre
157, Budhwar Peth, Opp. Ratan Talkies,
Pune 411002, Maharashtra
Tel : (020) 2445 8887 / 6602 2707, Fax : (020) 2445 8887

Pragati Book Centre
Amber Chamber, 28/A, Budhwar Peth,
Appa Balwant Chowk, Pune : 411002, Maharashtra,
Tel : (020) 20240335 / 66281669
Email : pbcpune@pragationline.com

Pragati Book Centre
676/B, Budhwar Peth, Opp. Jogeshwari Mandir,
Pune 411002, Maharashtra
Tel : (020) 6601 7784 / 6602 0855

PBC Book Sellers & Stationers
152, Budhwar Peth, Pune 411002, Maharashtra
Tel : (020) 2445 2254 / 6609 2463

MUMBAI
Pragati Book Corner
Indira Niwas, 111 - A, Bhavani Shankar Road, Dadar (W), Mumbai 400028, Maharashtra
Tel : (022) 2422 3526 / 6662 5254, Email : pbcmumbai@pragationline.com

Preface ...

This textbook **'Programming in Visual Basic'** designed for the students of **B.C.A. Semester IV** of Savitribai Phule Pune University. Visual basic is one of the most rapidly growing areas of Computer and Information Technology. Basically, Relational Database Management systems is nothing more than a computer based record keeping system that is a system whose overall purpose is to record and maintain information.

The objective of Programming in Visual Basic is to provide a convenient and effective method of defining, sorting and retrieving the information stored in the database.

A special word of thanks to Shri. Dineshbhai Furia, Mr. Jignesh Furia and Gautam Bapat for showing full faith in us to write this book. We also thank to Mahesh Swami, Mrs. Prachi Sawant and Vijay Shete of M/s Nirali Prakashan for their excellent co-operation.

Valuable suggestions communicated by the students and teachers are welcome.

AUTHORS

Syllabus ...

Unit 1 Getting Started with V. B.
    1.1   Object Oriented Concept
    1.2   Event Driven Programming Language
    1.3   Working with properties
        1.3.1   Studying the Events of a Form
        1.3.2   Working code for events
        1.3.3   Planning the Design

Unit 2 Constants, Variables, Operators, Control Structure, Looping & Array
    2.1   Constant
    2.2   Data Types
        2.2.1   Number , long ,Boolean ,doubles ,variant, String
        2.2.2   User defined data types
    2.3   Variables
    2.4   Operators
    2.5   Control Structures
        2.5.1   If
        2.5.2   If....Else
        2.5.3   Nested If....Else
        2.5.4   Select Case
    2.6   Looping
        2.6.1   Do Loop
        2.6.2   While Loop
        2.6.3   Until Loop
        2.6.4   For Loop
        2.6.5   With Statement
    2.7   Array
        2.7.1   Single Dimensional Array
        2.7.2   Multidimensional Array
        2.7.3   Control Array
    2.8   Functions(Built in and user defined)

Unit 3 Working with Controls
    3.1   Adding controls on form
    3.2   Working with Properties and Methods of each Controls
    3.3   Creating an application
    3.4   Creating MDI application
        3.4.1   Working with Multiple Forms
        3.4.2   Loading, Showing & Hiding Forms
        3.4.3   Setting the Startup form

- 3.4.4 Creating forms in Code
- 3.4.5 Using the MDI
- 3.4.6 Arranging MDI Child Window
- 3.4.7 Opening new MDI child window
- 3.4.8 Creating Properties in a form
- 3.4.9 Creating a method in a form

Unit 4 Working with ActiveX Controls & Menus
- 4.1 Creating Status Bar For your program
- 4.2 Working with Progress Bar
- 4.3 Working with Toolbar
- 4.4 Setting up the Image List Controls
    - 4.4.1 Adding and Deleting Images with code
    - 4.4.2 Study of Different Dialog Boxes
- 4.5 Menus
    - 4.5.1 Creating new Menu Item
    - 4.5.2 Modifying & Deleting Menu Item
    - 4.5.3 Adding Access Characters
    - 4.5.4 Adding Shortcut Keys
    - 4.5.5 Creating Sub Menus
- 4.6 Pop-up Menus
    - 4.6.1 Creating pop-up menu
    - 4.6.2 Displaying pop-up menu
- 4.7 Adding and Deleting Menus at Run-time
- 4.8 Adding Menu Items for MDI Child Form

Unit 5 Working With Database
- 5.1 Data Control
    - 5.1.1 Studying the Properties and methods of Data Control
    - 5.1.2 Connectivity with MS-Access
    - 5.1.3 Operations of database through coding
- 5.2 ADO Data Control
    - 5.2.1 Advantages of ADODC over DC
    - 5.2.2 Studying the properties and Methods of ADODC
    - 5.2.3 Connectivity with MS-Access
    - 5.2.4 Connectivity with Oracle
    - 5.2.5 Report Generation
- 5.3 Developing ADO application through ADODC and coding
- 5.4 Report Generation

Contents ...

UNIT 1

Getting Started with V. B.   1.1 –1.40

UNIT 2

Constants, Variables, Operators, Control Structure, Looping and Array

     2.1 – 2.74

UNIT 3

Working with Controls   3.1 –3.46

UNIT 4

Working with ActiveX Controls & Menus   4.1 –4.82

UNIT 5

Working With Database   5.1 –5.52

Chapter 1...

Getting Started With Visual Basic

Contents ...

This chapter includes basic concepts of Visual Basic such as :

1.1 INTRODUCTION

    1.1.1 Features of Visual Basic

    1.1.2 Terminology of Visual Basic

    1.1.3 Advantages

    1.1.4 Disadvantages

1.2 INSTALLING OF VISUAL BASIC

1.3 OBJECT-ORIENTED CONCEPTS

    1.3.1 Objects and Classes

    1.3.2 Encapsulation

    1.3.3 Polymorphism

    1.3.4 Inheritance

1.4 EVENT DRIVEN PROGRAMMING LANGUAGE

    1.4.1 Procedural Programming Vs. Event-Driven Programming

    1.4.2 Understanding the Event-driven Model

1.5 REVIEWING THE BASIC FORMS AND CONTROLS

    1.5.1 Integrated Development Environment (IDE))

    1.5.2 Properties in Visual Basic

    1.5.3 Controls in Visual Basic

1.6 STUDYING EVENTS OF A FORM

1.7 WORKING CODE FOR EVENTS

1.8 PLANNING THE DESIGN

    1.8.1 Steps for Designing an Application

  * Practice Questions

  * University Question & Answers

1.1 INTRODUCTION

- Visual Basic (VB) is an ideal programming language for developing sophisticated professional applications for Microsoft Windows. It makes use of Graphical User Interface (GUI) for creating robust and powerful applications.
- The Graphical User Interface as the name suggests, uses illustrations for text, which enable users to interact with an application. This feature makes it easier to comprehend things in a quicker and easier way.
- Coding in GUI environment is quite a transition to traditional, linear programming methods where the user is guided through a linear path of execution and is limited to small set of operations.
- In GUI environment, the number of options open to the user is much greater, allowing more freedom to the user and developer.
- Features such as easier comprehension, user-friendliness, faster application development and many other aspects such as introduction to ActiveX technology and Internet features make Visual Basic an interesting tool to work with.
- Visual Basic (VB) was developed from the BASIC programming language. In the 1970s, Microsoft started developing ROM-based interpreted BASIC for the early microprocessor-based computers.
- In 1982, Microsoft QuickBasic revolutionized Basic and was legitimized as a serious development language for MS-DOS environment. Later on, Microsoft Corporation created the enhanced version of BASIC called Visual Basic for Windows.
- Visual Basic (VB) is an event-driven programming language. This is called because programming is done in a graphical environment unlike the previous version BASIC where programming is done in a text only environment and executed sequentially in order to control the user interface. Visual Basic enables the user to design the user interface quickly by drawing and arranging the user elements. Due to this spent time is saved for the repetitive task.
- Visual Basic 6.0 provides a graphical environment in which you visually design the forms and controls that become the building blocks of your applications.
- Visual Basic 6.0 supports many useful tools that will help you be more productive.
- Visual Basic (VB) is the third-generation event-driven programming language and Integrated Development Environment (IDE) from Microsoft for its COM programming model.
- VB is also considered a relatively easy to learn and use programming language, because of its graphical development features and BASIC heritage. Visual Basic was derived from BASIC and enables the rapid application development (RAD) of Graphical User Interface (GUI) applications, access to databases using Data Access Objects (DAO), Remote Data Objects (RDO), or ActiveX Data Objects, and creation of ActiveX controls and objects.

- Scripting languages such as VBA and VBScript are syntactically similar to Visual Basic, but perform differently. A programmer can put together an application using the components provided with Visual Basic itself.
- Programs written in Visual Basic can also use the Windows API, but doing so requires external function declarations. Microsoft Visual Basic is the fastest and easiest way to create applications for Microsoft Windows®.
- Visual Basic provides the users with a complete set of tools to simplify rapid application development.
- Why Visual Basic? The "**Visual**" part refers to the method used to create the **Graphical User Interface** (**GUI**). Rather than writing numerous lines of code to describe the appearance and location of interface elements, the user simply adds prebuilt objects into place on screen. If the user has ever used a drawing program such as Paint or any other graphical package such as Corel Draw, AutoCAD etc., the user already has most of the skills necessary to create an effective user interface.
- The "**Basic**" part refers to the **BASIC** (**Beginners All-Purpose Symbolic Instruction Code**) language, a language used by more programmers than any other language in the history of computing. Visual Basic has evolved from the original BASIC language and now contains several hundred statements, functions and keywords, many of which related directly to the Windows GUI.

1.1.1 Features of Visual Basic

- The Visual Basic programming language is not unique to Visual Basic.
- The Visual Basic programming system, Applications Edition included in Microsoft Excel, Microsoft Access and many other Windows applications uses the same language.
- The Visual Basic Scripting Edition (VBScript) is a widely used scripting language and a subset of the Visual Basic language.
    1. **Data access:** These features allow you to create databases, front-end applications and scalable server-side components for most popular database formats including Microsoft SQL Server and other enterprise-level databases.
    2. **ActiveX technologies:** They allow you to use the functionality provided by other applications, such as Microsoft Word, Word processor, Microsoft Excel spreadsheet and other Windows **applications**. You can even automate applications and objects created using the Professional or Enterprise editions of Visual Basic.
    3. **Internet capabilities:** Make it easy to provide access to documents and applications across the Internet or **Intranet** from within your application or to create Internet server applications.
    4. **Simplicity:** Like the BASIC programming language, Visual Basic was designed to be easy to learn and use. The language not only allows programmers to create simple GUI applications, but can also develop complex applications. Programming in VB is a combination of visually arranging components or controls on a form, specifying attributes and actions of those components and writing additional lines of code for

more functionality. Since, default attributes and actions are defined for the components, a simple program can be created without the programmer having to write many lines of code. Performance problems were experienced by earlier versions, but with faster computers and native code compilation this has become less of an issue.

5. **Drag-and-drop techniques:** Forms are created using drag-and-drop techniques. A tool is used to place controls such as for example, text boxes, buttons, etc. on the form (window). Controls have attributes and event handlers associated with them. Default values are provided when the control is created, but may be changed by the programmer. Many attribute values can **be** modified during run time based on user actions or changes in the environment, providing a dynamic application. For example, code can be inserted into the form resize event handler to reposition a control so that it remains centered on the form, expands to fill up the form, etc. By inserting code into the event handler for a key press in a text box, the program can automatically translate the case of the text being entered, or even prevent certain characters from being inserted.

- Visual Basic can create executables (EXE files), ActiveX controls, or DLL files, but is primarily used to develop Windows applications and to interface database systems. Dialog boxes with less functionality can be used to provide pop-up capabilities. Controls provide the basic functionality of the application, while programmers can insert additional logic within the appropriate event handlers. For example, a drop-down combination box will automatically display its list and allow the user to select any element. An event handler is called when an item is selected, which can then execute additional code created by the programmer to perform some action based on which element was selected, such as populating a related list.
- Alternatively, a Visual Basic component can have no user interface, and instead provide ActiveX objects to other programs via Component Object Model (COM). This allows for server-side processing or an add-in module.
- The language is garbage collected using reference counting, has a large library of utility objects, and has basic object oriented support.
- Unlike many other programming languages, Visual Basic is generally not case sensitive, although it will transform keywords into a standard case configuration and force the case of variable names to conform to the case of the entry within the symbol table. String comparisons are case sensitive by default, but can be made case insensitive if so desired.
- The Visual Basic compiler is shared with other Visual Studio languages (C, C++), but restrictions in the IDE do not allow the creation of some targets (Windows model DLL's) and threading models.

1.1.2 Terminology of Visual Basic

- As with any programming language, using Visual Basic requires an understanding of some common terminology.
- The following table lists some key terms used in Visual Basic.

Sr. No.	Term	Definition
1.	Design Time	Any time an application is being developed in the Visual Basic environment.
2.	Run time	Any time application is running. At run time, the programmer interacts with the application as the user would.
3.	Forms	Windows that can be customized to serve as the interface for an application or as dialog boxes used to gather information from the user.
4.	Controls	Graphic representations of objects, such as buttons, list boxes, and edit boxes, that users manipulate to provide information to the application.
5.	Objects	A general term used to describe all the forms and controls that make up a program.
6.	Properties	The characteristics of an object such as size, caption, or color.
7.	Methods	The actions that an object can perform or that can be performed on the object.
8.	Events	Actions recognized by a form or control. Events occur as the user, operating system, or application interacts with the objects of a program.
9.	Events-driven programming	When a program is event-driven, its code executes in repose to events invoked by the user, operating system, or application. This differs from procedural programming, where the program starts at the first line of code and follows a defined path, calling procedures as needed.

1.1.3 Advantages

(April 14)

- The advantages of Visual Basic are :
  1. VB is very simple language. Things that may be difficult to program with other language, can be done in Visual Basic very easily.
  2. Advanced features such as easier comprehension, user-friendliness, faster application development and many other aspects such as introduction to ActiveX technology and Internet features make **Visual Basic** an interesting tool to work with.
  3. Robust and powerful application makes use of Graphical User Interface for creating robust and powerful applications.

1.1.4 Disadvantages

- The disadvantages of Visual Basic are :
  1. Visual Basic is powerful language, but it is not suit for programming really sophisticated games.
  2. VB is much more slower than other languages.

1.2 INSTALLING OF VISUAL BASIC

- In order to understand the application development process, it is helpful to understand some of the key concepts upon which Visual Basic is built in. Because Visual Basic is a Windows development language, some familiarity with the Windows environment is necessary. If you are new to Windows programming, you need to be aware of some fundamental differences between programming for Windows versus other environments.
- There are different edition of VB available in market. They are as given below.

Learning Edition	The Learning edition allows programmers to easily create powerful applications for the Windows and Windows NT operating systems.
Professional Edition	The Professional Edition adds to the capabilities of the Learning Edition allowing you to create client/server or inter-enabled applications.
Enterprise Edition	Developers in a corporate environment benefit by using the advanced features in the Enterprise Edition to create robust distributed applications in a team setting.

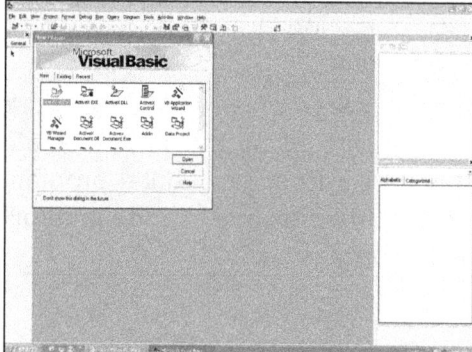

Fig. 1.1 : Visual Basic

- The easiest way to run Visual Basic under Windows XP or Windows NT is to use the program option on the start button.
- Select Microsoft Visual Basic 6.0, then click on Visual Basic 6.0. Clicking the Visual Basic 6.0 icon, we can view a copyright screen enlisting the details of the license holder of the copy of Visual Basic 6.0.
- Then it opens into a screen as shown below with the interface elements such as Menu bar, Tool bar, the New Project dialog box. These elements permit the user to build different types of Visual Basic applications.
- IDE is a term commonly used in the programming world to describe the interface and environment that we use to create our applications. It is called integrated be can access virtually all of the development tools that we need from one screen called an interface.
- The IDE is also commonly referred to as the design environment, or the program.

- For installation of Visual Basic we require Microsoft Visual Studio 6.0. Procedure to install Visual basic 6.0 is given below :

    1. **Take CD of Microsoft Visual Studio 6.0. Insert it in CD drive. Run Setup.exe.**

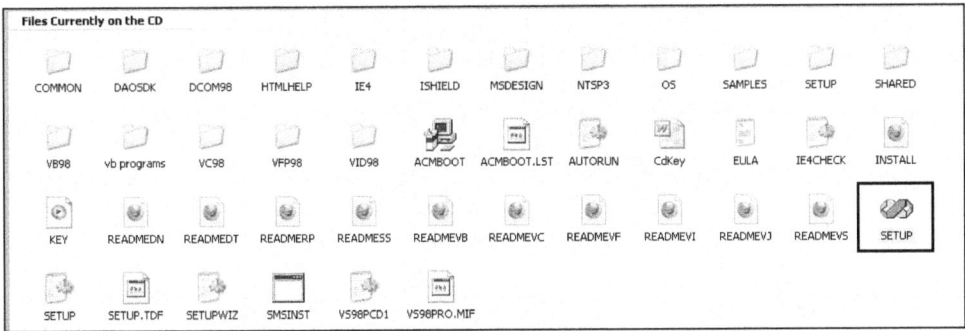

Fig. 1.2 : Microsoft visual studio 6.0 CD drive

    2. We see the following screen.

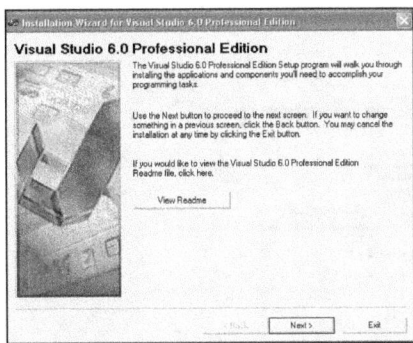

Fig. 1.3 : Installation Wizard

Click on **Next** button. Then the set up asked End User License Agreement. Click on **I Accept agreement** option button. Then he asked for product ID No. and company name. Enter the product Id no. and Company Name and click on **Continue** button. It give message as **"Setup is searching for installed Components"**

    3. For standalone PC, select **Install Visual Studio 6.0 Professional Edition :**

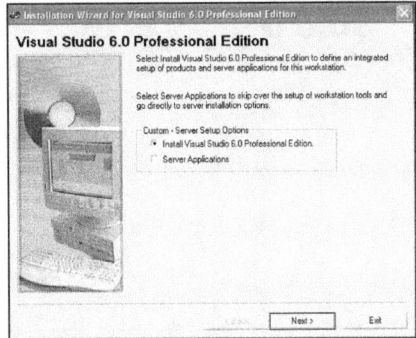

Fig. 1.4 : Professional Edition

4. Click on **Next** button. It will start installing Visual Studio 6.0 professional set.

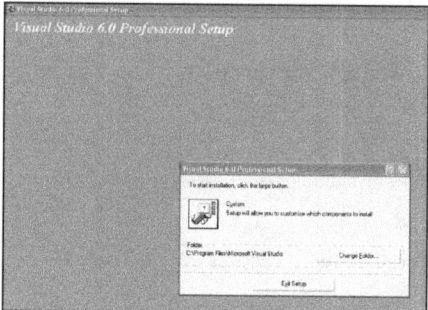

Fig. 1.5 : Professional setup

5. Click on [button] this button. It will continue installation on folder **C:\Program Files\Microsoft Visual Studio.** You get following screen.

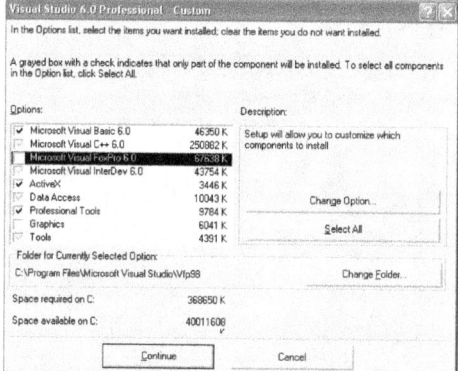

Fig. 1.6 : VB 6.0 professional custom

DeSelect whatever don't want and press continue. It will show message as "**Setup is checking for disk space**".

6. You see installation process. If you want to terminate the Setup click on **Cancel** button.

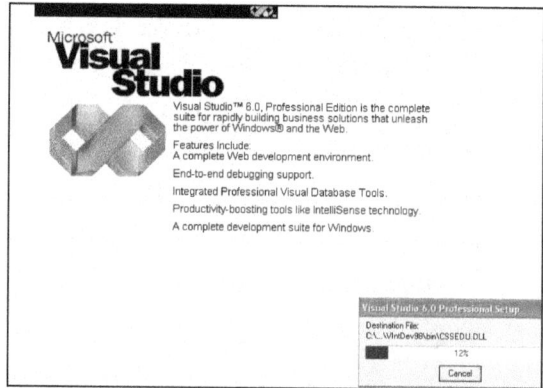

Fig. 1.7 : Installation process

After completing the setup, it give massage to Finish and asked for installation of MSDN help. If you want to install it press continue otherwise click on Finish button.

1.3 OBJECT-ORIENTED CONCEPTS (April 11)

- The basic idea behind object-oriented programming is to combine into a single unit both data and function that operate on that data. Such a unit is called an object.
- It ties data more closely to the functions that operate on it. If you want to read a data item in an object, you call a member function in the object. It will read the item and return the value to you.
- You can not access data directly. The data is protected from accidental modification. Data and its functions are said to be encapsulated into a single entity. If you want to modify that data in an object, you should know exactly what functions interact with it, the member functions in the object.
- No other functions can access the data. OOP (Object-oriented Programming) allows us to decompose entities called objects, which communicate with each other by calling one another's member functions.

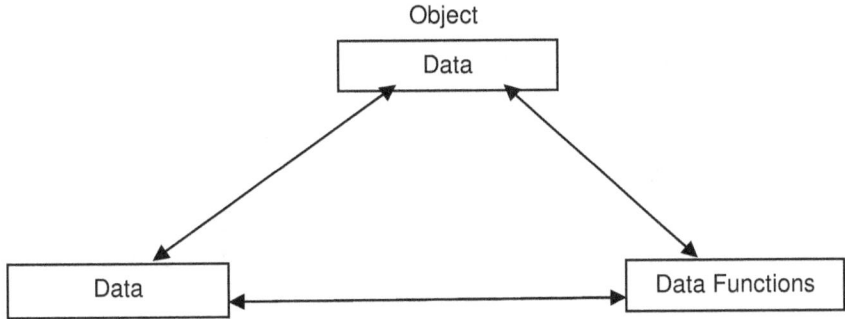

Fig. 1.8 : Object oriented concepts

- Visual Basic definitively is *not* a true OOP language and it won't be one until it possesses some essential OOP features, such as inheritance. But this deficit should not excuse your not learning in depth what classes and objects have to offer developers.
    1. Class modules can immensely improve your productivity, help you solve many common and intricate programming problems, and even permit you to perform tasks that would be extremely difficult, if not impossible, otherwise.
    2. Even if Visual Basic is not a full-fledged object-oriented programming language, you can still use its classes to better organize your code into truly reusable modules and design your applications entirely using concepts derived from the Object-Oriented Design discipline. In this sense, the inclusion of a tool such as Visual Modeler in the Enterprise Edition is a clear sign of Microsoft's will to pursue this goal.
- Most important, objects are the base on which almost every feature of Visual Basic is implemented. For example, without objects you can not do serious database programming, you can not deliver Internet applications, and you can not write components for COM, DCOM, or MTS.

1.3.1 Objects and Classes

- A *class* is a portion of the program (a source code file, in Visual Basic) that defines the properties, methods, and events in a word, behavior of one or more objects that will be created during execution.
- An *object* is an entity created at run time, which requires memory and possibly other system resources, and is then destroyed when it's no longer needed or when the application ends.

1.3.2 Encapsulation

- Encapsulation is probably the feature that programmers appreciate most in object-oriented programming.
- In a nutshell, an object is the sole owner of its own data. All data is stored inside a memory area that can not be directly accessed by another portion of the application, and all assignment and retrieval operations are performed through methods and properties provided by the object itself.
- This simple concept has at least two far-reaching consequences :
  1. You can check all the values assigned to object properties before they are actually stored in memory and immediately reject all invalid ones.
  2. You are free to change the internal implementation of the data stored in an object without changing the way the rest of the program interacts with the object. This means that you can later modify and improve the internal workings of a class without changing a single line of code elsewhere in the application.
- As with most OOP features, it's your responsibility to ensure that the class is well encapsulated.

1.3.3 Polymorphism

- Polymorphism is the ability of different classes to expose similar (or identical) interfaces to the outside. The most evident kind of polymorphism in Visual Basic is forms and controls.
- TextBox and PictureBox controls are completely different objects, but they have some properties and methods in common, such as Left, BackColor, and Move.
- This similarity simplifies your job as a programmer because you do not have to remember hundreds of different names and syntax formats.
- More important, it lets you manage a group of controls using a single variable (typed as Control, Variant or Object) and create generic procedures that act on all the controls on a form and therefore noticeably reduce the amount of code you have to write.

1.3.4 Inheritance

- Inheritance is the ability, offered by many OOP languages, to derive a new class, (the derived or inherited class) from another class, (the base class).
- The derived class automatically inherits the properties and methods of the base class.

- For example, you could define a generic Shape class with properties such as Color and Position and then use it as a base for more specific classes (For example, Rectangle, Circle, and so on) that inherit all those generic properties.
- You could then add specific members, such as Width and Height for the Rectangle class and Radius for the Circle class.
- It's interesting to note that, while polymorphism tends to reduce the amount of code necessary to use the class, inheritance reduces the code inside the class itself and therefore simplifies the job of the class creator.
- Unfortunately, Visual Basic does not support inheritance, at least not in its more mature form of implementation inheritance.

1.4 EVENT DRIVEN PROGRAMMING LANGUAGE (April 10,13; Oct. 10)

- Application written in Visual Basic are event-driven programming can best be understood by contrasting it to procedural programming.
- In an event-driven application, the code does not follow a predetermined path, it executes different code sections in response to events. Events can be triggered by the user's actions, by messages from the system or other applications, or even from the application itself.
- The sequence of these events determines the sequence in which the code executes. Thus, the path through the application's code differs each time the program runs.
- Because you can not predict the sequence of events, your code must make certain assumptions about the "State of the world" when it executes.
- When you make assumptions, you should structure your application in such a way as to make sure that the assumption will always be valid.
- Let us consider a textbox control and a few of its associated events to understand the concept of events driven programming.
- The textbox control supports various events such as Change, Click, MouseMove and many more that will be listed in the properties drop-down list in the code window for the textbox control.

1.4.1 Procedural Programming Vs. Event-Driven Programming

- Application written is procedural languages executes by proceeding logically through the program code, one line at a time.
- Logic flow can be temporarily transferred to other parts of the program through the GoTo, GoSub and Call statements, directing the program from beginning to end.
- In contrast, program statements in an event-driven application execute only when a specific event calls a section of code assigned to that event.
- Events can be triggered by keyboard input, mouse actions, the operating system or code in the application.
- For example: Consider what happens when the user clicks a command button named Command1 on a form. The mouse click is an event. When the Click event occurs, Visual

Basic executes the code in the Sub procedure named Command1_Click. When the code has finished running, Visual Basic waits for the next event.
- The event-driven nature of the application handles the logic required to direct program execution to the appropriate task in response to user actions.
- The programming logic required to implement the same type of application in a procedural language would be much more complicated and would involve many more lines of code.

1.4.2 Understanding the Event-driven Model (April 13)

- In traditional or "procedural" applications, the application itself controls which portions of code execute and in what sequence.
- Execution starts with the first line of code and follows a predefined path through the application, calling procedures as needed.
- In an event-driven application, the code does not follow a predetermined pat-it executes different code sections in response to events.
- Events can be triggered by the user's action, by messages from the system or other applications, or even from the application itself.
- The sequence of these events determines the sequence in which the code executes, thus the path through the application's code differs each time the program runs.
- The code can also be triggered by events during execution. For example, programmatically changing the text in a text box cause the text box's Change event to occur. This would cause the code, (if any) contained in the Change event to execute.
- If assumed that this event would only be triggered by user interaction, it might be seen unexpected results. It is for this reason that it is important to understand the event-driven model and keep it in mind when designing the application.

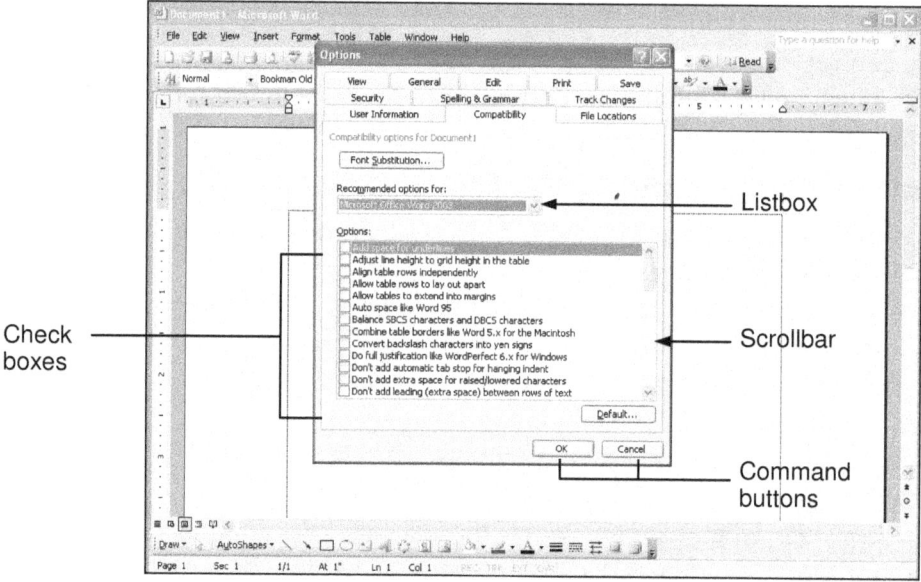

Fig. 1.9 : Windows Programs Respond to Event

- Fig. 1.9 shows a window from a Windows program. The window contains various kinds of Windows controls such as checkboxes Command buttons, and a scrollbar etc.
- These all windows controls are just a sample of the many Windows controls available for you within the Visual Basic programming environment to all to the programs that you write.
- Visual Basic requires these kinds of controls because, unlike programs written in older text-based languages, Windows programs must respond to event.
- An event is an activity that occurs during a program's execution, (mouse click or a keystroke).
- An event might come to a program for many of these controls. Events come in random order. Event-driven programming applies to programming that responds to Windows events.
- The user might perform several of these events in a different order each time the user runs the program. You must use event-driven programming techniques to respond properly to the user's actions and other activities that trigger event.
- Fig. 1.10 illustrates windows handles a few event but passes most to the programs currently running. Windows a multitasking operating system so more than one program can run simultaneously.
- Your program must handle any and all event appropriate at the time the events occur and ignore all the others.

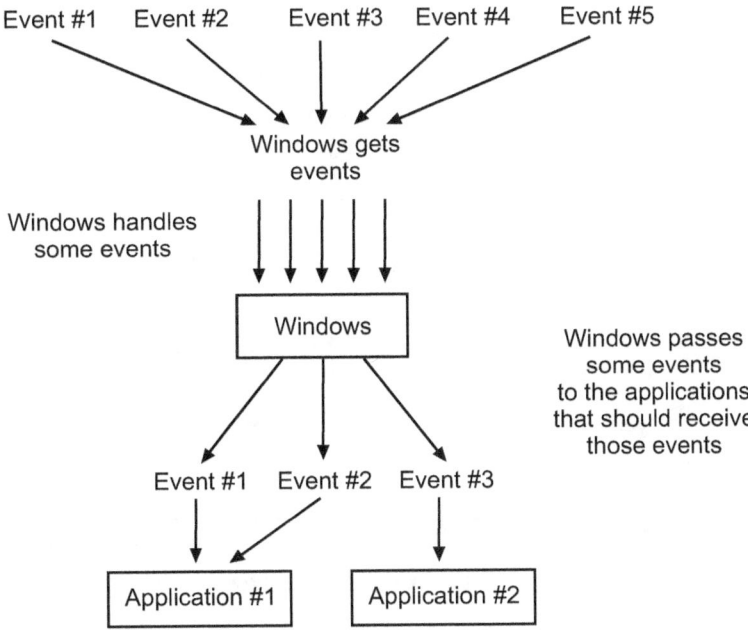

Fig. 1.10 : Your Programs must Responds to Some Event and Ignore Others

1.5 REVIEWING THE BASIC FORMS AND CONTROLS

1.5.1 Integrated Development Environment (IDE)) (Oct. 11, 13; April 12)

Fig. 1.11 shows following types of applications of Visual Basic.

1. **Standard EXE:** Most of the applications are made in this standard EXE. Standard EXE is a typical application.

2. **ActiveX EXE:** Active EXE projects are available with professional edition.

3. **ActiveX DLL:** This consists of ActiveX components which are basic code-building components that do not have a visible interface and that add special type of functionality of application.

4. **ActiveX Control:** ActiveX control consist of basic control elements such as Text Box, Command button etc. of use interface. ActiveX control projects are feature of the VB professional edition.

5. **ActiveX Document EXE and ActiveX Document DLL:** ActiveX Document EXE is necessary because, when user can run VB application in the environment of container that supports hyplerlinking.

6. **VB Application Wizard:** This application shows how to create a new document in VB. This application also gives steps for creating a new application.

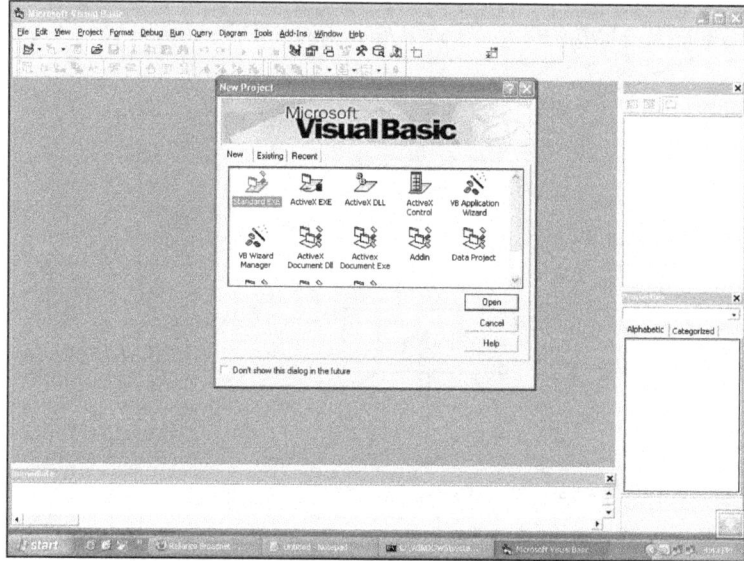

Fig. 1.11 : Application Wizard

7. **VB Wizard Manager:** Using Wizard Manager user can build or create his own wizard. Wizard is nothing but sequences of windows that collects information from the user.

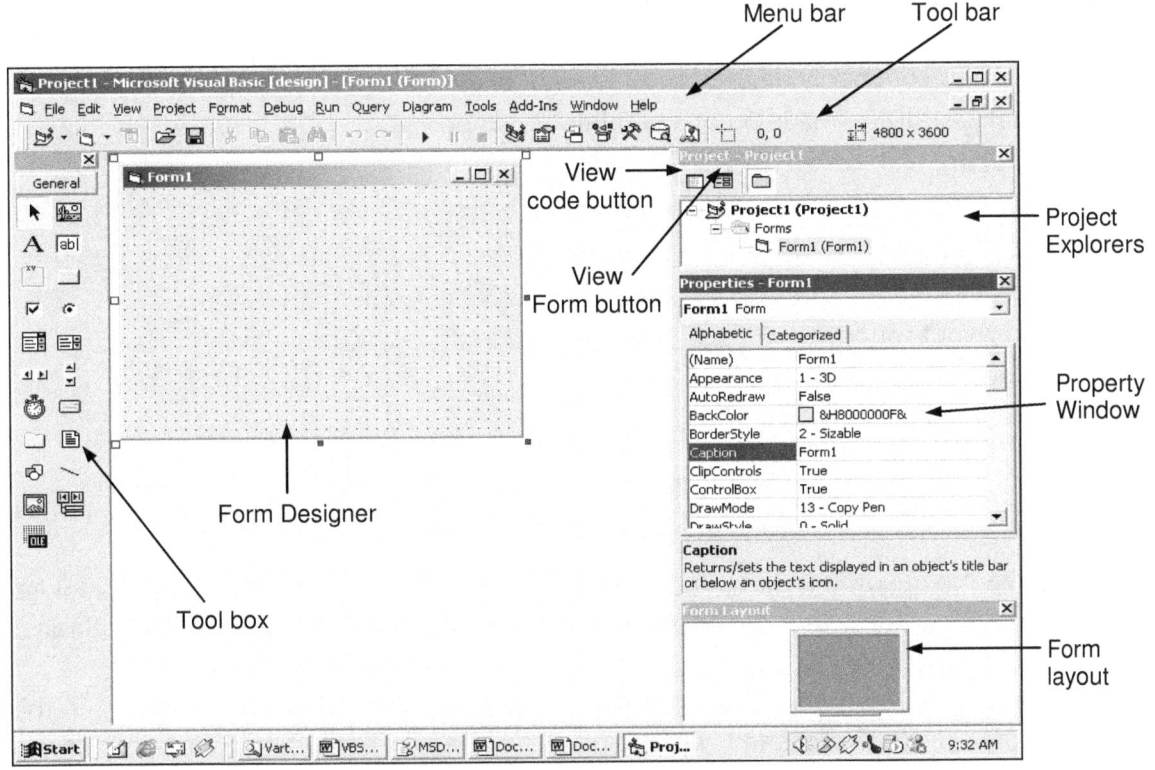

Fig. 1.12 : Integrated Development Environment

8. **DHTML Application :** This is a new application of VB that allows user can build or create dynamic HTML pages, that can be displayed in the browser's window on client system.

9. **IIS Application :** This is also new concept of VB that allows user to create applications that run on the web server and interact with client over the Internet with IIS, (Internet Information Server).

10. **Data Project :** Data project is a feature of Enterprise edition. Data project is identical to standard EXE projects, but it automatically adds the control which is used in accessing databases to the Toolbox.

11. **VB Enterprise Edition:** This is used for creating new standard EXE projects. Loads all the tools to Enterprise Edition of visual basic.

- The Visual Basic Integrated Development Environment (IDE) consists of the following elements. One of the most significant changes in Visual Basic 6.0 is the Integrated Development Environment (IDE).
- IDE is a term commonly used in the programming world to describe the interface and environment that we use to create our applications. It is called *integrated* because we can

access virtually all of the development tools that we need from one screen called an *interface*.

- The IDE is also commonly referred to as the *design environment*, or the *program*.
- The Visual Basic IDE is made up of a number of components :
    1. Menu bar,
    2. Tool bar,
    3. Project explorer,
    4. Properties window,
    5. Form layout window,
    6. Toolbox,
    7. Form designer, and
    8. Object browser.
- In previous versions of Visual Basic, the IDE was designed as a Single Document Interface (SDI).
- In a Single Document Interface, each window is a free-floating window that is contained within a main window and can move anywhere on the screen as long as Visual Basic is the current application.
- But, in Visual Basic 6.0, the IDE is in a Multiple Document Interface (MDI) format. In this format, the windows associated with the project will stay within a single container known as the parent.
- Code and form-based windows will stay within the main container form.

1. Menu Bar :

- It displays the commands to work with Visual Basic. Besides the standard File, Edit, View, Window, and Help menus, menus are provided to access functions specific to programming such as Project, Format or Debug. Fig. 1.13 shows menus in a menubar.
- Menu Bar displays the commands that are required to build an visual basic application. The main menu items have sub menu items that can be chosen when needed. The toolbars in the menu bar provide quick access to the commonly used commands and a button in the toolbar is clicked once to carry out the action represented by it.

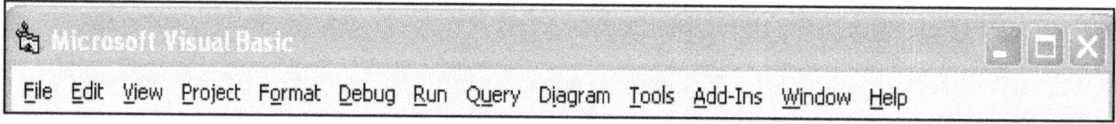

Fig. 1.13 : Menu bar

- The basic menus of Visual basic are given below.
    1. **File:** It contains command for:
        (i) Opening a project
        (ii) Saving project
        (iii) Creating executable files etc.

2. **Edit:** This consist of Editing commands such as :
   (i) Copy
   (ii) Paste
   (iii) Undo etc.
3. **View :** View consist of command for showing or hiding components of IDE.
4. **Format :** This menu consist of aligning commands for controls on the form.
5. **Debug :** This consist of Debugging commands.
6. **Run :** Run contain commands that start, break and end execution of the current application.
7. **Tools :** Tools consist of various types of ActiveX components and ActiveX controls.
8. **Window :** It contains commands to arrange window on the screen.
9. **Add – Ins :** It contains add-ins that user can add and remove as needed.
10. **Help :** It consist of information to help user as user works.
11. **Query :** It consist Structure Query Languages (SQL).
12. **Diagrams :** It consist commands for Editing database command.

2. Context Menus :

- It contain shortcuts to frequently performed actions. To open a context menu, click the right mouse button on the object that is using. The specific list of shortcuts available from context menus depends on the part of the environment where the right mouse button is clicked. For example, the context menu displayed when right click on the Toolbox lets the user display the Components dialog box, hide the Toolbox, dock or undock the Toolbox, or add a custom tab to the Toolbox.

3. Toolbars :

- Toolbar provide quick access to commonly used commands in the programming environment. A button is clicked on the toolbar once to carry out the action represented by that button. By default, the Standard toolbar is displayed when Visual Basic is started. Additional toolbars for editing, form design and debugging can be toggled on or off from the Toolbars command on the View menu.
- Toolbars can be docked beneath the menu bar or can "float" if the vertical bar is selected on the left edge and drag it away from the menu bar.

Fig. 1.14 : Standard Toolbar

Fig. 1.15 : Edit Toolbar

Fig. 1.16 : Debug Toolbar

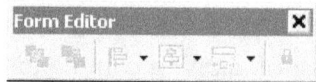

Fig. 1.17: Form editor Toolbar

4. **Toolbox :**

   The Toolbox contains a set of controls that are used to place on a Form at design time thereby creating the user interface area. Additional controls can be included in the toolbox by using the Components menu item on the Project menu. A Toolbox is represented in Fig. 1.18.

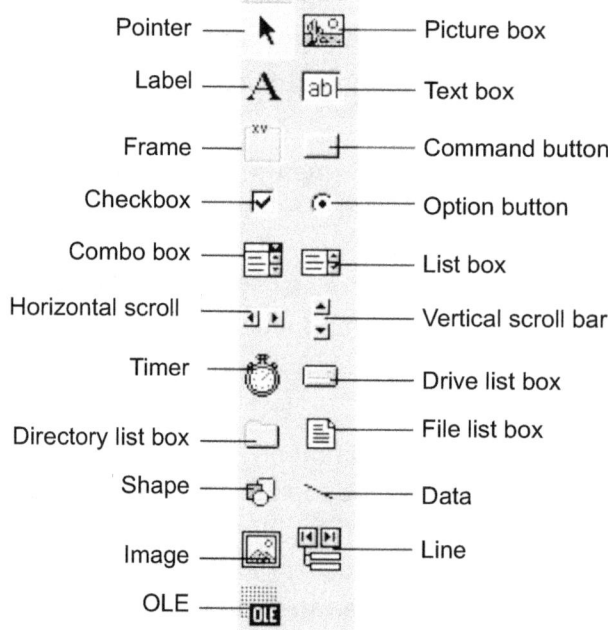

Fig. 1.18 : Tool box

Control	Description
Pointer	Provides a way to move and resize the controls form
PictureBox	Displays icons/bitmaps and metafiles. It displays text or acts as a visual container for other controls.
TextBox	Used to display message and enter text.

contd...

Frame	Serves as a visual and functional container for controls.
CommandButton	Used to carry out the specified action when the user chooses it.
CheckBox	Displays a True/False or Yes/No option.
OptionButton	OptionButton control which is a part of an option group allows the user to select only one option even it displays mulitiple choices.
ListBox	Displays a list of items from which a user can select one.
ComboBox	Contains a TextBox and a ListBox. This allows the user to select an ietm from the dropdown ListBox, or to type in a selection in the TextBox.
HScrollBar and VScrollBar	These controls allow the user to select a value within the specified range of values.
Timer	Executes the timer events at specified intervals of time.
DriveListBox	Displays the valid disk drives and allows the user to select one of them.
DirListBox	Allows the user to select the directories and paths, which are displayed.
FileListBox	Displays a set of files from which a user can select the desired one.
Shape	Used to add shape, (rectangle, square or circle) to a Form.
Line	Used to draw straight line to the Form.
Image	Used to display images such as icons, bitmaps and metafiles. But less capability than the PictureBox.
Data	Enables the use to connect to an existing **database** and display information from it.
OLE	Used to link or embed an object, display and manipulate data from other windows based applications.
Label	Displays a text that the user cannot modify or interact with.

- Provides a set of tools that you use at design time to place controls on a form. In addition to the default toolbox layout, selecting Add Tab from the context menu and adding controls to the resulting tab can create the custom layouts.

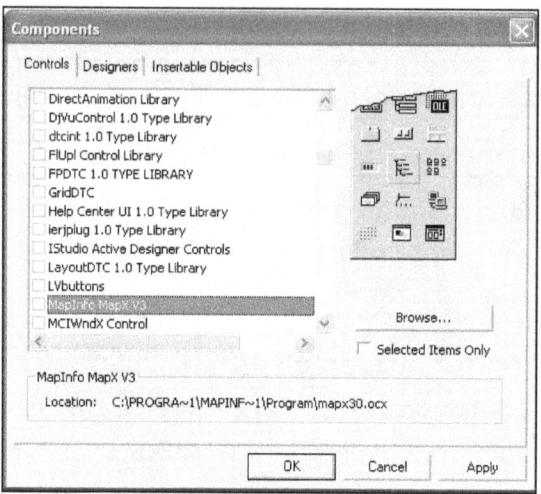

Fig. 1.19 : Components

5. **Project Explorer Window :**

    It lists the forms and modules in your current project. A ***project*** is the collection of files that is used to build an application.

    Docked on the right side of the screen, just under the toolbar, is the Project Explorer window. The Project Explorer as shown in Fig. 1.20 servers as a quick reference to the various elements of a project namely *form*, *classes* and *modules*. All of the object that make up the application are packed in a project. A simple project will typically contain one form, which is a window that is designed as part of a program's interface. It is possible to develop any number of forms for use in a program, although a program may consist of a single form. In addition to forms, the Project Explorer window also lists code modules and classes.

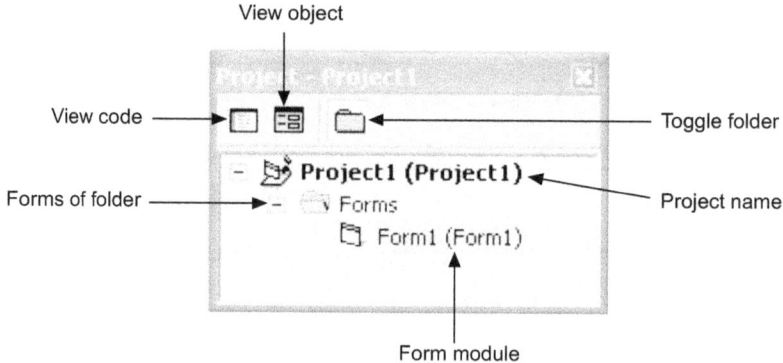

Fig. 1.20 : Project explorer window

6. **Properties Window**

    It lists the property settings for the selected form or control. A property is a characteristic of an object, such as size, caption or color. The Properties Window is docked under the Project Explorer window. The Properties Window exposes the various characteristics of selected objects.

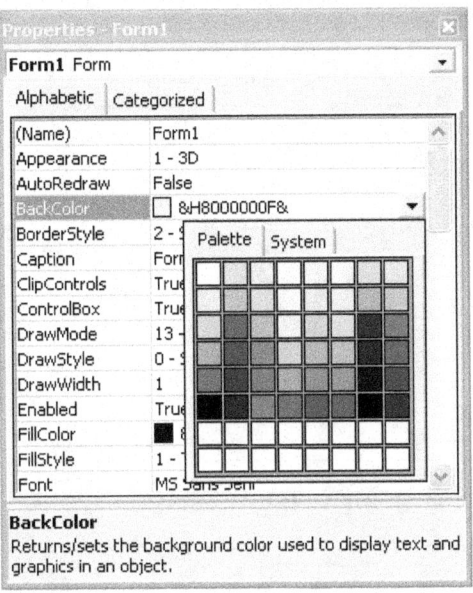

Fig. 1.21 : Property Window

Each and every form in an application is considered an object. Now, each object in Visual Basic has characteristics such as color and size. Other characteristics affect not just the appearance of the object but the way it behaves too. All these characteristics of an object are called its properties. Thus, a form has properties and any controls placed on it will have properties too. All of these properties are displayed in the Properties Window.

7. **Object Browser :**

The Object Browser allows us to browse through the various properties, events and methods that are made available to us. It is accessed by selecting Object Browser from the View menu or pressing the key F2. The left column of the Object Browser lists the objects and classes that are available in the projects that are opened and the controls that have been referenced in them. It is possible for us to scroll through the list and select the object or class that we wish to inspect. After an object is picked up from the Classes list, we can see its members (properties, methods and events) in the right column.

It lists objects available for use in the project and gives a quick way to navigate through the code. Object Browser can be used to explore objects in Visual Basic and other applications, see what methods and properties are available for those objects and paste code procedures into the application.

8. **Form Designer :**

It serves as a window that you customize to design the interface of any application. By adding controls, graphics and pictures to a form, the look can be created as per requirement. Each form in the application has its own form designer window.

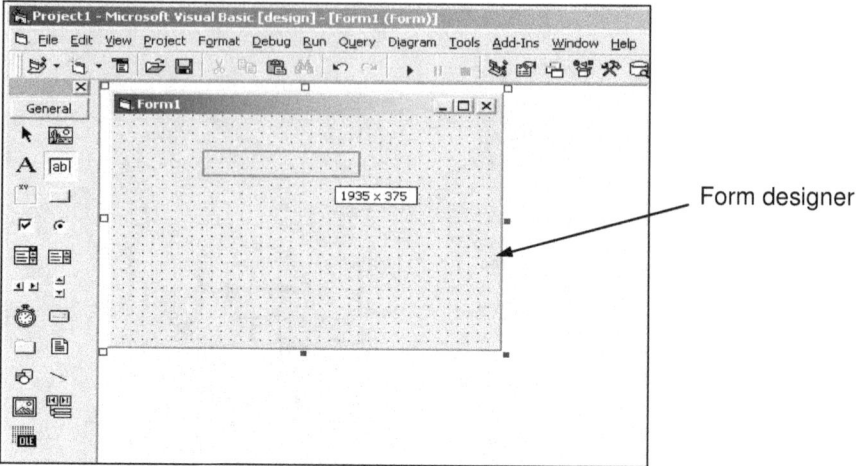

Fig. 1.22 : Form Design Layout

9. Code Editor Window :

It serves as an editor for entering application code. A separate code editor window is created for each form or code module in the application.

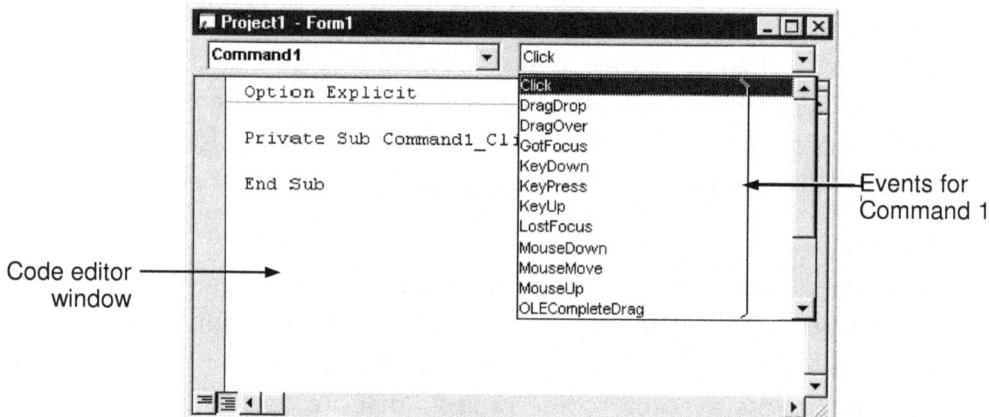

Fig. 1.23 : Code Editor Window

10. Form Layout Window :

The Form Layout window (Fig. 1.24) allows you to position the forms in the application using a small graphical representation of the screen.

Fig. 1.24 : The Form Layout Window

11. Immediate, Locals and Watch Windows :

These additional windows are provided for use in debugging your application. They are only available when the application is running within the IDE.

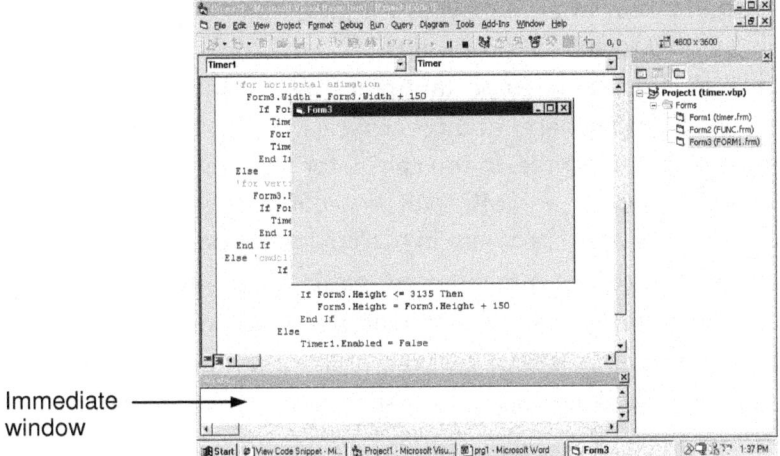

Immediate window

Fig. 1.25 : Immediate Window

1.5.2 Properties in Visual Basic

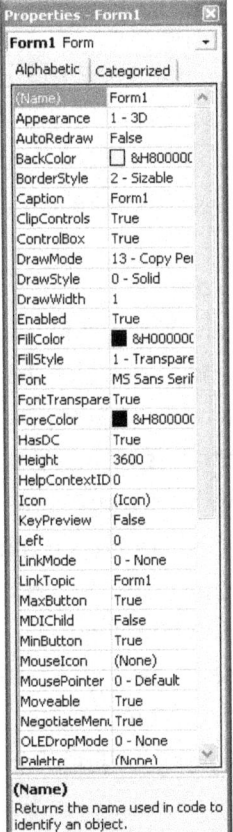

Fig. 1.26

- We would like to stress that knowing how and when to set the objects' properties is very important as it can help you to write a good program or you may fail to write a good program.
- So, we advice you to spend a lot of time playing with the objects' properties. We are not going into the details on how to set the properties.
- However, we would like to stress a few important points about setting up the properties.
  - You should set the Caption Property of a control clearly so that a user knows what to do with that command. For example, in the calculator program, all the captions of the command buttons such as +, – , MC, MR are commonly found in an ordinary calculator, a user should have no problem in manipulating the buttons.
  - A lot of programmers like to use a meaningful name for the Name Property may be because it is easier for them to write and read the event procedure and easier to debug or modify the programs later. However, it is not a must to do that as long as you label your objects clearly and use comments in the program whenever you feel necessary.
  - One more important property is whether the control is enabled or not.
  - Finally, you must also considering making the control visible or invisible at runtime, or when should it become visible or invisible.
- Visual Basic Consist of Following Properties :

1. **Name :** Name property sets the name of the control in which user can access the controls properties and method.
2. **Back color :** Using backcolor user can sets background color on which text is displayed.
3. **Appearance :** This property shows two values, 0 and 1. 0 shows a flat look and 1 shows 3-D look.
4. **Forecolor :** Forecolor sets text color.
5. **Font :** Using font property user can sets font face, attributes and size of the font.
6. **Caption :** This is very important property in visual basic. This property sets the text that is displayed on many controls that do not accept input.
7. **Text :** Text property sets the text that is displayed on the control and that accept input.
8. **Width :** Width properties sets control's width dimensions.
9. **Height :** Height properties sets control's height dimensions.
10. **Left, Top :** Using this property user can sets co-ordinates of the control's upper – left corner, expressed in the units of the container.
11. **Visible :** Visible property sets false to make a control invisible.
12. **Enabled :** Enabled property consist of two values :
    - (i) **True :** This is by default property of Enabled True means that the control can get the focus.
    - (ii) **False :** This sets disable the control.

Methods in Visual Basic
- Visual basic consist of the following methods :
    1. **Clear :** This method tells the control to discard its contents.
    2. **Move :** The syntax of the method is : Control name, Move left, Top, Width, Height.
    3. **AddItem :** Using this method user can adds contents item in control.
    4. **Remove Item:** This method used for remove contents item in the control.

1.5.3 Controls in Visual Basic (Oct. 10)

- When we create Visual Basic 6.0 standard project, the default controls are displayed in the Toolbox as shown in Fig. 1.27.
- Later, you can add more controls as you progress to more advanced programming.

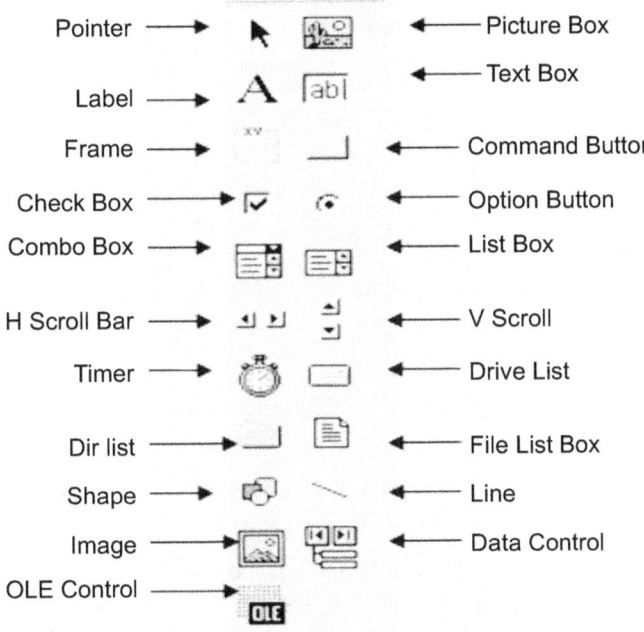

Fig. 1.27 : Controls in visual basic

- The icons in the Toolbox of the Visual Basic IDE and their names are shown below:

1. **Label :** Label control displays text on a Form that the user can not edit. It commonly identify other controls and can be transparent, so the text appears to be placed directly on the From. User set the label's text with the Caption property. The label is a very useful control for Visual Basic, as it is not only used to provide instructions and guides to the users, it can also be used to display outputs. One of its most important properties is Caption. Using the syntax `label.Caption`, it can display text and numeric data. You can change its caption in the properties window and also at runtime.

2. **TextBox** : TextBox control is a mini text editor. Its most important property is the Text property, which can set the text on the control or read the text that the user enters. TextBox control displays text that the user can edit. The text box is the standard control for accepting input from the user as well as to display the output. It can handle string (text) and numeric data but not images or pictures. String in a text box can be converted to a numeric data by using the function Val(text).

3. **PictureBox** : Picture Box control supports a number of methods for generating drawing. Picture Box control is used to display images and the images are set with the Picture property. The Picture Box is one of the controls that is used to handle graphics. You can load a picture at design phase by clicking on the picture item in the properties window and select the picture from the selected folder. You can also load the picture at runtime using the LoadPicture method. For example, the statement will load the picture grape.gif into the picture box.

```
Picture1.Picture=LoadPicture ("C:\VB program\Images\nature.gif")
```
(Oct. 10, April 12)

4. **CheckBox** : The CheckBox control's main property is Value, and it is 0 if the CheckBox is cleared and 1 if the CheckBox is checked. CheckBox control presents one or more choices that the user can select.

The Check Box control lets the user selects or unselects an option. When the Check Box is checked, its value is set to 1 and when it is unchecked, the value is set to 0. You can include the statements Check1.Value=1 to mark the Check Box and Check1.Value=0 to unmark the Check Box, as well as use them to initiate certain actions.

For example, the program will change the background color of the form to red when the check box is unchecked and it will change to blue when the check box is checked. You will learn about the conditional statement If....Then....Elesif in next lesson. VbRed and vbBlue are color constants and BackColor is the background color property of the form.

```
Private Sub Command1_Click()
If Check1.Value = 1 And Check2.Value = 0 Then
MsgBox "Apple is selected"
ElseIf Check2.Value = 1 And Check1.Value = 0 Then
MsgBox "Orange is selected"
Else
MsgBox "All are selected"
End If
End Sub
```

5. **Frame :** Frame control is used to draw boxes on the Form. It also used to group other elements.

6. **ListBox:** ListBox control contains a list of options form which the user can choose one or more. The selected item in a ListBox control is given by the Text property. Another important property of the ListBox control is the Sorted property, which determines whether the items in the list will be sorted.

   The function of the List Box is to present a list of items where the user can click and select the items from the list. In order to add items to the list, we can use the AddItem method. For example, if you wish to add a number of items to list box 1, you can key in the following statements

   ```
   Private Sub Form_Load ( )
         List1.AddItem "Unit1"
         List1.AddItem "Unit2"
         List1.AddItem "Unit3"
         List1.AddItem "Unit4"
   End Sub
   ```

   The items in the list box can be identified by the ListIndex property, the value of the ListIndex for the first item is 0, the second item has a ListIndex 1, and the second item has a ListIndex 2 and so on.

7. **Command Button :** A Command button represents an action that is carried out when the user clicks the button. The command button is one of the most important controls as it is used to execute commands. It displays an illusion that the button is pressed when the user click on it. The most common event associated with the command button is the Click event, and the syntax for the procedure is

   ```
   Private Sub Command1_Click ()
         Statements
   End Sub
   ```

8. **The Horizontal and Vertical ScrollBars :** Horizontal and Vertical scrollbars let the user specify a magnitude by scrolling the control's button between its minimum and maximum value.

9. **Option Button :** Option buttons or Radio buttons, appear in group. The user can choose only one of them. The Option button's main property is checked and it is True if the control is checked and False otherwise.

The Option button control also lets the user selects one of the choices. However, two or more Option buttons must work together because as one of the Option buttons is selected, the other Option buttons will be unselected. In fact, only one Option button can be selected at one time. When an option box is selected, its value is set to "True" and when it is unselected; its value is set to "False". In the following example, the shape control is placed in the form together with six Option button. When the user clicks on different option button, different shapes will appear. The values of the shape control are 0, 1, and 2, 3, 4, 5 which will make it appear as a rectangle, a square, an oval shape, a rounded rectangle and a rounded square respectively.

```
Private Sub Option1_Click ( )
      Shape1.Shape = 0
End Sub

Private Sub Option2_Click()
      Shape1.Shape = 1
End Sub

Private Sub Option3_Click()
      Shape1.Shape = 2
End Sub

Private Sub Option4_Click()
      Shape1.Shape = 3
End Sub

Private Sub Option5_Click()
      Shape1.Shape = 4
End Sub

Private Sub Option6_Click()
      Shape1.Shape = 5
End Sub
```

10. **Combo Box:** In ComboBox user can either choose an item from the list or enter a new string in the Edit field. This control is similar to the ListBox control, but it contains a text Edit field. The item selected from the list (or entered in the Edit field) is given by the control's Text property. The function of the Combo Box is also to present a list of items where the user can click and select the items from the list. However, the user needs to click on the small arrowhead on the right of the combo box to see the items which are presented in a drop-down list. In order to add items to the list, you can also use the AddItem method.

For example, if you wish to add a number of items to Combo box 1, you can key in the following statements,

```
Private Sub Form_Load ( )
   Combo1.AddItem "Item1"
   Combo1.AddItem "Item2"
   Combo1.AddItem "Item3"
   Combo1.AddItem "Item4"
End Sub
```

11. **Timer:** User can use this control to perform tasks at regular time intervals. The main property of the Timer control is Interval, which determines how often the Timer notifies User's application. If the Interval property is set to 10000.

12. **Image Box :** The Image Box is another control that handles images and pictures. It functions almost identically to the picture box. However, there is one major difference, the image in an Image Box is stretchable, which means it can be resized. This feature is not available in the Picture Box. Similar to the Picture Box, it can also use the `LoadPicture` method to load the picture. For example, the statement loads the picture grape.gif into the image box.

`Image1.Picture=LoadPicture ("C:\VB program\Images\nature.gif")`

13. **Drive ListBox :** The Drive ListBox is for displaying a list of drives available in your computer. When you place this control into the form and run the program, you will be able to select different drives from your computer as shown in Fig. 1.28.

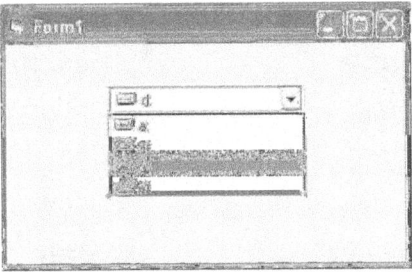

Fig. 1.28 : Drive ListBox

14. **Directory List Box:** The Directory List Box is for displaying the list of directories or folders in a selected drive. When you place this control into the form and run the program, you will be able to select different directories from a selected drive in your computer as shown in Fig. 1.29.

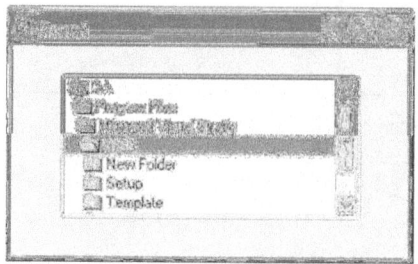

Fig. 1.29 : Directory ListBox

Sr. No.	Prefix	Object type
1.	frm	Form
2.	lbl	Label
3.	txt	Text box
4.	fil	File list box
5.	drv	Drive list box
6.	dir	Directory list box
7.	chk	Check box
8.	cbo	Combo box
9.	cmd	Command button
10.	lin	Line
11.	lst	List box
12.	mnu	Menu
13.	ole	OLE
14.	mod	Module
15.	hsb	Horizontal scrollbar
16.	opt	Option button
17.	grd	Grid
18.	fra	Frame
19.	img	Image
20.	pic	Picture box
21.	vsb	Vertical scrollbar
22.	shp	Shape
23.	typ	User defined data type
24.	tmr	Timer
25.	res	Resource

1.6 STUDYING EVENTS OF A FORM (April 10, 12, 14; Oct 11, 12, 13)

- Windows is an event-driven operating system i.e. it utilizes system events to react to the environment.
- Events are triggered by messages. Whenever we click a button, move the mouse, or anything else, Windows will generate a message that describes our action.
- This message then gets sent to the message queue. From here the message is sent to the appropriate control (from). When the control receives this message, it then generates an appropriate event.
- We can write our own code in an event to force a control to react precisely the way we want it to.

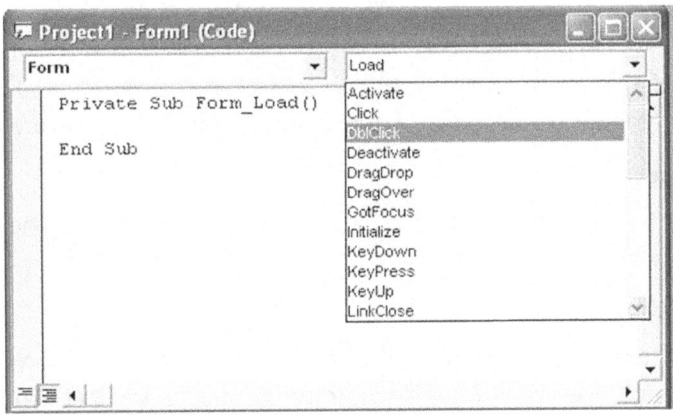

Fig. 1.30 : Event list of form

- Common events in visual basic are given below and the bold events are commonly in use.

Activate	KeyDown	LostFocus	OLESetData
Click	KeyPress	MouseDown	OLEStartDrag
DblClick	KeyUp	MouseMove	Paint
Deactivate	LinkClose	MouseUp	QueryUnload
DragDrop	LinkError	OLECompleteDrag	**Resize**
DragOver	LinkExecute	OLEDragDrop	Terminate
GotFocus	LinkOpen	OLEDragOver	**Unload**
Initialize	**Load**	OLEGiveFeedback	

- Just like properties of visual basic there are only a few of a form's events that are used a great deal of the time. Many of the events are rarely used, unless you are building a very complex application.
- The best way to view the event associated with a form is to double-click the form in design view to display the code window.

1. **Activate Event :**

   A form in Visual Basic is actually activated after it is initialized. The form then receives the focus after it has been activated.

   These subtle difference appear between all of them. The most important difference is the order in which they occur in an application. The order is as given below :

   - **Initialize :** Initialize event is triggered when a form is being configured before it is loaded.
   - **Load :** Load event is called after the form has been initialized, and before the form is displayed on the screen.
   - **Activate :** This event is triggered when the form has been loaded into memory and when it becomes the active form.
   - **GotFocus :** If it occurs at all, GotFocus event is triggered when the form gets the focus, either when it is loaded or when a user accesses the form with a mouse click.

2. **Deactivate Event :**

   The Deactivate event occurs when the form ceases to be active. The Deactivate event is the converse of Activate event.

3. **DragDrop Event :**

   DragDrop event takes place when a dragged control is dropped onto a form. To enable the DragDrop event, you must have something to drag and drop on the form in the first place.

4. **Load Event :**

   This event comes after the Initialize event, but load event comes before the Activate event as a form is loaded into memory from disk. This event is a particularly important one and is the one most frequently used. Load event extremely handy for specifying some of the contents of the form.

5. **Resize Event :**

   When the program code alters the size of a form, the Resize event occurs. Uses of resize events are:

   (i) User can set the form back to its original size.

   (ii) User can resize the controls on the form with code.

6. **Unload Event :**

   This event is, logically, the opposite of Load event. The most popular and common choice for an Unload event procedure is one that asks the user if they are sure they want to close the form.

- In visual basic Events determines the control's reaction to external condition. Following Table 1.1 shows events in Visual Basic.

Table 1.1 : Event in visual basic

S.N.	Event Name	Description
1.	**Mouse Event :**	**(April 12)**
	(i) Click	This event takes place when user clicks the left mouse button.
	(ii) DblClick	This event takes place when user double – clicks the left mouse button.
	(iii) MouseDown	When mouse button is pressed then Mouse Down event take place.
	(iv) MouseUp	When the pressed button is released then Mouse up event take place.
	(v) MouseMove	When mouse continuously move over a control then mouse move event take place.
2.	**Keyboard Event :**	**(April 12, Oct. 10)**
	(i) Key Press	When a key is pressed then Key Press event occurs.
	(ii) Key Up	When pressed key is released then key Up event is take place.
	(iii) Key Down	This event is triggered when a key is pressed.
3.	**Focus Event :** (i) Lost Focus (ii) Got Focus	When the focus of a control moved to another control then the first control receives Lost focus event and the second control is receives Got focus event.

1.7 WORKING CODE FOR EVENTS (Oct. 13)

- The 'look' of a Visual Basic application is determined by what controls are used, but the 'feel' is determined by the events.
- An event is something which can happen to a control. For example, a user can click on a button, change a text box, or resize a form.
- As explained in Creating a Visual Basic Application, writing a program is made up of three events :
    1. Select suitable controls,
    2. Set the properties, and
    3. Write the code.
- It is at the code writing stage when it becomes important to choose appropriate events for each control. To do this double click on the control the event will be used for, or click on the ▢ icon in the project window (usually top right of screen).

- A code window should now be displayed similar to the one shown in Fig. 1.31.

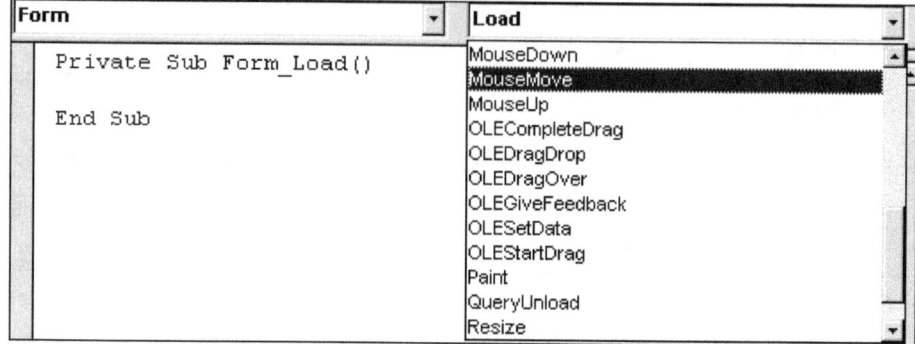

Fig. 1.31 : Event

- The left hand dropdown box provides a list of all controls used by the current form, the form itself, and a special section called General Declarations.
- The corresponding dropdown box on the right displays a list of all events applicable to the current control (as specified by the left hand dropdown box). Events displayed in bold signify that code has already been written for them, unbold events are unused.
- To demonstrate that different events can play a significant role in determining the feel of an application, a small example program will be written to add two numbers together and display the answer.
- The first solution to this problem will use the click event of a command button, while the second will the change event of two text boxes.
  1. Start Microsoft Visual Basic 6.0.
  2. On the opening dialog box, make sure Standard EXE is selected and click Open.
  3. On the main menu, click View → Code.
  4. In the empty window, type Private Sub Form_Click.

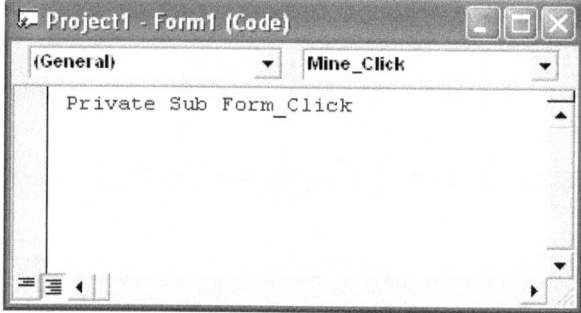

Fig. 1.32 : Form-click event

  5. Press Enter.
  6. Notice that Visual Basic added the parentheses and the End Sub line.
  7. In the Code window, notice that the Object combo box is displaying Form.

8. Click the arrow of the Object combo box to display its list :

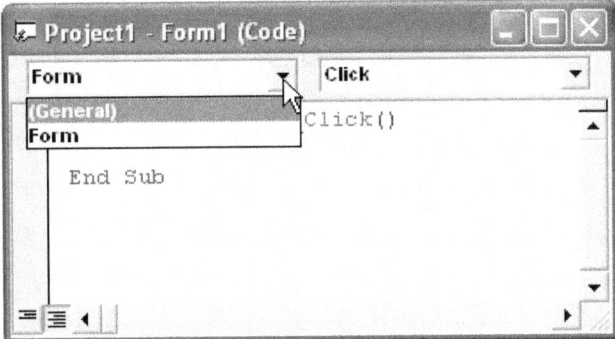

Fig. 1.33 : Object ComboBox

9. Click the arrow of the Procedure combo box and, in the list, click MouseDown.
10. Notice the section of the MouseDown event. Also notice that this event has a few arguments.

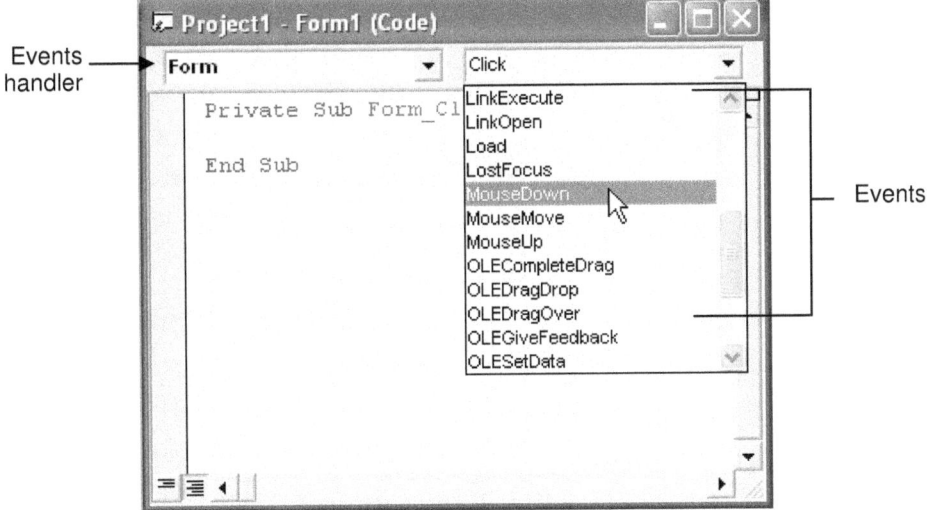

Fig. 1.34 : Event handler and event

11. We will eventually learn what the writings of these arguments mean. In the Object combo box, notice that Text1 is still displaying.
12. In the Code window, click on one of the form events.
13. Notice that the Object combo box has automatically changed.

1. **Program for Load event :**

```
Private Sub Form_Load ( )
  Form1.show
  Print "Welcome to Visual Basic"
End Sub
```

Output :

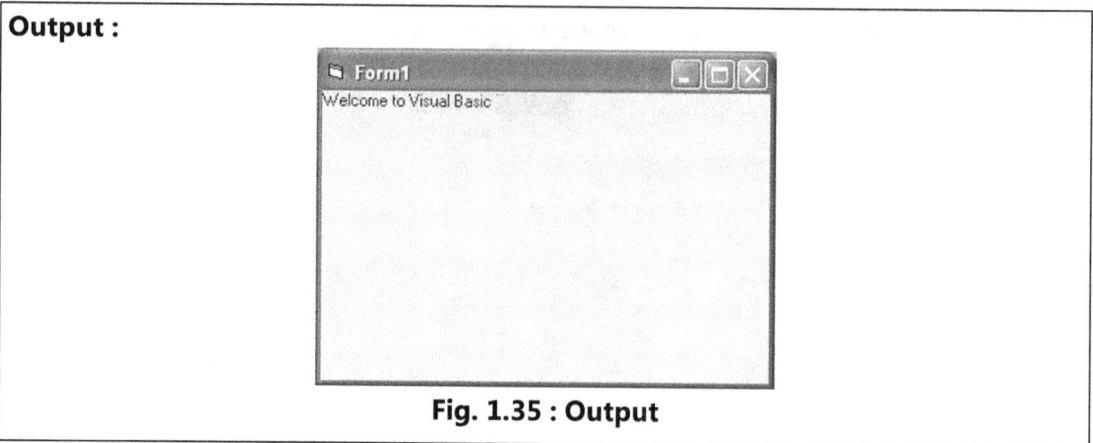

Fig. 1.35 : Output

2. **Program for Activate event :**

```
Private Sub Form_Activate ( )
    Print 20 + 10
    Print 20 - 10
    Print 20 * 10
    Print 20 / 10
End Sub
```

Output :

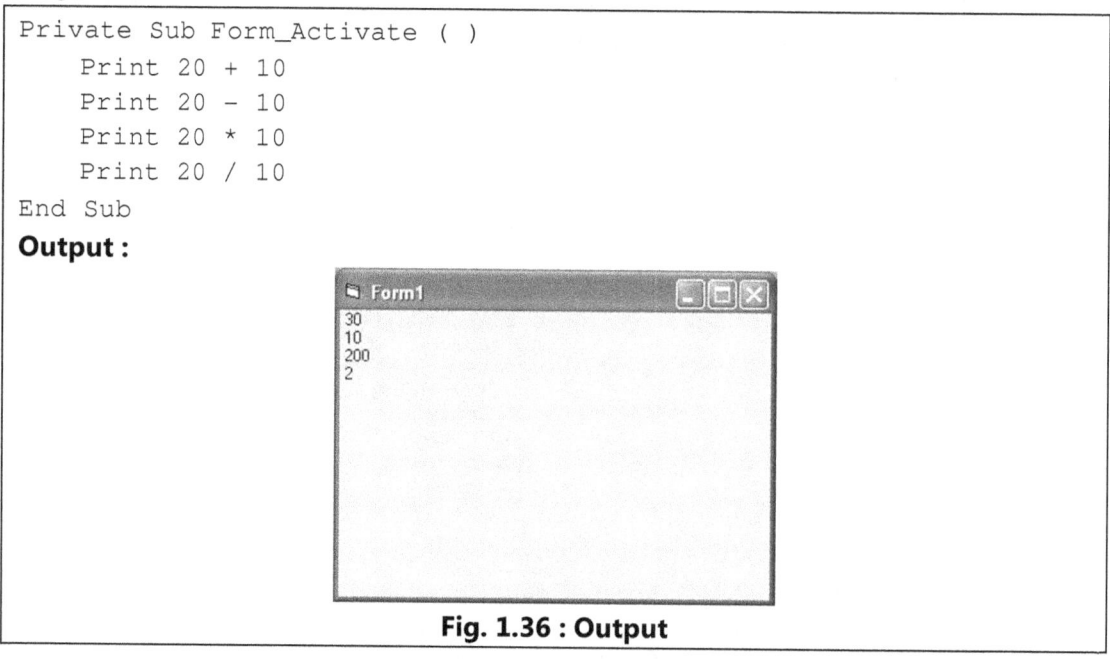

Fig. 1.36 : Output

3. **Program for click event :**

   Before any events can be coded it is necessary to design the interface from suitable controls. As shown in the screen shot below use: 2 text boxes to enter the numbers, a label for the '+' sign, a command button for the '=' sign, and another label for the answer.

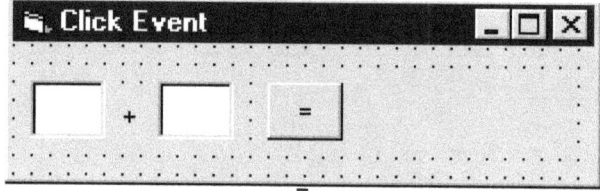

Fig. 1.37 : Click Event

Making the click event is very simple just select the button with the mouse and double click visual basic will generate click event.

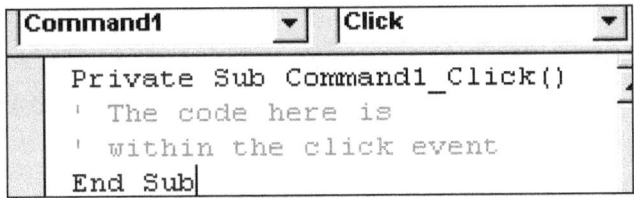

Fig. 1.38 : Code of click event

You can see on the top right there is a 'click' dropdown list this is known as a event handler. In this program, two text boxes are inserted into the form together with a few labels. The two text boxes are used to accept inputs from the user and one of the labels will be used to display the sum of two numbers that are entered into the two text boxes.

Besides, a command button is also programmed to calculate the sum of the two numbers using the plus operator. The program use creates a variable sum to accept the summation of values from text box 1 and text box 2.

The procedure to calculate and to display the output on the label is shown below. The output is shown in Fig. 1.39.

```
Private Sub Command1_Click()
   'To add the values in text box 1 and text box 2
   Sum = Val(Text1.Text) + Val(Text2.Text)
   'To display the answer on label 1
   Label1.Caption = Sum
End Sub
```

Output :

Fig. 1.39 : Output

1.8 PLANNING THE DESIGN

- There are three main phases are used for designing an application structure, the three phases are given below :
   1. **User Interface :** User interface displays what user will see in his interface to the application. The interface may be distribute to multiple servers.
   2. **Classes :** Classes defines basic business logic of the application.

3. **Database :** Database displays the contents of the application, as well as it deployed on a database server.
- The structure of the application consist of object model and data structure.
- The object model and database model may be deployed on different servers.
- In form Interface design is user may changes in object model it also make that changes in database model.

1.8.1 Steps for Designing an Application

1. Implement top-level object model for the system.
2. Implement Database structure, which holds persistent data from the object model.
3. Design stored procedures in the database for performing basic functions such as, ADD, INSERT, and DELETE etc.
4. Design the database in a data environment in VB.
5. Implement a prototype user interface for the system or application.
6. Implement appropriate reports for the system.
7. Design / implement the functionality logic of the system.
8. Test the system.
9. Deploy the system.

- When the functionality takes place used need to debug testing, user testing etc. In Visual Basic class Builder tool is useful for creating **object model**. User can also utilize the form **design tool**.

Practice Questions

1. What are the features of Visual Basic?
2. What is meant by Event driven programming language?
3. Explain Integrated Development Environment of visual basic.
4. Explain advantages of VB.
5. What are properties, methods and events?
6. What are the components contained in the VB project?
7. What is meant by object oriented languages?
8. What is meant by object?
9. What is Dockable window?
10. What is GUI? Explain in brief.
11. What is the use of Visual Basic for building application softwares?
12. Visual Basic is used as a front end. Justify.
13. What are various interfacing element of Visual Basic?
14. What is an event?

15. Describe design steps for developing on application
16. Describe installation steps of VB.
17. With suitable diagram describe VB controls.

University Questions & Answers

April 2010

1. What is event driven programming language? [4 M]
Ans. Please refer to Section 1.4.
2. Discuss various events related with form control. [4 M]
Ans. Please refer to Section 1.5.

Oct. 2010

1. Write short notes on:
   (i) Event driven programming [4 M]
Ans. Please refer to Section 1.4.
   (ii) Picture box [4 M]
Ans. Please refer to Section 1.5.

April 2011

1. Write short notes on: Object Oriented Programming. [4 M]
Ans. Please refer to Section 1.3.

Oct. 2011

1. Write short notes on:
   (i) Keyboard events. [4 M]
Ans. Please refer to Section 1.6.
   (ii) Integrated development environment. [4 M]
Ans. Please refer to Section 1.5.1.

April 2012

1. Write short notes on: Picture box. [4 M]
Ans. Please refer to Section 1.5.
2. Discuss various events related with mouse and keyboard. [4 M]
Ans. Please refer to Section 1.6.

Oct. 2012

1. What is an Event? Explain various Events of a Form. [4 M]
Ans. Please refer to Section 1.6.

April 2013

1. Why visual basic is called as GUI Applications? [4 M]
Ans. Please refer to Section 1.4.

2. What is Event Driven Programming in VB? Explain with example. [4 M]
Ans. Please refer to Section 1.4.2.

Oct. 2013

1. Property used to specify text to be displayed when the mouse is paused over the control. [4 M]
Ans. Please refer to Section 1.7.

2. Explain any two from events. [4 M]
Ans. Please refer to Section 1.6.

3. Attempt the following: Integrated Development environment.
Ans. Please refer to Section 1.5.1.

April 2014

1. Explain the features of Visual Basic. [4 M]
Ans. Please refer to Section 1.1.3.

2. Explain the various events related to form. [4 M]
Ans. Please refer to Section 1.6.

❖❖❖

Chapter 2

Constants, Variables, Operators, Control Structure, Looping & Array

Contents ...

This chapter includes

2.1 CONSTANT
2.2 DATA TYPES
    2.2.1 String
    2.2.2 Boolean
    2.2.3 Numeric Data Types
    2.2.4 Other Data Types
    2.2.5 User Defined Data Types
2.3 VARIABLES
    2.3.1 Declaring Variables
    2.3.2 Rules for Writing Variables
    2.3.3 Implicit Declaration
    2.3.4 Explicit Declaration
    2.3.5 Scope of Variables
2.4 OPERATORS
    2.4.1 Uses of Operators
    2.4.2 Operator Precedence
2.5 CONTROL STRUCTURES
    2.5.1 If...Then Statement
    2.5.2 If...Then...Else Statement
    2.5.3 Nested If...Then...Else Statement
    2.5.4 Select...Case Statement
2.6 LOOPING
    2.6.1 Do .... Loop
    2.6.2 Do While .... Loop / Do Until ...... Loop
    2.6.3 Do ...... Loop While / Do ...... Loop Until

2.6.4 For ...... Next Loop
2.6.5 For Each......Next Loop
2.6.6 While .....Loop / While .....Wend Loop
2.6.7 Exit Statement
2.7 ARRAY
2.7.1 Single Dimensional Arrays
2.7.2 Multidimensional Arrays
2.7.3 Control Array
2.8 FUNCTIONS (BUILT IN AND USER DEFINED)
2.8.1 Function Creation
2.8.2 Calling a Function
2.8.3 Built-in Functions
2.8.4 User Defined Functions
* Practice Questions
* University Question & Answers

2.1 CONSTANT (Oct. 12)

- Many applications require data that is used if it were variable in nature but is actually unchanged during the program's execution.
- A constant is defined in the application and is assigned a value during its declaration.
- Then, as the program executes the constant's value can be used anywhere, a variable could be used, but its value cannot be changed by the program's code.
- A value that cannot change during program execution, including literal numbers, strings and symbolic constants and is defined with **const** statement.
- Constants improve the readability of your code and make it easier to maintain.
- Constants are values those do not change from program to program.
- The constants are preferred for two reasons :
  1. Constants can not change value. This is a safety feature. Once, a constant has been declared, you cannot change its value in subsequent statement, and you can be sure that the value specified in the constant's declaration will take effect in the rest of the program.
  2. Constants are processed faster than variables. When the program is running, the values of constants do not have to be looked up. The compiler substitutes constant names with their values and the program executes faster.
- A constant statement has scope like variable declaration and the same rules apply.
- To create a constant that exist within a procedure, declare it within that procedure.
- To create a constant available to all procedures within a module but not to any code outside module, declare it in the declaration section of the module.

- To create a constant available throughout the application, declare the constant in the declaration section of a standard module, and place the Public keyword before it.
- Public constants cannot be declared in a form or class module.
- Visual Basic uses constants extensively to define the various arguments of its methods and the setting of the various control properties.
- The value of a CheckBox, control, can be :
    ```
    0 (unchecked), 1 (checked) or 2 (grayed)
    check1.value = 0
    check2.value  = 2
    ```
    use the built-in constants vbUnchecked and vbGrayed :
    ```
    check1.value = vbUnchecked
    check2.value = vbGrayed.
    ```
- The syntax of a constant's declaration is as follows :
    ```
    [Public|Private] Const ConstName [As DataType] = Value
    ```
    Ex. const Pi AS double = 3.142
- The same naming conventions apply to constants as to variables. The constant's name must begin with a letter of the alphabet and can not contain any punctuation other than the underscore character. Constant names must be 255 characters or less in length.
- The same scoping rules apply to constants and variables. Constants defined in standard modules are public throughout, the application by default. Constants defined within form modules are private to the form in which their declarations appear by default.
- If the data type is not provided in a constant's declaration, Visual Basic assumes the data type from the data used to initialize the constant's value. Any data type except objects and user-defined types can be used to initialize constants.
- Constants can even be defined in terms of other constants :
    ```
    Const conversion = "5.1"
    Const conVerDate = "13-Nov-99" & conversion
    ```
- The following constant declaration generates a compile-time error :
    ```
    Const conVerDate = Date()
    ```

2.2 DATA TYPES (April 13)

- When you decide to use a variable, you are in fact asking the computer to use a certain amount of space to hold that variable.
- Since, different variables will be used for different purposes, you should specify the kind of variable you intend to use, then the computer will figure out how much space is needed for a particular variable.
- Each variable you use will utilize a certain amount of space in the computer's memory.
- Before declaring or using a variable, first decide what kind of role that variable will play in your program. Different variables are meant for different situations.

- The kind of variable you want to use is referred to as a data type. To specify the kind of variable you want to use, you type the **As** keyword on the right side of the variable's name.
- The syntax to declare such a variable is :
  ```
  Dim VariableName As DataType
  ```
- Once, you know what kind of variable you will need, choose the appropriate data type. Data types are organized in categories such as numbers, characters, or other objects.
- Data type is a characteristics of a variable that determines its attributes and kind of data it can hold.
- The following table shows the fundamental data types supported by Visual Basic, and type declaration suffix, storage size, and range of each data type.

Data type	Suffix	Storage size	Range
Integer	%	2 bytes	– 32,768 to 32,767
Long (long integer)	&	4 bytes	– 2,147,483,648 to 2,147,483,647
Single (single-precision floating point)	!	4 bytes	For negative values : $-3.402823E38$ to $-1.401298E-45$ For positive values : $1.401298E-45$ to $3.402823E38$
Double (double-precision floating point)	#	8 bytes	For negative values : $-1.79769313486232E308$ to $-4.94065645841247E324$ For positive values : $4.94065645841247E-324$ to $1.79769313486232E308$
Currency (scaled integer)	@	8 bytes	–9,22,337,203,685,477.5808 to 922,337,203,685,477.5807
String (variable-length)	$	10 bytes + String length	0 to approximately 2 billion.
String (fixed length)	$	Length of string	1 to approximately 65,400
Byte	None	1 byte	0 to 255
Boolean	None	2 bytes	True or False
Date	None	8 bytes	Jan 1,1997 to Dec. 31,1999
Object	None	4 bytes	Any object reference

Contd...

Variant	None	As appropriate	Null, Error, or any numeric value upto the range of a Double or any character text, object or array.
User-defined (using Type)	None	Number required by elements	The range of each element is the same as the range of its fundamental data type, listed above.
Decimal	None	12 bytes	With a 28-decimal places, the largest value is /– 7.9228162514264337593543950335 and the smallest, non-zero is +/– 0.0000000000000000000000000001

- For example, X% is an integer, X! is a single-precision floating point number, X$ is a string.

2.2.1 String   (Oct. 13)

- A string is an empty text, a letter, a word or a group of words considered.
- To declare a string variable, use the String data type. Here is an example :

```
Private Sub Form_Load()
    Dim CountryName As String
End Sub
```

- After declaring the variable, you can initialize. If you want its area of memory to be empty, you can assign it two double-quotes.
- Here, is an example :

```
Private Sub Form_Load()
  Dim CountryName As String
    CountryName = ""
End Sub
```

- If you want to store something in the memory space allocated to the variable, assign it a word or group of words included between double-quotes. Here is an example :

```
Private Sub Form_Load()
  Dim CountryName As String
    CountryName = "India"
End Sub
```

- You can also initialize a string variable with another.

2.2.2 Boolean

- A Boolean variable is one whose value can be only either True or False. To declare such a variable, use the Boolean keyword. Here is an example :

```
Private Sub Form_Load()
    Dim IsMarried As Boolean
End Sub
```

- After declaring a Boolean variable, you can initialize by assigning it either True or False. Here is an example :

```
Private Sub Form_Load()
    Dim IsMarried As Boolean
    IsMarried = False
End Sub
```

- Like any other variable, after initializing the variable, it keeps its value until you change its value again.

2.2.3 Numeric Data Types

- A natural number is one that contains only one digit or a combination of digits and no other character, except those added to make it easier to read.
- Examples of natural numbers are 122, 8, and 2864347. When a natural number is too long, such 3253754343, to make it easier to read, the thousands are separated by a special character.
- This character depends on the language or group of language and it is called the thousands separator. The thousands separator symbol is mainly used only to make the number easier to read.
- To support different scenarios, Microsoft provides different types of natural numbers.

1. **Byte :**
- A byte is a small natural positive number that ranges from 0 to 255. A variable of byte type can be used to hold small values such as a person's age, the number of fingers on an animal etc.
- To declare a variable for a small number, use the Byte keyword. Here is an example :

```
Private Sub Form_Load()
    Dim StudentAge As Byte
End Sub
```

2. **Integer :**
- An integer is a natural number larger than the **Byte**. It can hold a value between – 32,768 and 32,767. Examples of such ranges are : the number of pages of a book.
- To declare a variable of type integer, use the **Integer** keyword. Here is an example :

```
Private Sub Form_Load()
    Dim MusicTracks As Integer
End Sub
```

3. Long Integer :

- A long integer is a natural number whose value is between –2,147,483,648 and 2,147,483,642. Examples are the population of a city, the distance between places of different countries, the number of words of a book.
- To declare a variable that can hold a very large natural number, use the **Long** keyword. Here is an example :

```
Private Sub Form_Load( )
    Dim Population As Long
End Sub
```

4. Single :

- A single is a decimal number whose value can range from –3.402823e38 and –1.401298e-45 if the number is negative, or 1.401298e-45 and 3.402823e38 if the number is positive.
- To declare a variable that can hold small decimal numbers with no concern for precision, use the **Single** data type. Here is an example :

```
Private Sub Form_Load()
        Dim CountryName As String
        Dim IsMarried As Boolean
        Dim StudentAge As Byte
        Dim Tracks As Integer
        Dim Population As Long
        Dim Distance As Single
End Sub
```

5. Double :

- While the **Single** data type can allow large numbers, it offers less precision. For an even larger number, Microsoft Visual Basic provides the **Double** data type. This is used for a variable that would hold numbers that range from 1.79769313486231e308 to – 4.94065645841247e–324 if the number is negative or from 1.79769313486231E308 to 4.94065645841247E–324 if the number is positive.
- To declare a variable that can store large decimal numbers with a good level of precision, use the **Double** keyword. Here is an example of declaring a **Double** variable :

```
Private Sub Form_Load()
     Dim Distance As Double
End Sub
```

6. Currency :

- The **Currency** data type is used for a variable that can hold monetary values. To declare such a variable, use the **Currency** keyword. Here is an example :

```
Private Sub Form_Load()
    Dim CountryName As String
    Dim IsMarried As Boolean
    Dim StudentAge As Byte
    Dim Tracks As Integer
    Dim Population As Long
    Dim Distance As Single
    Dim StartingSalary As Currency
End Sub
```

2.2.4 Other Data Types

1. Date :

- A date is a numeric value that represents the number of days that have elapsed since a determined period. A time is a numeric value that represents the number of seconds that have elapsed in a day.
- To declare a variable that can hold either date values, time values, or both, use the **Date** keyword. After the variable has been declared, you will configure it to the appropriate value. Here are example :

```
Private Sub Form_Load()
    Dim CountryName As String
    Dim IsMarried As Boolean
    Dim StudentAge As Byte
    Dim Tracks As Integer
    Dim Population As Long
    Dim Distance As Single
    Dim StartingSalary As Currency
    Dim DateOfBirth As Date
    Dim KickOffTime As Date
End Sub
```

2. Variant :

- A Variant can be used to declare any kind of variable. You can use a variant when you can not make up your mind regarding a variable but, as a beginning programmer, you should avoid it.

2.2.5 User Defined Data Types

(Oct. 13)

- When data consists of different types, variables of several different types can be combined to create User-defined type.
- **Declaring User-defined types :** User-defined types are declared with **Type** statement in the declaration section of a module and can be defined as Private or Public. Variables declared as a user-defined type can be public, module-level, local in other modules.

Syntax :
```
[Public] [Private] Type typename
         fieldname1 As type
         fieldname2 As type
    ......
    ......
         fieldnamen A type
End Type
```

For example :
```
Type system
    CPU As Variant
    Memory As Long
    Cost As Currency
    PurchaseDate As Variant
End Type
Dim MySystem As System, YourSystem As System
```

- Assigning and Retrieving values from elements :
```
MySystem.CPU = "486"
YourSystem = MySystem    'assigning all elements
```

- Applications create variables to store Single values. Most programs store sets of data of different types. For example, a program for balancing your checkbook must store several pieces of information for each check : the check's number, its amount, the date and so on. All these pieces of information are necessary to process the checks and ideally, they should be stored together.

- A structure for storing multiple values (of the same or different type) is called a *record*. For example, each check in a checkbook-balancing application is stored in a separate record, as shown below. When you recall a given check, you need all the information stored in the record.

Record Structure :

CheckNumber	CheckDate	CheckAmount
Array of Records		
240	04/12/97	104.25
245	04/12/97	48.76
248	04/14/97	200.00
290	04/21/97	430.00

- The declaration for the record structure shown below :
  ```
  Type CheckRecord
      CheckNumber As Integer
      CheckDate As Date
      CheckAmount As Single
  End Type
  ```
- User can think of the record as an object and its fields as properties. Here, are the assignments statements for a check :
  ```
  check2.CheckNumber = 240
  check2.CheckDate = #02/12/97#
  check2.CheckAmount = 104.25
  ```
- User can also create arrays of records with a statement such as the following :
  ```
  Dim Checks(100) As CheckRecord
  ```
- To access the fields of the third element of the array, use the following notation :
  ```
  Check(2).CheckNumber = 240
  Check(2).CheckDate = #04/12/97#
  Check(2).CheckAmount = 104.25
  ```
  Records are used frequently to read from and write to random access files.

2.3 VARIABLES (April, 10, 14)

- Variables are used to temporarily store values during the execution of an application.
- Variables have a name, (the word that is used to refer to the value the variable contains) and a data type, (which determines the kind of data the variable can store).
- For example, the student roll no, student's name these values are going to vary at each time. Thus, a variable can be used where value is not fixed.
- A variable is the named storage location that can contain data that can be modified during program execution.
- Each variable has a name that uniquely identifies it within its level of scope.

Storing and Retrieving Data in Variables

- Assignment statements can be used to perform calculations and assign the result to a variable :
  ```
  ApplesSold = 10     ' The value 10 is passed to the ' variable.
  ApplesSold = ApplesSold + 1   ' The variable is 'incremented.
  ```

2.3.1 Declaring Variables

- Declaration of a variable is being done with the **Dim** statement, supplying a name for the variable :

  Dim variablename [**As** type]

- Variables declared with the Dim statement within a procedure exist only as long as the procedure is executing. When the procedure finishes, the value of the variable disappears.
- Means these variables are local for that procedure — that is, a variable can not be accessed in one procedure from another procedure.
- These characteristics allow to use the same variable names in different procedures without worrying about conflicts or accidental changes.
- A variable name :
  - Must begin with a letter.
  - Can not contain an embedded period or embedded type-declaration character.
  - Must not exceed 255 characters.
  - Must be unique within the same *scope,* which is the range from which the variable can be referenced — a procedure, a form and so on.
- The optional As *type* clause in the Dim statement allows to define the data type or object type of the variable that are declaring.
- Data types define the type of information the variable stores. Some examples, of data types include String, Integer and Currency.
- Variables can also contain objects from Visual Basic or other applications.
- Examples of Visual Basic object types or classes, include Object, Form1, and TextBox. Such as text box always contains the String data type. So whenever, the value in the text box is used for calculation, then it has to be converted into integer with available conversion functions.
- There are other ways to declare variables :
  1. Declaring a variable in the Declarations section of a form, standard or class module, rather than within a procedure, makes the variable available to all the procedures in the module.
  2. Declaring a variable using the Public keyword makes it available throughout your application.
  3. Declaring a local variable using the Static keyword preserves its value even when a procedure ends.

2.3.2 Rules for Writing Variables

1. The first character must be alphabet. The remaining character may be alphabets or digits, underscore character (_).
2. The underscore character (_) must be embedded between characters.
3. Variable name cannot exceed 225 characters.
4. Keyboards that have special meaning such as **Sub**, **Print** and **End** cannot be used as names.
5. Case insensitive but all characters are significant.
   For example :   Base =   base = bAse = BASE
   　　　　　　　　Base ≠ Base1 ≠ Base_1

6. Mixed case is recommended while naming. First letter of the all words forming name to be capital.

   For example : `SumAll, MaxLimit`.
7. Visual Basic corrects case changes automatically.
8. Variable name must be unique within its scope.

2.3.3 Implicit Declaration

- There is no need to declare a variable before using it. For example, a below function is using a variable without declaring "TempVal" before using it :

```
Function SafeSqr(num)
    TempVal = Abs(num)
    SafeSqr = Sqr(TempVal)
End Function
```

- Visual Basic automatically creates a variable with that name. While this is convenient, it can lead to subtle errors in the code if misspell of a variable name. For example, suppose that this was the function you wrote :

```
Function SafeSqr(num)
    TempVal = Abs(num)
    SafeSqr = Sqr(TemVal)
End Function
```

- At first glance, this looks the same. But because the TempVal variable was misspelled on the next-to-last line, this function will always return zero. When Visual Basic encounters a new name, it can not determine whether it actually meant to implicitly declare a new variable, so it creates a new variable with that name.

2.3.4 Explicit Declaration

- To avoid the problem of misnaming variables, explicit declaration is being used.
- To explicitly declare variables : Place this statement in the Declarations section of a class, form, or standard module :

    `Option Explicit`

    – or –

- From the **Tools** menu, choose **Options**, click the **Editor** tab and check the **Require Variable Declaration** option. This automatically inserts the Option Explicit statement in any new modules, but not in modules already created; therefore, you must manually add Option Explicit to any existing modules within a project.
- Had this statement been in effect for the form or standard module containing the SafeSqr function, Visual Basic would have recognized `TempVal` and `TemVal` as undeclared variables and generated errors for both of them.

- The way it is explicitly declared `TempVal` as :
  ```
  Function SafeSqr(num)
      Dim TempVal
      TempVal = Abs(num)
      SafeSqr = Sqr(TemVal)
  End Function
  ```
- Now Visual Basic would display an error message for the incorrectly spelled `TemVal`. Because the Option Explicit statement helps to catch these kinds of errors, it's a good idea to use it with all the code.

> **Note :** The Option Explicit statement operates on a per-module basis; it must be placed in the Declarations section of every form, standard and class module for which Visual Basic to enforce explicit variable declarations. Option Explicit should be manually added to any existing modules within a project.

2.3.5 Scope of Variables
- The scope of a variable defines which parts of your code are aware of its existence.
- When you declare a variable within a procedure, only code within that procedure can access or change the value of that variable; it has a scope that is local to that procedure.
- Sometimes, however, you need to use a variable with a broader scope, such as one whose value is available to all the procedures within the same module, or even to all the procedures in your entire application. Visual Basic allows you to specify the scope of a variable when you declare it.

2.3.5.1 Scoping Variables
- Depending on how it is declared, a variable is scoped as either a procedure-level (local) or module-level variable.

Scope	Private	Public
Procedure-level	Variables are private to the procedure in which they appear.	Not applicable. You cannot declare public variables within a procedure.
Module-level	Variables are private to the module in which they appear.	Variables are available to all modules.

2.3.5.2 Variables Used Within a Procedure
- Procedure-level variables are recognized only in the procedure in which they are declared. These are also known as **local variables**.
- You declare them with the Dim or Static keywords. For example :
  ```
  Dim intTemp As Integer
  ```

– OR –
```
Static intPermanent As Integer
```
- Values in local variables declared with Static exist the entire time your application is running while variables declared with Dim exist only as long as the procedure is executing.
- Local variables are a good choice for any kind of temporary calculation. For example, you can create a dozen different procedures containing a variable called **intTemp**.
- As long as each `intTemp` is declared as a local variable, each procedure recognizes only its own version of `intTemp`.
- Any one procedure can alter the value in its local `intTemp` without affecting `intTemp` variables in other procedures.

2.3.5.3 Variables Used Within a Module

- By default, a module-level variable is available to all the procedures in that module, but not to code in other modules. You create module-level variables by declaring them with the Private keyword in the Declarations section at the top of the module. For example :
```
Private intTemp As Integer
```
- At the module level, there is no difference between Private and Dim, but Private is preferred because it readily contrasts with Public and makes your code easier to understand.

2.3.5.4 Variables Used by All Modules

- To make a module-level variable available to other modules, use the Public keyword to declare the variable. The values in public variables are available to all procedures in your application. Like all module-level variables, public variables are declared in the Declarations section at the top of the module. For example :
```
Public intTemp As Integer
```

2.4 OPERATORS (Oct. 13; April 14)

- In this chapter you will learn how to use variables to store data temporarily in your program and how to use mathematical operators to perform tasks such as addition and multiplication.
- You will also learn how to use mathematical functions to perform calculations involving numbers. This chapter also gives the clear idea of visual basic constant and expressions.

2.4.1 Uses of Operators

- An operation is an action performed on one or more values either to modify one value or to produce a new value by combining existing value.
- Therefore, an operation is performed using at least one symbol and one value.
- The symbol used in an operation is called an operator.
- A variable or a value involved in an operation is called an operand.

1. Arithmetical Operators :

Operators	Description	Example	Result
+	Add	5+5	10
−	Substract	10-5	5
/	Divide	25/5	5
\	Integer Division	20\3	6
*	Multiply	5*4	20
^	Exponent (power of)	3^3	27
Mod	Remainder of division	20 Mod 6	2
&	String concatenation	"Amar"&" "&"Salunke"	"Amar Salunke"

2. Relational Operators :

Operators	Description	Example	Result
>	Greater than	10>8	True
<	Less than	10<8	False
>=	Greater than or equal to	20>=10	True
<=	Less than or equal to	10<=20	True
<>	Not Equal to	5<>4	True
=	Equal to	5=7	False

3. Logical Operators :

Operators	Description
OR	Operation will be true if either of the operands is true
AND	Operation will be true only if both the operands are true

I. Arithmetic Operators :

(a) Addition + Operator :

The addition is performed with the + sign. It is used to add one value to another. To add two numbers, such as 225 and 64, you could use 225 + 64. The result would be 289. + operator used to sum two numbers.

Syntax :

```
result = number1 + number2
```

The + operator syntax has following parts :

Part	Description
result	Required; any numeric variable.
number1	Required; any numeric expression.
number2	Required; any numeric expression.

The addition is also used to add the values of two variables. For example, you could use CDbl(txtMondayHours) + CDbl(txtTuesdayHours) to get a total number of hours worked on Monday and Tuesday. The result could be stored in another control.

1. Consider the following table :

Control	Caption	Name
Label	First Name:	
TextBox		txtOperand1
Label	Last Name:	
TextBox		txtOperand2
CommandButton	Addition	cmdAddition
Label	Result:	
TextBox		txtResult

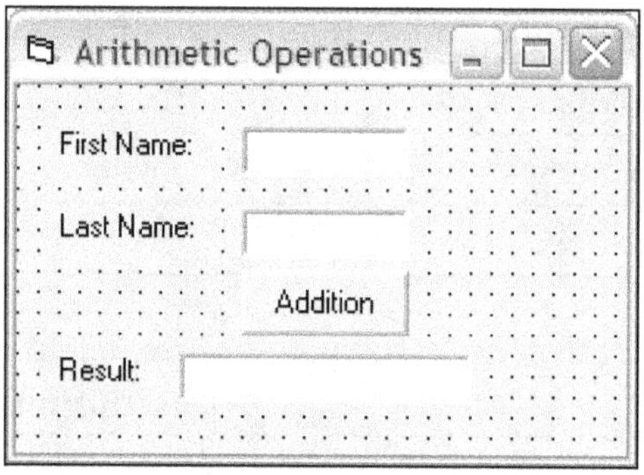

Fig. 2.1

2. Double-click the Addition button and change its code as follows : (April 10)

```
Private Sub cmdAddition_Click()
   Dim dblOperand1 As String
   Dim dblOperand2 As String
   Dim dblResult As String
   dblOperand1 = txtOperand1
   dblOperand2 = txtOperand2
   dblResult = dblOperand1 + " " + dblOperand2
   txtResult = dblResult
End Sub
```

3. Test the application. Enter a name one the First Name text box and another name in the Last Name text box then click Addition.

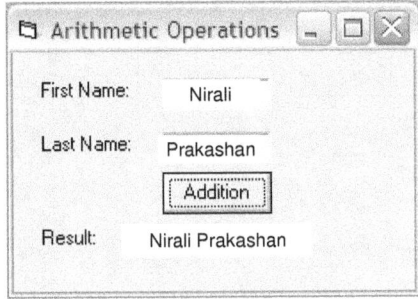

Fig. 2.2

4. After using the form, close it.

(b) Subtraction – Operator :

The subtraction operation is performed using the – sign. This operation produces the difference of two or more numbers. It could also be used to display a number as a negative value. To subtract 28 from 65, you express this with 65 – 28. The subtraction can also be used to subtract the values of two values.

Operator used to find the difference between tow numbers or to indicate the negative value of a numeric expression.

Syntax 1 :
```
result = number1 - number2
```
Syntax 2 :
```
- number
```
The – operator syntax has these parts :

Part	Description
result	Required; any numeric variable.
number	Required; any numeric expression.
number1	Required; any numeric expression.
number2	Required; any numeric expression.

In syntax 1, the – operator is the arithmetic subtraction operator used to find the difference between two numbers. In syntax 2, the – operator is used as the unary negation operator to indicate the negative value of an expression.

1. Change the design of the form as follows :

Control	Caption	Name
Label	Number 1:	
TextBox		txtOperand1
Label	Number 2:	

TextBox		txtOperand2
CommandButton	Subtraction	cmdSubtraction
Label	Result:	
TextBox		txtResult

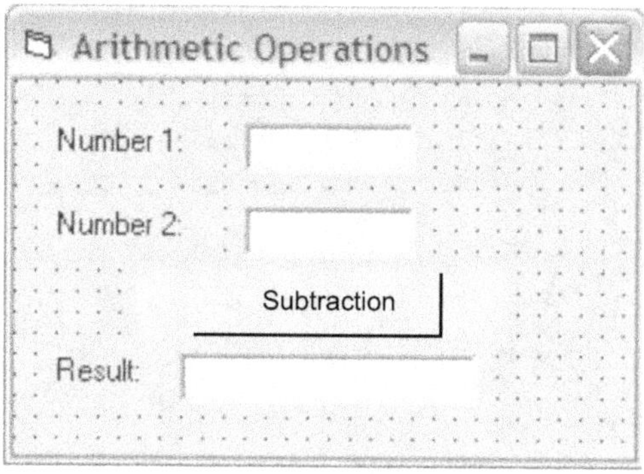

Fig. 2.3

2. Double-click the Subtraction button and change its code as follows :

```
Private Sub cmdSubtration_Click()                              (April 10)
    Dim dblOperand1 As Double
    Dim dblOperand2 As Double
    Dim dblResult   As Double
    dblOperand1 = txtOperand1
    dblOperand2 = txtOperand2
    dblResult = dblOperand1 - dblOperand2
    txtResult = dblResult
End Sub
```

3. Test the application. Enter a number one the Number text box and another number in the Number text box then click Subtraction

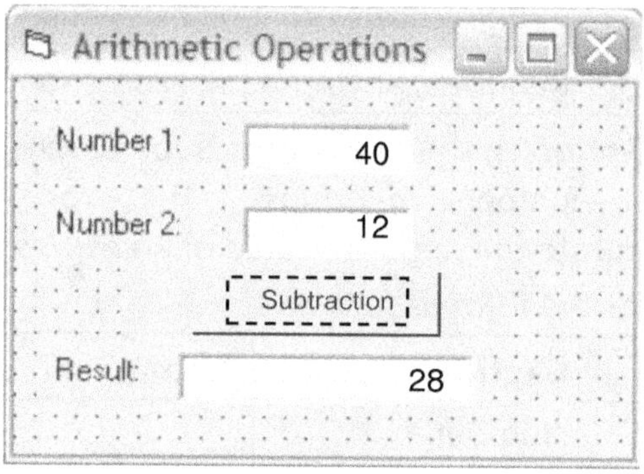

Fig. 2.4

4. After using the form, close it.

(c) Multiplication * operator

The multiplication operation allows you to add a number to itself a certain number of times set by another number. The multiplication operation is performed using the * sign. For example, to add 25 to itself 3 times, you would perform the operation as 25 * 3.

*Operator used to multiplication two numbers.

Syntax :
```
result = number1* number2
```
The *operator syntax has these parts :

Part	Description
result	Required; any numeric variable.
number1	Required; any numeric expression.
number2	Required; any numeric expression.

1. Add a new CommandButton as Multiplication.
2. Change its Name to cmdMultiplication and its Caption to Multiplication.

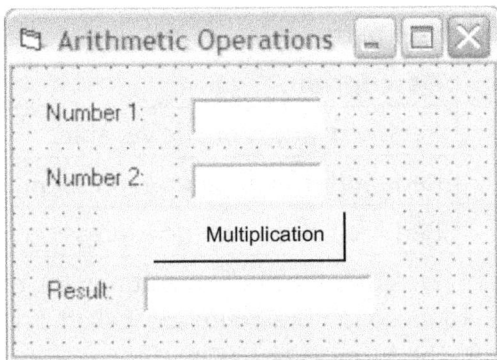

Fig. 2.5

3. Double-click the Multiplication button and change its code as follows : **(April 10)**

```
Private Sub cmdMultiplication_Click()
    Dim dblOperand1 As Double
    Dim dblOperand2 As Double
    Dim dblResult   As Double
    dblOperand1 = txtOperand1
    dblOperand2 = txtOperand2
    blResult = dblOperand1 * dblOperand2
    txtResult = dblResult
End Sub
```

4. Test the application. Enter a number one the Number text box and another number in the Number text box then click Multiplication

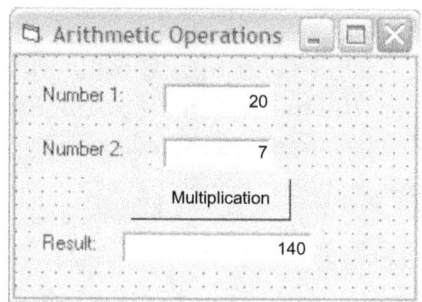

Fig. 2.6

5. After using the form, close it

(d) Integer Division \ Operator :

Dividing an item means cutting it in pieces or fractions of a set value. Therefore, the division is used to get the fraction of one number in terms of another. Operator used to divide two numbers and return an integer result.

Syntax :

```
result = number1\number2
```

The \ operator syntax has these parts :

Part	Description
result	Required; any numeric variable.
number1	Required; any numeric expression.
number2	Required; any numeric expression.

Microsoft Visual Basic provides two types of operations for the division. If you want the result of the operation to be a natural number, called an integer, use the backlash operator "\" as the divisor. The formula to use is :

```
Value1 \ Value2
```

This operation can be performed on two types of valid numbers, with or without decimal parts. After the operation, the result would be a natural number.

Create CommandButton for division operation.

Change its Name to cmdDivision and its Caption to Division.

Fig. 2.7

3. Double-click the Division button and change its code as follows :

```
Private Sub cmdDivision_Click()
    Dim dblOperand1 As Double
    Dim dblOperand2 As Double
    Dim dblResult   As Double
    dblOperand1 = txtOperand1
    dblOperand2 = txtOperand2
    dblResult = dblOperand1 \ dblOperand2
    txtResult = dblResult
End Sub
```

4. Test the application. Enter a number one the Number text box and another number in the Number text box then click Division

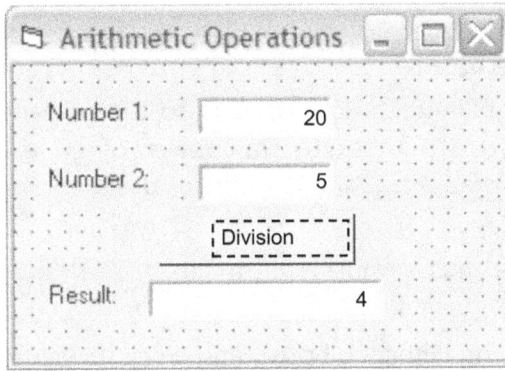

Fig. 2.8

5. After using the form, close it.

(e) Decimal Division / Operator :

The second type of division results in a decimal number. It is performed with the forward slash "/". Its formula is :

```
Value1 / Value2
```

Operator used to divide two numbers and returns a floating-point result.

Syntax :

```
result = number1/number2
```

The /operator syntax has these parts :

Part	Description
result	Required; any numeric variable.
number1	Required; any numeric expression.
number2	Required; any numeric expression.

After the operation is performed, the result is a decimal number.

For example :

```
Private Sub cmdDivision_Click()
    Dim dblOperand1 As Double
    Dim dblOperand2 As Double
    Dim dblResult   As Double

    dblOperand1 = txtOperand1
    dblOperand2 = txtOperand2
    dblResult = dblOperand1 / dblOperand2

    txtResult = dblResult
End Sub
```

(f) Exponentiation ^ Operator :

Exponentiation is the ability to raise a number to the power of another number. ^ Operator used to raise a number to the power of an exponent. This operation is performed using the ^ operator (Shift + 6). It uses the following formula :

$$y^x$$

In Microsoft Visual Basic, this formula is written as :

$$y\text{^}x$$

and means the same thing. Either or both y and x can be values, variables, or expressions, but they must carry valid values that can be evaluated. When the operation is performed, the value of y is raised to the power of x.

Syntax :

```
result = number^exponent
```

The ^ operator syntax has these parts :

Part	Description
result	Required; any numeric variable.
number	Required; any numeric expression.
exponent	Required; any numeric expression.

1. To start a new application, on the main menu, click File → New Project...
2. In the New Project dialog box, double-click Standard EXE
3. To save the project, on the main menu, click File → Save Project
4. Click the Create New Folder button. Type **Exponentiation** and press Enter twice to display it in the Save In combo box
5. Click Save twice to save the form and the project

6. Using the controls on the Toolbox, design the form as follows :

Control	Caption	Name
Label	This number:	
TextBox		txtNumber
Label	to the power of	
TextBox		txtPower
CommandButton	is	cmdCalculate
TextBox		txtResult

Fig. 2.9

7. Double-click the is button and implement its event as follows :

```
Option Explicit
Private Sub cmdCalculate_Click()
      Dim dblNumber As Double
      Dim dblPower As Double
      Dim dblResult As Double
      dblNumber = txtNumber
      dblPower = txtPower
      dblResult = dblNumber ^ dblPower
      txtResult = dblResult
End Sub
```

8. Press F5 to test the application. Enter two numbers in the left two text boxes and click the is button

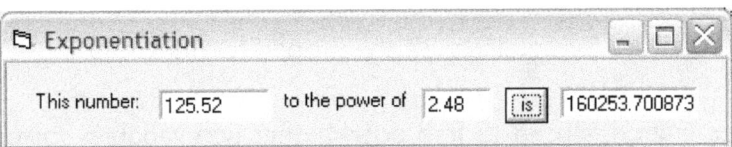

Fig. 2.10

9. After using it, close the form

(g) Mod Operator :

Mod Operator used to divide two numbers and return only the remainder.

Syntax :

```
result = number1 Mod number2
```

The Mod operator syntax has these parts :

Part	Description
result	Required; any numeric variable.
number1	Required; any numeric expression.
number2	Required; any numeric expression.

(II) Relational Operators :

Sometimes, while a person is using your program, you may need to check whether something is true or it is false. This type of operation is performed using operators referred to as comparison operators. Visual basic provides various operators that can be used in appropriate types of comparisons.

Syntax :

```
result = expressional comparisonoperator expression2
result = object1 Is object2
result = string Like pattern
```

Part	Description
result	Required; any numeric variable.
expression	Required; any expression.
comparisonoperator	Required; any comparison operator.
object	Required; any object name.
string	Required; any string expression.
pattern	Required; any string expression or range of characters.

(a) Equality = Operator

To compare two values for equality, use the = operator. Its syntax is :

```
Value1 = Value2
```

The equality operation is used to find out whether two variables (or one variable and a constant) hold the same value. From our formula, the compiler would compare the value of Value1 with that of Value2. If Value1 and Value2 hold the same value, the comparison produces a true result. If they are different, the comparison renders false or 0.

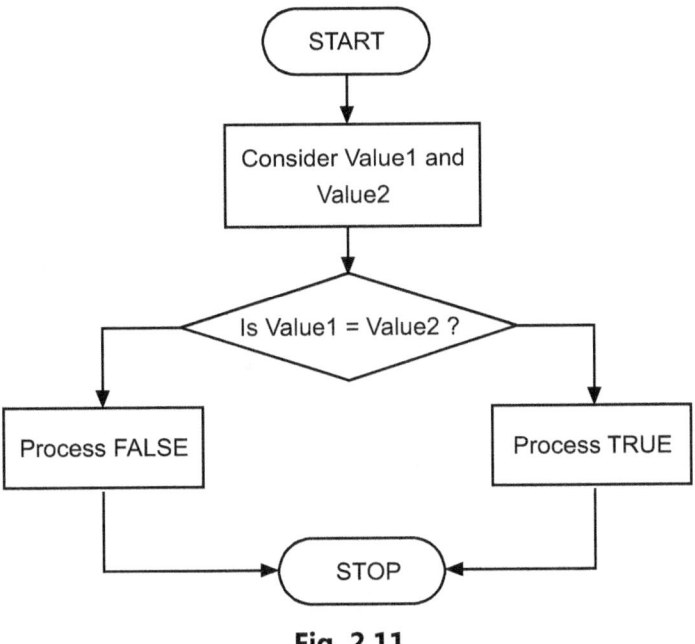

Fig. 2.11

For example :
```
Private Sub Command1_Click()
   Dim value As Integer
   value = 15
   Text1.Text = "Comparison of Value=32 produces"&(value=32)
End Sub
```

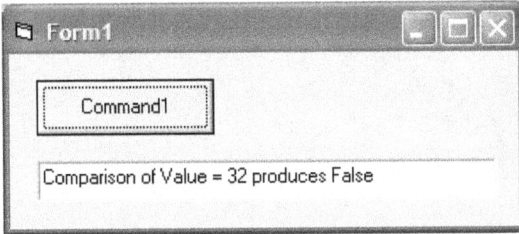

Fig. 2.12

The result of a comparison can also be assigned to a Boolean variable. Here is an example :
```
Private Sub Command1_Click()
   Dim value1 As Integer
   Dim value2 As Boolean
   value1 = 15
   value2 = (value1 = 32)
   Text1.Text = "Comparison of Value = 32 produces " & value2
End Sub
```

(b) Inequality <> operator :

Visual Basic provides an operator used to compare two values for inequality. Its syntax is :

```
Value1 <> Value2
```

<> is a binary operator (like all logical operators except the logical **NOT**, which is a unary operator) that is used to compare two values. The values can come from two variables as in Variable1 <> Variable2. Upon comparing the values, if both variables hold different values, the comparison produces a true or positive value. Otherwise, the comparison renders false or a null value.

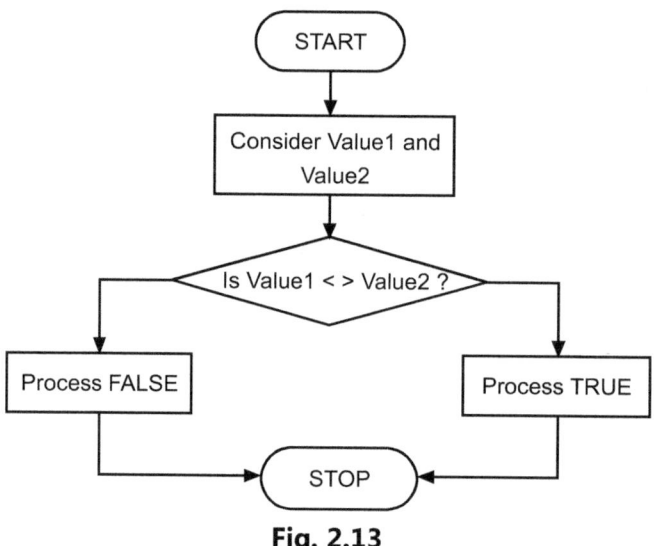

Fig. 2.13

For Example :

```
Private Sub Command1_Click()
   Dim value1 As Integer
   Dim value2 As Integer
   Dim value3 As Boolean
   value1 = 212
   value2 = -46
   value3 = (value1 <> value2)
   Text1.Text = value1 & " <> " & value2 & " = " & value3
End Sub
```

Output :

Fig. 2.14

The inequality is obviously the opposite of the equality.

(c) Less Than < operator :

To find out whether one value is lower than another, use the < operator. Its syntax is :

```
Value1 < Value2
```

The value held by Value1 is compared to that of Value2. As it would be done with other operations, the comparison can be made between two variables, as in Variable1 < Variable2. If the value held by Variable1 is lower than that of Variable2, the comparison produces a true or positive result.

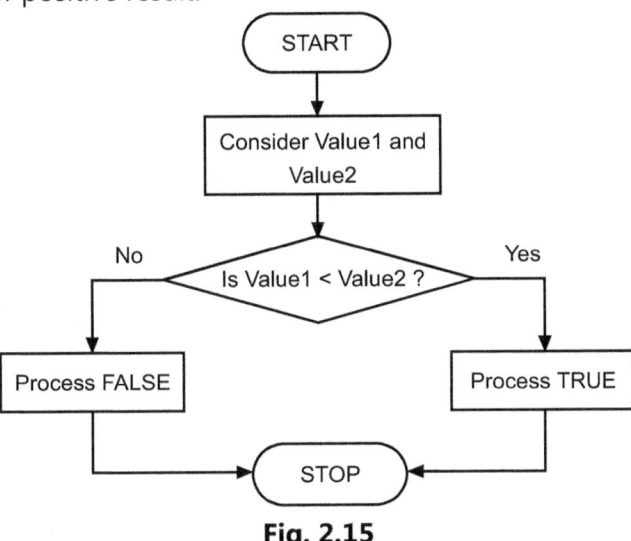

Fig. 2.15

For example :

```
Private Sub Command1_Click()
    Dim value1 As Integer
    Dim value2 As Integer
    Dim value3 As Boolean
    value1 = 212
    value2 = -46
    value3 = (value1 < value2)
    Text1.Text = value1 & " < " & value2 & " = " & value3
End Sub
```

Output :

Fig. 2.16

(d) Less Than Or Equal <= Operator :

The previous two operations can be combined to compare two values. This allows you to know if two values are the same or if the first is less than the second. The operator used is <= and its syntax is :

```
Value1 <= Value2
```

The <= operation performs a comparison as any of the last two. If both Value1 and Value2 hold the same value, the result is true or not null. If the left operand, in this case Value1, holds a value lower than the second operand, in this case Value2, the result is still true.

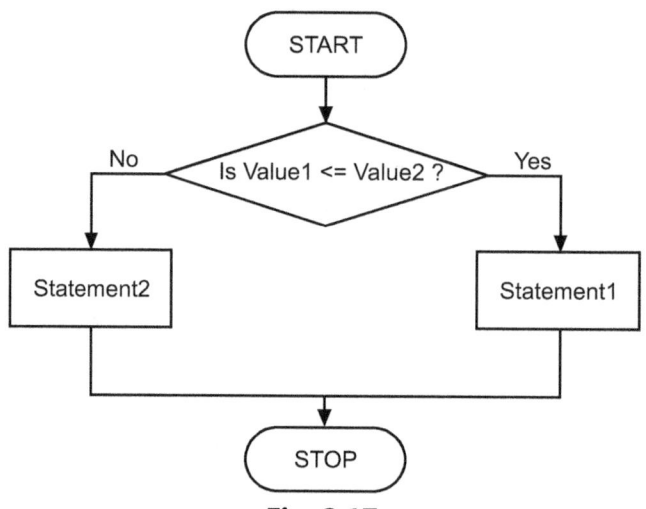

Fig. 2.17

For example :

```
Private Sub Command1_Click()
    Dim value1 As Integer
    Dim value2 As Integer
    Dim value3 As Boolean
    value1 = 212
    value2 = -46
    value3 = (value1 <= value2)
    Text1.Text = value1 & " <= " & value2 & " = " & value3
End Sub
```

Output :

Fig. 2.18

(e) Greater Than > Operator :

When two values of the same type are distinct, one of them is usually higher than the other. Visual Basic provides a logical operator that allows you to find out if one of two values is greater than the other. The operator used for this operation uses the > symbol. Its syntax is :

```
Value1 > Value2
```

Both operands, in this case Value1 and Value2, can be variables or the left operand can be a variable while the right operand is a constant. If the value on the left of the > operator is greater than the value on the right side or a constant, the comparison produces a true or positive value. Otherwise, the comparison renders false or null. This can be illustrated as follows :

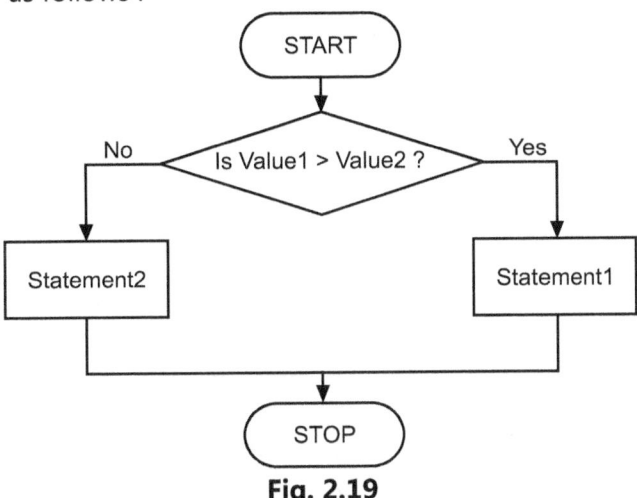

Fig. 2.19

For example :

```
Private Sub Command1_Click()
    Dim value1 As Integer
    Dim value2 As Integer
    Dim value3 As Boolean
    value1 = 212
    value2 = -46
    value3 = (value1 > value2)
    Text1.Text = value1 & " > " & value2 & " = " & value3
End Sub
```

Output :

```
212 > -46 = True
```

Fig. 2.20

(f) Greater Than or Equal >= Operator :

The greater than or the equality operators can be combined to produce an operator as >=. This is the "greater than or equal to" operator. Its syntax is :

```
Value1 >= Value2
```

A comparison is performed on both operands i.e. Value1 and Value2. If the value of Value1 and that of Value2 are the same, the comparison produces a true or positive value. If the value of the left operand is greater than that of the right operand, the comparison produces true or positive also. If the value of the left operand is strictly less than the value of the right operand, the comparison produces a false or null result. This can be illustrated as follows :

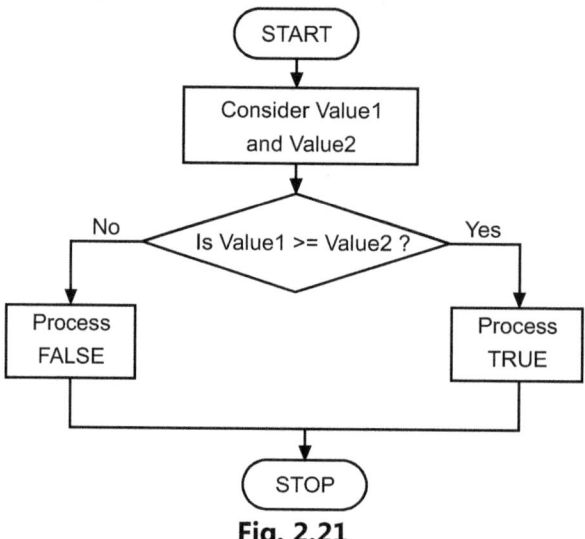

Fig. 2.21

For example :

```
Private Sub Command1_Click( )
   Dim value1 As Integer
   Dim value2 As Integer
   Dim value3 As Boolean
   value1 = 212
   value2 = -46
   value3 = (value1 >= value2)
   Text1.Text = value1 & " >= " & value2 & "produces" & value3
End Sub
```

Output:

Fig. 2.22

(g) Is Operator :

This used to compare two object reference variables.

Syntax :

```
result = object1 Is object2
```

The **Is** operator syntax has these parts :

Part	Description
result	Required; any numeric variable.
object1	Required; any object name.
object2	Required; any object name.

Remarks : If object1 and object2 both refer to the same object, result is **True**; if they do not, result is **False**. Two variables can be made to refer to the same object in several ways.

In the following example, A has been set to refer to the same object as B :

```
Set A = B
```

The following example makes A and B refer to the same object as C :

```
Set A = C
Set B = C
```

(h) Like Operator

This operator is used to compare two strings.

Syntax :

```
result = string Like pattern
```

The **Like** operator syntax has these parts :

Part	Description
result	Required; any numeric **variable**.
string	Required; any **string expression**.
pattern	Required; any string expression conforming to the pattern-matching conventions described in Remarks.

(III) Logical Operators :

A logical operation is one that is performed on one or two expressions to check the truthfulness or falsity. Logical operators are performed only on conditional statements.

(a) AND Operator :

A logical conjunction is an operation used to check two conditions for absolute truthfulness. This operation uses the **AND** keyword. The syntax to use the **AND** operator is :

```
Condition1 AND Condition2
```

The left condition, Condition1, is first checked. If it is False, the whole expression is rendered False and the checking process stopped. If the left condition is True, then the right condition, Condition2, is checked. If the right condition is False, the whole expression is False, even if the first is True. In the same way, if both conditions are false, the whole expression is False. Only if both conditions are True is the whole condition true. This can be resumed as follows :

Condition1	Condition2	Condition1 AND Condition2
False	Don't Care	False
Don't Care	False	False
True	True	True

(b) OR Operator :

A logical disjunction is performed on two conditions for a single truthfulness. This operation uses the OR keyword on the following syntax :

```
Condition1 OR Condition2
```

The left condition, Condition1, is first checked. If Condition1 is True, then the whole expression is true, regardless of the outcome of the second. If Condition1 is False, then Condition2 is checked. If Condition2 is True, the whole expression is True even if Condition1 is False. In the same way, if both conditions are True, the whole expression is True. The whole expression is false only if both Condition1 and Condition2 are False. This can be resumed as follows :

Condition1	Condition2	Condition1 OR Condition2
True	Don't Care	True
Don't Care	True	True
True	True	True
False	False	False

(c) NOT Operator :

When a variable is declared and receives a value, (this could be done through initialization or a change of value) in a program, it becomes alive. It can then participate in any necessary operation. The compiler keeps track of every variable that exists in the program being processed. When a variable is not being used or is not available for processing, (in visual programming, it would be considered as disabled) to make a variable, (temporarily) unusable, you can nullify its value. To render a variable unavailable during the evolution of a program, apply the logical not operator which is NOT.

Its syntax is :

```
NOT Value
```

There are two main ways you can use the logical NOT operator. As we will learn when studying conditional statements, the most classic way of using the logical NOT operator is to check the state of a variable.

To nullify a variable, you can write NOT to its left. When used like that, you can display its value. You can even assign it to another variable. Here is an example :

```
Private Sub Command1_Click()
    Dim value1 As Integer
    Dim value2 As Boolean
    value1 = 250
    value2 = Not value1
    Text1.Text = value2
End Sub
```

When a variable holds a value, it is "alive". To make it not available, you can "not" it. When a variable has been "notted", its logical value has changed. Therefore, you can inverse the logical value of a variable by "notting" or not "notting" it. This is done by typing Not to its left.

2.4.2 Operator Precedence

- When several operations occur in an expression, each part is evaluated and resolved in a predetermined order called operator precedence.
- When expressions contain operators from more than one category, arithmetic operators are evaluated first, comparison operators are evaluated next, and logical operators are evaluated last.
- Comparison operators all have equal precedence; that is, they are evaluated in the left-to-right order in which they appear.
- Arithmetic and logical operators are evaluated in the following order of precedence :

Arithmetic	**Comparison**	**Logical**
Exponentiation (^)	Equality (=)	NOT
Negation (−)	Inequality (<>)	AND
Multiplication and division (*, /)	Less than (<)	OR
Integer division (\)	Greater than (>)	XOR
Modulus arithmetic (**Mod**)	Less than or equal to (<=)	Equi
Addition and subtraction (+, −)	Greater than or equal to (>=)	Imp
String concatenation (&)	**Like**	
	Is	

- When multiplication and division occur together in an expression, each operation is evaluated as it occurs from left to right.
- When addition and subtraction occur together in an expression, each operation is evaluated in order of appearance from left to right.
- Parentheses can be used to override the order of precedence and force some parts of an expression to be evaluated before others.
- Operations within parentheses are always performed before those outside. Within parentheses, however, operator precedence is maintained.
- The string concatenation operator (**&**) is not an arithmetic operator, but in precedence, it does follow all arithmetic operators and precede all comparison operators.
- The **Like** operator is equal in precedence to all comparison operators, but is actually a pattern-matching operator. The **Is** operator is an object reference comparison operator. It does not compare objects or their values; it checks only to determine if two object references refer to the same object.

2.5 CONTROL STRUCTURES

- The flow of the program during execution is not always sequential only. It is a combination of the following :
    1. **Sequential :** Sequential execution of statements from top to bottom.
    2. **Decision :** Selecting a particular block of statements.
    3. **Iteration/Repetition :** Repetitive execution of a block of statements.
- Control structures allows us to control the flow of our program's execution. Control structures are statements controlling decisions and loops.
- The control structures define flow of a program.

2.5.1 If...Then Statement (Oct. 12)

- The If...Then statement performs an indicated action only when the condition is True; otherwise the action is skipped.
- Syntax of the If...Then statement,

    ```
    If <condition> Then
    statement
    End If
    ```

    For example :

    ```
    If average>75 Then
    txtGrade.Text = "A"
    End If
    ```

    1. In the Code Editor, click the arrow of the Object combo box and select Form.
    2. Click the arrow of the Procedure combo box and select Click.

3. Implement the events as follows :
```
Private Sub Form_Click()
  If BackColor = vbRed Then BackColor = vbBlue
       End Sub
 Private Sub Form_Load()
       BackColor = vbRed
       End Sub
```
4. Press F5 to test the application.
5. Click somewhere in the form to change its color.
6. After using the form, close it and return to MSVB.

1. To use the new expression, change the form's Click event as follows :
```
Private Sub Form_Click()
    If BackColor = vbRed Then
        BackColor = vbBlue
    ElseIf BackColor = vbBlue Then
        BackColor = vbGreen
    ElseIf BackColor = vbGreen Then
        BackColor = vbBlack
    Else
        BackColor = vbRed
    End If
End Sub
```
2. Test the application
3. Close it and return to MSVB.

2.5.2 If...Then...Else Statement (Oct. 10, 11; April 10)

- The If...Then...Else statement allows the programmer to specify that a different action is to be performed when the condition is True than when the condition is False.
- Syntax of the If...Then...Else statement are given below :
    ```
    If <condition > Then
    statements
    Else
    statements
    End If
    ```

For example :
```
If average>50 Then
txtGrade.Text = "Pass"
Else
txtGrade.Text = "Fail"
End If
```

- To use the new condition, change the form's Click event as follows :
  ```
  Private Sub Form_Click( )
         If BackColor = vbRed Then
            BackColor = vbBlue
        Else
           BackColor = vbRed
          End If
     End Sub
  ```
- Press F5 to test the application.
- Click the form a few times to change its color.
- Close the form and return to MSVB.

2.5.3 Nested If...Then...Else Statement

- Nested If...Then...Else statement test for multiple cases by placing If...Then...Else selection structures inside If...Then...Else structures.
- You can use Nested If either of the methods as shown below :

Method 1 :
```
If < condition 1 > Then
statements
ElseIf < condition 2 > Then
statements
ElseIf < condition 3 > Then
statements
Else
Statements
End If
```

Method 2 :
```
If < condition 1 > Then
statements
Else
If < condition 2 > Then
statements
Else
If < condition 3 > Then
statements
Else
Statements
End If
End If
EndIf
```

For example : Assume you have to find the grade using nested if and display in a text box

```
If average > 75 Then
txtGrade.Text = "A"
ElseIf average > 65 Then
txtGrade.Text = "B"
ElseIf average > 55 Then
txtGrade.text = "C"
ElseIf average > 45 Then
txtGrade.Text = "S"
Else
txtGrade.Text = "F"
End If
```

2.5.4 Select...Case Statement

- Select...Case structure is an alternative to If...Then...Else If for selectively executing a single block of statements from among multiple block of statements. Select...Case is more convenient to use than the If...Else...End If.
- The following program block illustrate the working of Select...Case.
- Syntax of the Select...Case selection structure Statements is given below :
  ```
  Select Case Index
  Case 0
  Statements
  Case 1
  Statements
  End Select
  ```
- **For example :** Assume you have to find the grade using select...case and display in the text box.

```
Dim average as Integer
average = txtAverage.Text
Select Case average
Case 100 To 75
txtGrade.Text ="A"
Case 74 To 65
txtGrade.Text ="B"
Case 64 To 55
txtGrade.Text ="C"
Case 54 To 45
txtGrade.Text ="S"
Case 44 To 0
txtGrade.Text ="F"
Case Else
MsgBox "Invalid average marks"
End Select
```

Program 3.1 : To use a Select ......case Statement.

```
Private Sub Form_Click()
   Select Case BackColor
  Case vbRed
           BackColor = vbBlue
      Case vbBlue
           BackColor = vbGreen
   Case vbGreen
           BackColor = vbBlack
     Case Else
        BackColor = vbRed
   End Select
End Sub
```

- Some case statements can be followed by multiple values, which are separated by commas.

    For example,

    Select Case WeekDay (Date)

        Case 1, 2, 3, 4, 5

            Message "Working Days"

        Case 6, 7

            Message "Holiday"

- In the above example, there is no Case Else statement because all values are examined in the Case Statements. If number values are more than one, (continuous range), they are to be separated by - symbol.

    For example,
    ```
    Select Case WeekDay (Date)
       Case 1 - 5
    ```
            Message "Working Days"

        Case 6 - 7
    ```
        Message "Holiday" End Select
    ```

> **Note :** If more than one case value matches the expression, only the statement block associated with the first matching case executes.

2.6 LOOPING   (April, 10, 11, 12; Oct. 10, 11, 12, 13)

- The loop statements allow us to execute a piece of code (one or more lines) repetitively.
- The number of repetitions could be definite (specific) or indefinite.
- The loop structures that Visual Basic supports are :
    1. Do .... Loop
    2. For .... Next
    3. For Each .... Next
    4. While .... Wend

2.6.1 Do .... Loop

- If a particular code is to be executed number of times and number of repetitions are not known (indefinite), you can use **Do .... Loop** statement. Number of repetitions are decided by the state of a condition.
- There are several variants of **Do .... Loop.**

   Syntax :
   ```
   Do
       statements
   Loop
   ```
- Number of repetitions are truly indefinite. The only way to come out of a loop is to use **Exit Do** inside loop.

   For example :
   ```
   Do
       sum = sum + i
       Exit Do
   Loop
   ```

2.6.2 Do While .... Loop / Do Until ...... Loop

- The **Do** loop executes a block of statements for as long as a condition is **True**. Visual Basic evaluates, an expression, and if it's True, the statements are executed.

If the expression is not True, the program continues, and the statement following the loop is executed.

Syntax for Do While ...... Loop :
```
Do While ......condition
    statement-block
Loop
```

Syntax for Do Until ...... Loop :
```
Do Until  condition
    statement-block
Loop
```

- The loop is executed either **while** the condition is **True** or **Until** the condition becomes **True.** If the condition is False, the Do While or Do Until loop is skipped.
- When the Loop statement is reached, Visual Basic evaluates the expression again and repeats the statement-block of the Do While loop if the expression is True or repeats the statements of the Do Until loop if the expression is False.

For example :
```
1.  Do While i < 10
        sum = sum + i
    Loop
    Debug . Print sum
2.  Do Until counter < 30
        counter = counter + 2
    Loop
```

2.6.3 Do ...... Loop While / Do ...... Loop Until

- The **Do** loop executes the statements first and evaluates the condition after each execution.
- The syntax of **Do** Loop While :
    ```
    Do
        statements
    Loop While condition
    ```
- The syntax of Do Loop .... Until as,
    ```
    Do
        statements
    Loop Until condition
    ```
- The statements in this type of loop executes at least once, since the condition is examined at the end of the loop.

    For example :
    ```
            Do
    counter = counter + 1
    while counter < 15
    ```

2.6.4 For ...... Next Loop

- If you want to execute a particular code specific/number of times, you can use **For..... Next** loop.
- The For ..... Next loop uses a variable (it's called the loop's counter) that increases or decreases in value during each repetition of the loop.

    Syntax :

    For counter = start, To End [Step increment]

    statements
    ```
    Next [counter]
    ```
- The arguments counter, start end and increment are all numeric. The argument increment can be either positive or negative.
- To execute the statements in For ...... Next loop,
    1. If increment is positive, start must be less than or equal to end.
    2. If increment is negative, start must be greater than or equal to end.
       If step is not set, then increment defaults to 1.
    3. Sets counter equal to start.
    4. Tests to see if counter is greater than end. If so, it exits the loop. If increment is negative, Visual Basic tests to see if counter is less than end, in which case it exits the loop.
    3. Executes the statements in the block.
    4. Increments counter by the amount specified with the increment argument. If the increment argument is not specified, counter is incremented by 1.

5. Repeats the statements.
   For example :
   ```
   For i = 0 To 10
   Debug. Print i
            i=i+1
   Next i
   ```
- Finally, the counter variable need not be listed after the Next statement, but it makes the code easier to read, especially when For .... Next loops are nested within each other.
   ```
   Dim intLoopIndex, Total
   Total = 0
   For intLoopIndex = 1 to 10
      Total = Total + 1
   Next intLoopIndex
   ```

2.6.5 For Each......Next Loop
- A For Each.....Next Loop is similar to For Next loop. It repeats a group of statements for each element in a collection of objects or an array.
- This is especially useful if you do not know how many elements are there is a collection.

   Syntax :
   ```
   For Each element In Group
       statements
   Next elements
   ```

   For example :
   ```
   Dim ObjDb As Database
   Set ObjDb = OpenDatabase("c:\vb\biblio.mdb",True, False)
   For Each TableDef In ObjDb.Table Defs
   ```
   List1.AddItem TableDef.Name
   Next TableDef.

2.6.6 While .....Loop / While .....Wend Loop
- The While .....Wend loop executes a block of statements while a condition is True.
- The While .... Wend loop has the following syntax :
   ```
   While condition
       statement
   wend
   ```
- If condition is True, all statements are executed, and when the Wend statement is reached, control is returned to the While statement, which evaluates condition again. If

condition is still True, the process is repeated. If condition is False, the program resumes with the statement following the **Wend statement.**

For example :
```
number = 0
While number = 0
    total = total + number
            number = InputBox ("Enter another value")
Wend
```

```
Dim intInput
IntInput = -1

while intInput < 0
    intInput = InputBox ("Enter a positive number")
Wend
```

2.6.7 Exit Statement

- The Exit statement allows you to exit directly from a control structure, a sub procedure, or a function procedure.

    Syntax is,

    1. `Exit For`

        for a For loop

    2. `Exit Do`

        for a Do loop

    3. `Exit Sub`

        for a Sub procedure

    4. `Exit Function`

        for a Function procedure.

- Suppose you have a For.....Next loop that calculates the square root of a series of numbers. Because the square root of negative numbers can not be calculated.

    For example :
```
        For    i = 0 To Ubound (nArray( ) )
            If nArray (i) < 0 Then
            Exit For
            nArray(i)=sqr (nArray (i))
            Next
```

- If a negative element is found in this loop, the program exits the loop and continues with the statement following the Next statement.

2.7 ARRAY (Oct. 11)

- Arrays allow to refer to a series of variables by the same name and to use a number (an index) to tell them apart.
- Arrays have both upper and lower bounds, and the elements of the array are contiguous within those bounds. Because Visual Basic allocates space for each index number, avoid declaring an array larger than necessary.
- All the elements in an array have the same data type. Of course, when the data type is Variant, the individual elements may contain different kinds of data (objects, strings, numbers, and so on).
- In Visual Basic there are two types of arrays : a **fixed-size array** which always remains the same size, and a **dynamic array** whose size can change at run-time.

Declaring Fixed-Size Arrays

- There are three ways to declare a fixed-size array :
   1. To create a **public array**, use the Public statement in the Declarations section of a module to declare the array.
   2. To create a **module-level array**, use the Private statement in the Declarations section of a module to declare the array.
   3. To create a **local array**, use the Private statement in a procedure to declare the array.

Setting Upper and Lower Bounds

- When declaring an array, follow the array name by the upper bound in parentheses. The upper bound cannot exceed the range of a Long data type (–2,147,483,648 to 2,147,483,647).

    For example, these array declarations can appear in the Declarations section of a module:
    ```
    Dim Counters(14) As Integer    ' 15 elements.
    Dim Sums(20) As Double         ' 21 elements.
    ```
- To create a public array, simply use Public in place of Dim :
    ```
    Public Counters(14) As Integer
    Public Sums(20) As Double
    ```
- The same declarations within a procedure use Dim :
    ```
    Dim Counters(14) As Integer
    Dim Sums(20) As Double
    ```
- The first declaration creates an array with 15 elements, with index numbers running from 0 to 14. The second creates an array with 21 elements, with index numbers running from 0 to 20. The default lower bound is 0.
- To specify a lower bound, provide it explicitly (as a Long data type) using the To keyword :

```
Dim Counters(1 To 15) As Integer
Dim Sums(100 To 120) As String
```
- In the preceding declarations, the index numbers of `Counters` range from 1 to 15, and the index numbers of `Sums` range from 100 to 120.

Arrays that Contain Other Arrays

- It's possible to create a Variant array and populate it with other arrays of different data types. The following code creates two arrays, one containing integers and the other strings.
- It then declares a third Variant array and populates it with the integer and string arrays.

```
Private Sub Command1_Click()
  Dim intX As Integer
  ' Declare counter variable
  ' Declare and populate an integer array
  Dim countersA(5) As Integer
        For intX = 0 To 4
        countersA(intX) = 5
     Next intX
  'Declare and populate a string array
  Dim countersB(5) As String
     For intX = 0 To 4
        countersB(intX) = "hello"
Next intX
Dim arrX(2) As Variant
           ' Declare a new two-member
           ' array.
     ArrX(1) =  countersA()
              ' Populate the array with
              ' other arrays.
     ArrX(2) =  countersB()
       MsgBox arrX(1)(2)    ' Display a member of each
                            ' array.
     MsgBox arrX(2)(3)
End Sub
```

2.7.1 Single Dimensional Arrays

- A single dimension is a direction in which you can vary the specification of an array's elements. An array that holds the sales total for each day of the month has one dimension (the day of the month). An array that holds the sales total by department for each day of the month has two dimensions (the department number and the day of the month). The number of dimensions an array has is called its *rank*.

Working with Dimensions

- You specify an element of an array by supplying an *index* or *subscript* for each of its dimensions. The elements are contiguous along each dimension from index 0 through the highest index for that dimension.
- The following illustrations show the conceptual structure of arrays with different ranks. Each element in the illustrations shows the index values that access it. For example, you can access the first element of the second row of the two-dimensional array by specifying indexes (1, 0).

One-dimensional array

(0)	(1)	(2)	(3)	(4)

One Dimension

- Many arrays have only one dimension, such as the number of people of each age. The only requirement to specify an element is the age for which that element holds the count. Therefore, such an array uses only one index. The following example declares a variable to hold a *one-dimensional array* of age counts for ages 0 through 120.

    ```
    Dim ageCounts(120) As UInteger
    ```

2.7.2 Multidimensional Arrays

- Sometimes, keeping track of related information should be stored in an array. For example, to keep track of each pixel on the computer screen, its X and Y coordinates should be referred. This can be done using a multidimensional array to store the values.
- For example, the following statement declares a two-dimensional 10-by-10 array within a procedure :
    ```
    Static MatrixA(9, 9) As Double
    ```
- Either or both dimensions can be declared with explicit lower bounds :
    ```
    Static MatrixA(1 To 10, 1 To 10) As Double
    ```
- This can be extended to more than two dimensions. For example :
    ```
    Dim MultiD(3, 1 To 10, 1 To 15)
    ```
- This declaration creates an array that has three dimensions with sizes 4 by 10 by 15. The total number of elements is the product of these three dimensions or 600.

Using Loops to Manipulate Arrays

- A multidimensional array can be efficiently process by using nested for loops.
- For example, these statements initialize every element in MatrixA to a value based on its location in the array :
    ```
    Dim I As Integer, J As Integer
    Static MatrixA(1 To 10, 1 To 10) As Double
    For I = 1 To 10
    For J = 1 To 10
      MatrixA(I, J) = I * 10 + J
    Next J
    ```

```
Next I
```

Dynamic Arrays

- Sometimes, size of an array is not known. It should have capability of changing the size of the array at run time.
- A dynamic array can be resized at any time. Dynamic arrays are among the most flexible and convenient features in Visual Basic and they help to manage memory efficiently. For example, a large array can be used for a short time and then free up memory to the system when array are not using more.
- The alternative is to declare an array with the largest possible size and then ignore array elements it would not need. However, this approach, if overused, might cause the operating environment to run low on memory.

To Create a Dynamic Array

1. Declare the array with a Public statement, (if the array is to be public) or Dim statement at the module level, (if the array is to be module level), or a Static or Dim statement in a procedure, (if the array is to be local). Declare, the array as dynamic by giving it an empty dimension list.
2. `Dim DynArray( )`
3. Allocate the actual number of elements with a ReDim statement.
4. `ReDim DynArray(X + 1)`

- The ReDim statement can appear only in a procedure. Unlike the Dim and Static statements, ReDim is an executable statement, it makes the application carry out an action at run-time.
- The ReDim statement supports the same syntax used for fixed arrays. Each ReDim can change the number of elements, as well as the lower and upper bounds, for each dimension. However, the number of dimensions in the array cannot change.

```
ReDim DynArray(4 to 12)
```

For example : The dynamic array `Matrix1` is created by first declaring it at the module level :

```
Dim Matrix1() As Integer
```
A procedure then allocates space for the array :
```
Sub CalcValuesNow()
    .
    .
    .
    ReDim Matrix1(19, 29)
End Sub
```

- The ReDim statement shown here allocates a matrix of 20 by 30 integers, (at a total size of 600 elements). Alternatively, the bounds of a dynamic array can be set using variables :

```
ReDim Matrix1(X, Y)
```

Preserving the Contents of Dynamic Arrays

- Each time the ReDim statement is executed, all the values currently stored in the array are lost. Visual Basic resets the values to the Empty value (for Variant arrays), to zero, (for numeric arrays), to a zero-length string (for string arrays), or to Nothing, (for arrays of objects).
- This is useful when the array is to be prepared for new data or when shrinking of the size of the array to take up minimal memory. Sometimes, the size of the array should be changed without losing the data in the array. By using ReDim with the Preserve keyword. For example, an array has been enlarged by one element without losing the values of the existing elements using the Ubound function to refer to the upper bound :

    ```
    ReDim Preserve DynArray(Ubound(DynArray) + 1)
    ```
- Only the upper bound of the last dimension in a multidimensional array can be changed when you use the Preserve keyword; if changing of any of the other dimensions or the lower bound of the last dimension, a run-time error occurs.
- Thus, code can be used like this :

    ```
    ReDim Preserve Matrix(10, Ubound(Matrix, 2) + 1)
    ```
    But this code can not used like :
    ```
    ReDim Preserve Matrix(Ubound(Matrix, 1) + 1, 10)
    ```

2.7.3 Control Array (Oct. 10, 11, April 12, 13)

- A control array is a list of controls with the same name. Therefore, instead of using five command buttons with separate five names, you can place a command button control array on the form, and that control array holds five command buttons.
- The control array can have a single name, and you will distinguish the control from each other with a subscript.
- One of the best reasons to use control array from that first control, all the elements in the control array take on the same property values, you then can change those properties that need to be changed without having to set every property for each control individually.
- Control arrays have a lot in common with data arrays.
- A control array has one array, and you distinguish all the array's controls from each other with the zero-based subscript, (The index property holds the controls subscript number).
- All of the control elements must be the same data type. As soon as you place a control on a form that has the same name as an existing control, Visual Basic makes sure you that you want to begin a control array by issuing the warning message to show that the control is already in use.

- This is used as a built in safety so that you do not over right an existing control by putting it some where else on the same form. If you answer the warning box with a no button, Visual Basic uses a default control name for the placed control.
- All event procedures that use control from a control array require a special argument value passed to them that the determines which control is being worked on.

  For example if your application contains a single control command button named cmdtotal the click ( ) event begins and ends as follows :
  ```
  Private sub cmdtotal_click( )
  End Sub
  ```
- If however you create a control array named the same name as before (cmdtotal) it will end up like this
  ```
  Private sub cmdtotal_click (index as integer)
  End sub
  ```
- The procedure uses the index argument as the control index number, (the subscript) that the user clicked, Therefore, if you want to change the clicked command buttons caption property inside the cmdtotal_click ( ) the procedures you would need are as Cmdtoal (index).caption = "A caption name".
- The index value holds the command button's index the user click to generate the event procedures so you will always respond to the proper control clicked if you use Index after the control array name.

2.8 FUNCTIONS (BUILT IN AND USER DEFINED) (April 13)

- Function is used to perform an assignment.
- The main difference between a sub routine and a function is that, after carrying its assignment, a function gives back a result.
- We also say that a function "returns a value". To distinguish both, there is a different syntax you use for a function.
- Display the form and change its design as follows :

Control	Name	Caption	Additional Properties
Label		Length:	
TextBox	txtLength	0.00	Alignment: 1-Right Justify
Label		Height:	
TextBox	txtHeight	0.00	Alignment: 1-Right Justify
Button		Calculate	
Label		Perimeter:	
TextBox	txtPerimeter	0.00	Alignment: 1-Right Justify

Label		Area:	
TextBox	txtArea	0.00	Alignment: 1-Right Justify

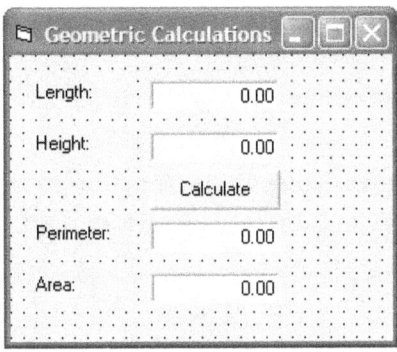

Fig. 2.23

- Save all

2.8.1 Function Creation

- To create a function, you use the Function keyword followed by a name and parentheses. Unlike a sub routine, because a function returns a value, you should/must specify the type of value the function will produce.
- To give this information, on the right side of the closing parentheses, type the As keyword, followed by a data type. To indicates where a function stops, type End Function. Based on this, the minimum syntax used to create a function is:

    Function FunctionName() As DataType

    End Function

- The name of a function follows the same rules and suggestions we reviewed for sub routines. The *DataType* factor indicates the type of value that the function will return. If the function will produce a word or a group of words, you can create it as String.
- If the function will check something and determine whether it produce a true or a false value, you can create it as Boolean. The other data types are also valid in the contexts we reviewed them.
- As mentioned already, the section between the Function and the End Function lines is the body of the function. It is used to describe what the function does.
- As done on a sub routine, one of the actions you can perform in a function is to declare a (local) variable and use it as you see fit. Here is an example :

```
Function CallMe() As String
    Dim Salute As String
    Salute = "You can call me Al"
End Function
```

- After performing an assignment in a function, to indicate the value it returns, somewhere after the assignment and before the End Function line, type the name of the function, followed by the = sign, followed by the value the function returns. Here, is an example in which a function returns a name :

```
Function CallMe() As String
    CallMe = "You can call me Al"
End Function
```

- You can also use some local variables in the function to perform an assignment and then assign their result to the name of the function. Here is an example :

```
Function CallMe() As String
    Dim Salute As String
    Salute = "You can call me Al"
    CallMe = Salute
End Function
```

1. Display the Routines module and delete (only) the previously implemented routines
2. To create a new function, at the end of the file, type **function RectPerimeter** and press Enter
3. To create another function, on the main menu, create Tools -> Add Procedure...
4. In the Name edit box, type **RectArea**
5. In the Type section, click Function

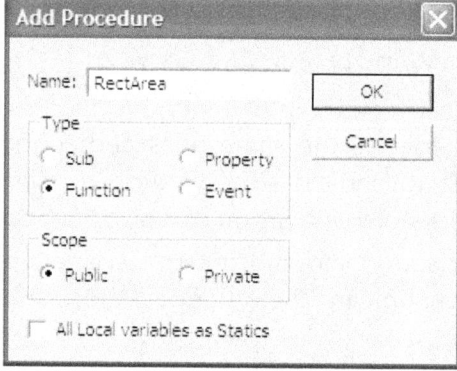

Fig. 2.24

6. Press Enter
7. Implement both functions as follows :

```
Function RectPerimeter()
    Dim dblLength As Double
    Dim dblHeight As Double
    dblLength = Form1.txtLength.Text
    dblHeight = Form1.txtHeight.Text
    RectPerimeter = (dblLength + dblHeight) * 2
```

```
End Function
Public Function RectArea()
     Dim dblLength As Double
     Dim dblHeight As Double
     dblLength = Form1.txtLength.Text
     dblHeight = Form1.txtHeight.Text
     RectArea = dblLength * dblHeight
End Function
```

8. Save all.

2.8.2 Calling a Function

- As done for the sub routines, in order to use a function in your program, must call it.
- Like a sub routine, to call a function, you can simply type its name in the desired section of the program. Here is an example :

```
Private Sub Form_Load()
    CallMe
End Sub
```

- Since, the primary purpose of a function is to return a value, to better take advantage of such a value, you can assign the name of a function to a property or a variable in the section where you are calling the function.
- In the following example, the return value of the CallMe function is assigned to the Caption property of the form from its own Load event :

```
Private Sub Form_Load()
    Caption = CallMe
End Sub
```

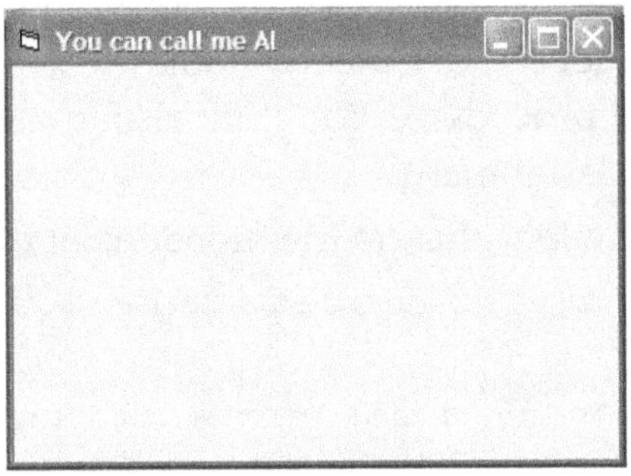

Fig. 2.25

1. Display the form and double-click the Calculate button
2. Implement its event as follows :

```
Private Sub cmdCalculate_Click()
    txtPerimeter = RectPerimeter
```

```
            txtArea = RectArea
End Sub
```

3. Test the application

Arguments and Parameters

- So far, to use a value in a procedure, we had to declare it. In some cases, a procedure may need an external value in order to carry its assignment. A value that is supplied to a procedure is called an argument. When creating a procedure that will use an external value, declare the argument that represents that value between the parentheses of the procedure. For a sub routine, the syntax you use would be :

```
Sub ProcedureName(Argument)
End Sub
```

- If you are creating a function, the syntax would be :

```
Function ProcedureName(Argument)
Function Sub
```

- The argument must be declared as a normal variable, omitting only the Dim keyword, Here, is an example that creates a function that takes a string as argument :

```
Function CalculatePayroll(strName As String) As Double
Function Sub
```

- A certain procedure can take more than one argument. In this case, in the parentheses of the procedure, separate the arguments with a comma. Here, is an example of a sub routine that takes two arguments :

```
Sub EvaluateInvoice(strEmplName As String, dblHourlySalary As Currency)
End Sub
```

- In the body of a procedure that takes one or more arguments, use the argument(s) as you see fit as if they were locally declared variables. For example, you can involve them with values inside of the procedure. You can also exclusively use the values of the arguments to perform the assignment.

1. To pass arguments to a function, change the functions in the Routines module as follows:

```
        Function RectPerimeter(dblLength As Double, dblHeight As
                                                            Double)
            RectPerimeter = (dblLength + dblHeight) * 2
        End Function
        Public Function RectArea(dblLength As Double, dblHeight As
                                                            Double)
            RectArea = dblLength * dblHeight
        End Function
```

2. Save.

Passing Arguments (By Value)

- To call a procedure that takes an argument, type its name and a space, followed by value for each argument. The value provided for an argument is also called a parameter. If there is more than one argument, separate them with a comma.
- Here, is an example :

```
Private Sub txtResult_GotFocus()
    Dim dblHours As Double
    Dim dblSalary As Double
    dblHours = txtHours
    dblSalary = txtSalary
    CalcAndShowSalary dblHours, dblSalary
End Sub
Sub CalcAndShowSalary(Hours As Double, Salary As Double)
    Dim dblResult As Double
    dblResult = Hours * Salary
    txtResult = dblResult
    End Sub
```

- Alternatively, you can use the **Call** keyword to call a sub routine. In this case, when calling a procedure using **Call**, you must include the argument(s) between the parentheses. using **Call**, the above **GotFocus** event could call the **CalcAndShowSalary** as follows :

```
Private Sub txtResult_GotFocus()
    Dim dblHours As Double
    Dim dblSalary As Double
    dblHours = txtHours
    dblSalary = txtSalary
    Call CalcAndShowSalary(dblHours, dblSalary)
End Sub
```

- If you use the above technique to call a procedure that takes more than one argument, you must provide the values of the arguments in the exact order they are listed inside of the parentheses of the function.
- Fortunately, you don't have to. If you know the name of the arguments, you can type them in any order and provide a value for each. To do that, on the right side of each argument, type the := operator followed by the desired value for the argument. Here, is an example :

```
Function DisplayName(FirstName As String, LastName As String)
                        As String Dim FullName As String
```

```
        FullName = FirstName & " " & LastName
        DisplayName = FullName
End Function
Private Sub Form_Load()
    Caption = DisplayName(LastName:="Salunkhe", _
                            FirstName:="Sarika")
    End Sub
```

- Display the form and double-click the Calculate button.
- To call the above functions, change the button's event as follows :

```
Private Sub cmdCalculate_Click()
    Dim dblLen As Double
    Dim dblHgt As Double
    Dim dblPerim As Double
    Dim dblAreaG As Double
    dblLen = txtLength.Text
    dblHgt = txtHeight.Text
    dblPerim = RectPerimeter(dblLen, dblHgt)
    dblArea = RectArea(dblLen, dblHgt)
    txtPerimeter.Text = dblPerim
    txtArea.Text = dblArea
End Sub
```

- Test the application

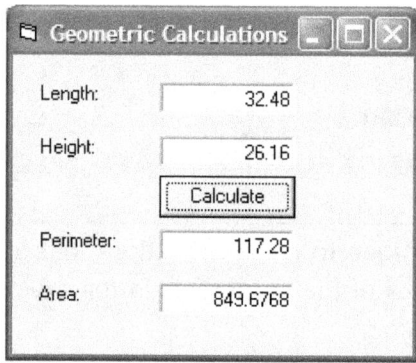

Fig. 2.26

- Close the form and return to MSVB.

Passing Arguments By Reference

- When calling a procedure that took an argument, we were supplying a value for that argument. When this is done, the procedure that is called makes a copy of the value of the argument and make that copy available to calling procedure. That way, the argument itself is not accessed. This is referred to as passing an argument by value. This can be reinforced by typing the **ByVal** keyword on the left side of the argument. Here is an example :

```
Sub GetFullName(ByVal FullName As String)
    FullName = "Salunkhe, Yogita"
End Sub
```

- If you create a procedure that takes an argument by value and you have used the **ByVal** keyword on the argument, when calling the procedure, you do not need to use the **ByVal** keyword; just the name of the argument is enough, as done in the examples on arguments so far. Here, is an example :

```
Private Sub Form_Load()
    Dim FName As String
    FName = "Deepika Ramchandra Jagtap"
    GetFullName FName
    Caption = FName
End Sub
```

Output :

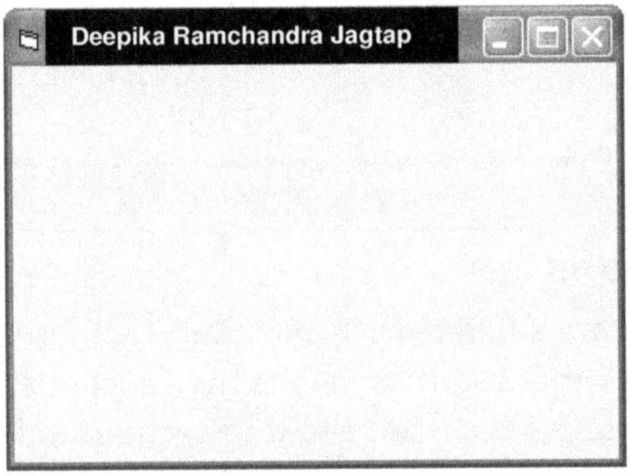

Fig. 2.27

- An alternative to this technique is to pass the address of the argument to the called procedure. When this is done, the called procedure does not receive a simple copy of the value of the argument: the argument is accessed at its root.
- That is, at its memory address. With this technique, any action carried on the argument will be kept. That is, if the value of the argument is modified, the argument would now have the new value, dismissing or losing the original value it had. This technique is referred to as passing an argument by reference.
- To pass an argument by reference, on its left, type the **ByRef** keyword. This is done only when creating the function. When the called procedure finishes with the argument, the

argument would keep whatever modification was made on its value. Now consider the following :

```
Private Sub Form_Load()
    Dim FName As String
    FName = "Deepika Ramchadra Jagtap"
    GetFullName FName
    Caption = FName
End Sub
Sub GetFullName(ByRef FullName As String)
    FullName = "Salunkhe,Yogita"
End Sub
```
Output :

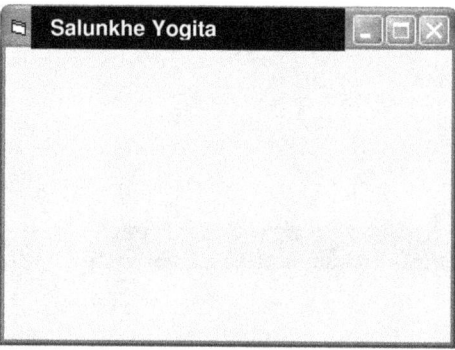

Fig. 2.28

2.8.3 Built-in Functions

- Many built-in functions are offered by Visual Basic fall under various categories. These functions are procedures that return a value. The functions fall into the following basic categories that will be discussed in the following sections at length.
    1. Date and Time Functions,
    2. Format Functions and
    3. String Functions

1. Date and Time Functions :

- Microsoft Visual Basic provides various functions to perform date and time related operations. These functions allow you to add dates or times, find the difference between dates or times, or add constant values to dates or times.
- The current date is represented by a function called **Date**. The **Date( )** function is used to get the system date of the computer. You can use it to display today's date, provided your computer has the correct date.
- The current time of the computer is represented by a function called **Time**. The **Time( )** function is used to get the system time of the computer.

- The **Date( )** and **Time( )** functions can be combined and are represented by a function called **Now**.

2. **Format Function :**
- Returns a **Variant** (**String**) containing an expression formatted according to instructions contained in a format expression.

   Syntax :
   ```
   Format(expression[, format[, firstdayofweek[,firstweekofyear]]])
   ```
   The **Format** function syntax has these parts :

Part	Description
expression	Required. Any valid expression.
Format	Optional. A valid named or user-defined format expression.
firstdayofweek	Optional. A **constant** that specifies the first day of the week.
firstweekofyear	Optional. A constant that specifies the first week of the year.

Settings :

- The firstdayofweek **argument** has these settings :

Constant	Value	Description
vbUseSystem	0	Use NLS API setting.
vbSunday	1	Sunday (default)
vbMonday	2	Monday
vbTuesday	3	Tuesday
vbWednesday	4	Wednesday
vbThursday	5	Thursday
vbFriday	6	Friday
vbSaturday	7	Saturday

- The firstweekofyear argument has these settings :

Constant	Value	Description
vbUseSystem	0	Use NLS API setting.
vbFirstJan1	1	Start with week in which January 1 occurs (default).
vbFirstFourDays	2	Start with the first week that has at least

		four days in the year.
vbFirstFullWeek	3	Start with the first full week of the year.

(i) Tab Function :

Syntax :

```
Tab (n); x
```

- The item x will be displayed at a position that is n spaces from the left border of the output form. There must be a semicolon in between Tab and the items you intend to display, (VB will actually do it for you automatically).

For Example :

```
Private Sub Form_Activate
   Print "I"; Tab(5); "like"; Tab(10); "to"; Tab(15); "learn"; Tab(20); "VB"
   Print
   Print Tab(10); "I"; Tab(15); "like"; Tab(20); "to";Tab(25); "learn"; Tab(20); "VB"
   Print
   Print Tab(15); "I"; Tab(20); ; "like"; Tab(25);"to"; Tab(30); "learn"; Tab(35); "VB"
End sub
```

Output :

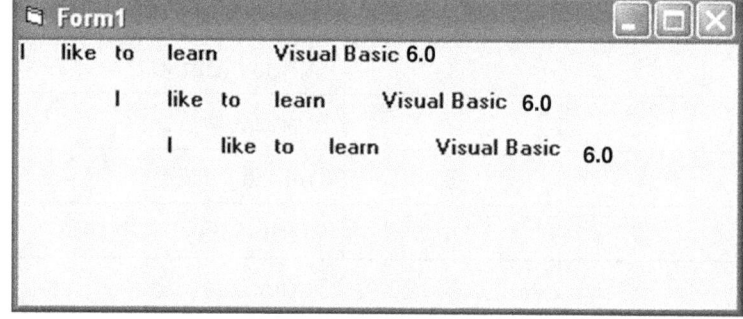

Fig. 2.29

(ii) Space Function :

- The **Space** function is very closely linked to the Tab function. However, there is a minor difference. While Tab (n) means the item is placed n spaces from the left border of the screen, the Space function specifies the number of spaces between two consecutive items. For example, the procedure,

For Example :

```
Private Sub Form_Activate()
    Print "Visual"; Space(10); "Basic"
End Sub
```

- Means that the words Visual and Basic will be separated by 10 spaces.

(iii) Format Functions :

- The **Format** function is a very powerful formatting function which can display the numeric values in various forms. There are two types of Format function, one of them is the built-in or predefined format while another one can be defined by the users.
- The format of the predefined Format function is,

    Format (n, "style argument")

    where, n is a number and the list of style arguments is given in the table

Style argument	Explanation	Example
General Number	To display the number without having separators between thousands.	Format(8972.234, "General Number")=8972.234
Fixed	To display the number without having separators between thousands and rounds it up to two decimal places.	Format(8972.2, "Fixed")=8972.23
Standard	To display the number with separators or separators between thousands and rounds it up to two decimal places.	Format(6648972.265, "Standard")=6,648,972.27
Currency	To display the number with the dollar sign in front, has separators between thousands as well as rounding it up to two decimal places.	Format(6648972.265, "Currency")=$6,648,972.27
Percent	Converts the number to the percentage form and displays a % sign and rounds it up to two decimal places.	Format(0.56324, "Percent")=56.32 %

For Example :

```
    Private Sub Form_Activate()
    Print Format (8972.234, "General Number")
    Print Format (8972.2, "Fixed")
    Print Format (6648972.265, "Standard")
    Print Format (6648972.265, "Currency")
    Print Format (0.56324, "Percent")
    End Sub
```

Output :

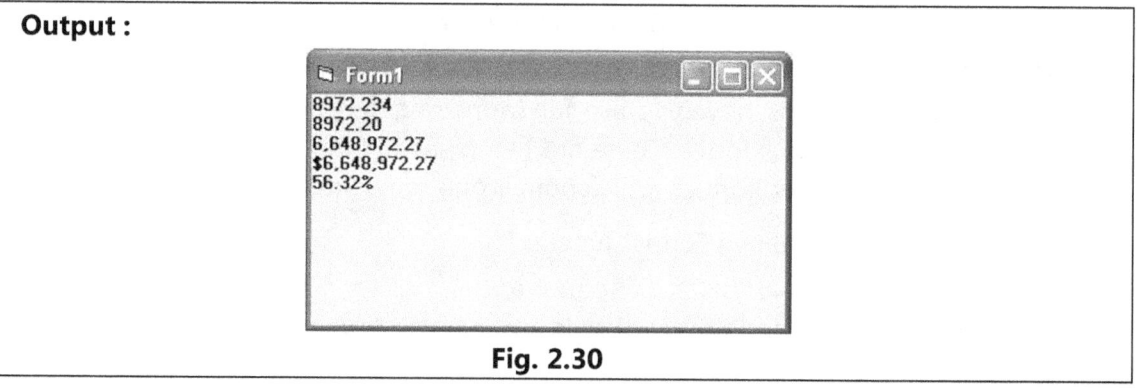

Fig. 2.30

3. String Functions : (April 10, 11)

- A string-based function is one that deals with functions; either it manipulates them or returns them. Microsoft Visual Basic allows you to be specific about the return value you are expecting. Some of the functions you will be using can be configured to return exactly a sting. Such functions use the $ suffix that states it clearly.

Compare two strings.	StrComp
Convert strings.	StrConv
Convert to lowercase or uppercase.	Format, Lcase, Ucase
Create string of repeating character.	Space, String
Find length of a string.	Len
Format a string.	Format
Justify a string.	Lset, Rset
Manipulate strings.	InStr, Left, Ltrim, Mid, Right, Rtrim, Trim
Set string comparison rules.	Option Compare
Work with ASCII and ANSI values.	Asc, Chr

(a) StrComp Function :

Returns a **Variant (Integer)** indicating the result of a string comparision.

Syntax :

    StrComp(string1, string2[, compare])

For Example :

- This example uses the **StrComp** function to return the results of a string comparison. If the third argument is 1, a textual comparison is performed; if the third argument is 0 or omitted, a binary comparison is performed.

```
Dim MyStr1, MyStr2, MyComp
MyStr1 = "ABCD": MyStr2 = "abcd"        ' Define variables.
MyComp = StrComp(MyStr1, MyStr2, 1)     ' Returns 0.
MyComp = StrComp(MyStr1, MyStr2, 0)     ' Returns -1.
MyComp = StrComp(MyStr2, MyStr1)        ' Returns 1
```

(b) Mid Function :

Returns a **Variant** (**String**) containing a specified number of characters from a string.

Syntax :
```
Mid(string, start[, length])
```
For example :

- The first example uses the **Mid** function to return a specified number of characters from a string.

```
Dim MyString, FirstWord, LastWord, MidWords
MyString = "Mid Function Demo"      ' Create text string.
FirstWord = Mid(MyString, 1, 3)     ' Returns "Mid".
LastWord = Mid(MyString, 14, 4)     ' Returns "Demo".
MidWords = Mid(MyString, 5)         ' Returns "Function Demo".
```

- The second example use MidB and a user-defined function (MidMbcs) to also return characters from string. The difference here is that the input string is ANSI and the length is in bytes.

```
Function MidMbcs(ByVal str as String, start, length)
MidMbcs = StrConv(MidB(StrConv(str,vbFromUnicode),start,
                       length),vbUnicode)
End Function
Dim MyString
MyString = "AbCdEfG"
' Where "A", "C", "E", and "G" are DBCS and "b", "d",
' and "f" are SBCS.
MyNewString = Mid(MyString, 3, 4)
' Returns ""CdEf"
MyNewString = MidB(MyString, 3, 4)
' Returns ""bC"
MyNewString = MidMbcs(MyString, 3, 4)
' Returns "bCd"
```

(c) LTrim, RTrim and Trim Functions :

Returns a **Variant** (**String**) containing a copy of a specified string without leading spaces (**LTrim**), trailing spaces (**RTrim**), or both leading and trailing spaces (**Trim**).

Syntax :

```
LTrim(string)
RTrim(string)
Trim(string)
```

The required *string* argument is any valid string expression. If *string* contains NULL, **NULL** is returned.

For Example :

This example uses the **LTrim** function to strip leading spaces and the **RTrim** function to strip trailing spaces from a string variable. It uses the **Trim** function to strip both types of spaces.

```
Dim MyString, TrimString
MyString = "   <-Trim->   "   ' Initialize string.
TrimString = LTrim(MyString)     ' TrimString = "<-Trim->   ".
TrimString = RTrim(MyString)     ' TrimString = "   <-Trim->".
TrimString = LTrim(RTrim(MyString))    ' TrimString = "<-Trim->".
' Using the Trim function alone achieves the same result.
TrimString = Trim(MyString)     ' TrimString = "<-Trim->".
```

(d) InStr Function :

Returns a **Variant** (**Long**) specifying the position of the first occurrence of one string within another.

Syntax :

```
InStr([start, ]string1, string2[, compare])
```

For example :

This example uses the **InStr** function to return the position of the first occurrence of one string within another.

```
Dim SearchString, SearchChar, MyPos
SearchString ="XXpXXpXXPXXP"    ' String to search in.
SearchChar = "P"   ' Search for "P".
' A textual comparison starting at position 4. Returns 6.
MyPos = Instr(4, SearchString, SearchChar, 1)
' A binary comparison starting at position 1. Returns 9.
MyPos = Instr(1, SearchString, SearchChar, 0)
' Comparison is binary by default (last argument is omitted).
```

```
MyPos = Instr(SearchString, SearchChar)    ' Returns 9.
MyPos = Instr(1, SearchString, "W")        ' Returns 0.
```

(e) Left Function :

Returns a **Variant** (**String**) containing a specified number of characters from the left side of a string.

Syntax :
```
Left(string, length)
```

For Example :

This example uses the **Left** function to return a specified number of characters from the left side of a string.

```
Dim AnyString, MyStr
AnyString = "Hello World"         ' Define string.
MyStr = Left(AnyString, 1)        ' Returns "H".
MyStr = Left(AnyString, 7)        ' Returns "Hello W".
MyStr = Left(AnyString, 20)       ' Returns "Hello World".
```

(f) Right Function :

Returns a **Variant** (**String**) containing a specified number of characters from the right side of a string.

Syntax :
```
Right(string, length)
```

For Example :

This example uses the **Right** function to return a specified number of characters from the right side of a string.

```
Dim AnyString, MyStr
AnyString = "Hello World"           ' Define string.
MyStr = Right(AnyString, 1)         ' Returns "d".
MyStr = Right(AnyString, 6)         ' Returns " World".
MyStr = Right(AnyString, 20)        ' Returns "Hello World".
```

(g) Len Function :

Returns a **Long** containing the number of characters in a string or the number of bytes required to store a **variable**.

Syntax :
```
Len(string | varname)
```

For Example :

The first example uses **Len** to return the number of characters in a string or the number of bytes required to store a variable. The **Type...End Type** block defining

CustomerRecord must be preceded by the keyword **Private** if it appears in a class module. In a standard module, a **Type** statement can be **Public**.

```
Type CustomerRecord        ' Define user-defined type.
    ID As Integer          ' Place this definition in a
    Name As String * 10    ' standard module.
    Address As String * 30
End Type
Dim Customer As CustomerRecord   ' Declare variables
Dim MyInt As Integer, MyCur As Currency
Dim MyString, MyLen
MyString = "Hello World"    ' Initialize variable
MyLen = Len(MyInt)          ' Returns 2
MyLen = Len(Customer)       ' Returns 42
MyLen = Len(MyString)       ' Returns 11
MyLen = Len(MyCur)          ' Returns 8
```

The second example uses **LenB** and a user-defined function (**LenMbcs**) to return the number of byte characters in a string if ANSI is used to represent the string.

```
Function LenMbcs (ByVal str as String)
    LenMbcs = LenB(StrConv(str, vbFromUnicode))
End Function
Dim MyString, MyLen
MyString = "ABc"
' Where "A" and "B" are DBCS and "c" is SBCS.
MyLen = Len(MyString)
' Returns 3 - 3 characters in the string.
MyLen = LenB(MyString)
' Returns 6 - 6 bytes used for Unicode.
MyLen = LenMbcs(MyString)
' Returns 5 - 5 bytes used for ANSI.
```

(h) String Function :

Returns a **Variant** (**String**) containing a repeating character string of the length specified.

Syntax :

```
String(number, character)
```

For example :

This example uses the **String** function to return repeating character strings of the length specified.

```
Dim MyString
MyString = String(5, "*")      ' Returns "*****".
MyString = String(5, 42)       ' Returns "*****".
MyString = String(10, "ABC") ' Returns "AAAAAAAAAA".
```

(i) LSet Statement :

Left aligns a string within a string **variable**, or copies a variable of one **user-defined type** to another variable of a different user-defined type.

Syntax :
```
LSet stringvar = string
LSet varname1 = varname2
```

This example uses the **LSet** statement to left align a string within a string variable. Although **LSet** can also be used to copy a variable of one user-defined type to another variable of a different, but compatible, user-defined type, this practice is not recommended. Due to the varying implementations of data structures among platforms, such a use of **LSet** can not be guaranteed to be portable.

```
Dim MyString
MyString = "0123456789"      ' Initialize string.
Lset MyString = "<-Left"     ' MyString contains "<-Lef
```

(j) Asc Function :

Returns an **Integer** representing the **character code** corresponding to the first letter in a string.

Syntax :
```
Asc(string)
```

The required *string* **argument** is any valid **string expression**. If the *string* contains no characters, a **run-time error** occurs.

For Example :

This example uses the **Asc** function to return a character code corresponding to the first letter in the string.
```
Dim MyNumber
```

4. Message Boxes : (April 10, 11, 12; Oct. 10, 11)

A message box is a special form used to display a piece of information to the user. As opposed to a regular form, the user cannot type anything on the box. There are usually two kinds of dialog boxes you will create: one that simply displays information and one that expects the user to make a decision.

To create a message box, you can use the **MsgBox** function. There are two techniques to use it. To display a simple message with just an OK button, use the **MsgBox** method whose syntax is,

```
MsgBox Message
```
The parameter, Message, is the string to present to the user. As a normal, it should be passed in double-quotes. Here is an example :

```
Private Sub Form_Load()
   MsgBox "Welcome to Microsoft Visual Basic"
End Sub
```

When the above version of the MsgBox function is used, a rectangular form, (we will learn later on that this type of form is called a dialog box) is presented to the user, display a string message and an OK button.

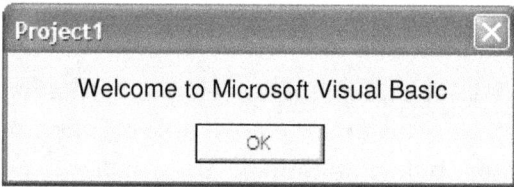

Fig. 2.31

5. **Input Box :** (Oct. 10)

Like a message box, an input box is a (relatively) small form (in reality, it is a dialog box) that displays a message to the user. Unlike a message box, an input box presents a small text box that expects the user to enter a value. After using it, the user can either send the form with the new value or dismiss it without any change.

To create an input box, you can use the **InputBox** function procedure prompts the user to enter some information in a message box, and the function will return the content of that box.

6. **Logical Functions :**

(a) **Is it Empty ?**

A logical function is one that checks whether an expression is true or false and then return a Boolean value. The **IsEmpty** function check whether a field is empty. Its syntax is :

```
IsEmpty(Expression)
```

In this case, the Expression argument will be checked. If it is empty, the IsEmpty function returns True. If the expression or field is not empty, that is, if it contains something, the function returns False.

(b) **Is it Null ?**

Another problem you may encounter when involving an operation or the contents of a control is whether it has never contained a value. This operation is sometimes confused with that of checking whether a field is empty.

To check whether an expression or the value of a control is null, you can call the **IsNull( )** function. Its syntax is :

```
IsNull(Expression)
```

Also used on fields, the IsNull() function checks the state of a field (remember, this functions does not check whether a field is empty or not; it checks if the field has ever contained a value). If the field it null, this function returns True. If the field is not null, this function returns False.

7. **Conversion Functions :**

The first action you should take when dealing with a value or an expression is to convert it to the appropriate type. There are various conversion functions adapted to the different possible kinds of values. The general syntax of the conversion functions is :

```
ReturnType = FunctionName(Expression)
```

The Expression could be of any kind. For example, it could be a string or value the user would have entered in a form. It could also be the result of a calculation performed on another field or function. The conversion function would take such a value, string or expression and attempt to convert it. If the conversion is successful, the function would return a new value that is of the type specified by the ReturnType in our syntax. The conversion functions are given below :

Functions		Description
Name	**Return Type**	
CBool	Boolean	Converts an expression into a Boolean value.
CByte	Byte	Converts an expression into Byte number.
CDate	Date	Converts and expression into a date or time value.
CDbl	Double	Converts an expression into a flowing-point (decimal) number.
CInt	Integer	Converts an expression into an integer (natural) number.
CCur	Currency	Converts an expression into a currency (monetary) value.
CLng	Long	Converts an expression into a long integer (a large natural) number.
CSng	Single	Converts an expression into a flowing-point (decimal) number.
CStr	String	Converts an expression into a string.

8. **Mathematical Functions :**

Various mathematical functions used Visual Basic. They on given below :

(i) **Atn( ) :**

It returns the arctangent of a numerical expression which is supplied as a argument to Atn( ) function.

Syntax :

```
Atn (dbiExpression)
```
dbiExpression is an expression for which user want arctangent.

For example : Consider following code,
```
Dim dblAngle      As      Double
Dim dblRatio      As      Double
dbiAngle = Atn (dbiRatio)
```

(ii) Abs( ) :

Abs( ) returns the absolute value of a number.

`Abs(numExpression)`

The Abs() function returns the unsigned value of the supplied numerical expression.

For example : `Abs (240) and Abs(-240)` both will return the value 240.

(iii) Sin( ), Cos( ), Tan( ) :

Sin( ) : The sin( ) returns sine of an angle supplied to it as an argument.

Cos( ) : Returns cosine of an angle.

Tan( ) : Returns tangent of an angle supplied to it as an argument.

Syntax :

`Sin(dblAngle)`

`Cos(dblAngle)`

`Tan (dblAngle)`

For example :

```
Dim dblSinResult As Double
Dim dblCosResult As Double
Dim dblTanResult As Double
dblSinResult    =   Sin(4.93)
dblCosResult = Cos (4.93)
dblTanResult = Tan (4.93)
```

(iv) Oct Function :

Similar to Hex function we have Oct function in VB to generate Octal Value Oct function returns a variant or string, which is Octal format of the supplied numerical expression :

`Oct (numExpression)`

NumExpression is an expression, which is to be converted into Octal format.

For example :

Consider strOctal as a string variable and we have the following statement.

```
strOctal = Oct(100)
strOctal variable will contain the Octal value of 100.
```

(v) Hex Function :

These functions return a string that represents the value of numerical expression in hexadecimal format.

Syntax :

`Hex (numExpression)`

For example :
```
Dim A asInteger
Dim B asString
A = 140
B = Hex (A)
```
Above example places a string "8C" which is a hexadecimal value of variable A into B. Hexadecimal is often used to display Memory addresses.

(vi) Val Function :
Val function returns the numerical value of the supplied string expression.

Syntax :
```
Val(strExpression)
```

For example :
```
Dim A as Double, B as Double
A = Val ("2352")
B = Val ("2352")
```
The above two lines will assign a value 2352 to A and B variables.

(vii) Sqr Function :
This function calculates the square root of a number.

Syntax :
```
sqr(dblExpression)
```
dblExpression is a numerical expression of which user want the square root.

For example :
```
Dim dblResult as Double
DbiResult = sqr(64)
```
The above code uses Sqr function. 64 is the value of which you want square root. The dblResult will contain value 8.

2.8.4 User Defined Functions

The general format of a function is as follows :

Public Function functionName (Arg As dataType, ...) As dataType

- OR -

Private Function functionName (Arg As dataType,....) As dataType

Public indicates that the function is applicable to the whole project and Private indicates that the function is only applicable to a certain module or procedure.

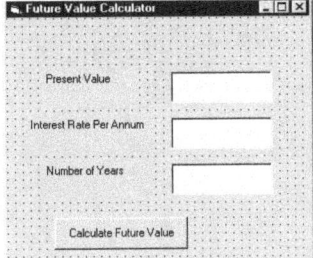

Fig. 2.32

For Example : In this example, a user can calculate the future value of a certain amount of money he has today based on the interest rate and the number of years from now, supposing he will invest this amount of money somewhere. The calculation is based on the compound interest rate.

```
Public Function FV(PV As Variant, i As Variant, n As Variant)
                                                         As Variant
'Formula to calculate Future Value(FV)
'PV denotes Present Value
FV = PV * (1 + i / 100) ^ n
End Function
Private Sub compute_Click()
'This procedure will calculate Future Value
Dim FutureVal As Variant
Dim PresentVal As Variant
Dim interest As Variant
Dim period As Variant
PresentVal = PV.Text
interest = rate.Text
period = years.Text
'calling the funciton
FutureVal = FV(PresentVal, interest, period)
MsgBox ("The Future Value is " & FutureVal)
   End Sub
```

- The following program will automatically compute examination grades based on the marks that a student obtained.

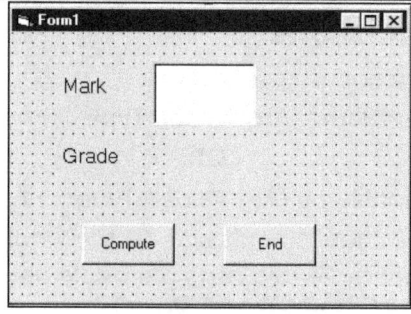

Fig. 2.33

```
Public Function grade(mark As Variant) As String
Select Case mark
Case Is >= 80
grade = "A"
Case Is >= 70
grade = "B"
```

```
Case Is >= 60
grade = "C"
Case Is >= 50
grade = "D"
Case Is >= 40
grade = "E"
Case Else
grade = "F"
End Select
End Function
Private Sub compute_Click()
grading.Caption = grade(mark)
   End Sub
```

Practice Questions

1. What is meant operator in Visual Basic ?
2. Explain uses of operators.
3. What is data types ?
4. Describe string and number data types with example.
5. What is user defined data types ?
6. Explain the term constant.
7. How to declare a variable ?
8. What is an expression ?
9. What is a variable ?
10. Enlist two types of variable conversion with examples.
11. What are the arithmetic operators used in visual basic ?
12. What is control structure ?
13. Describe If ...... Then statement with example.
14. What is an array ?
15. With suitable example describe select case statement.
16. Explain for loop with syntax.
17. Describe while loop with syntax.
18. Explain until loop with syntax and example.
19. What is a function?
20. How to create an array ?
21. How to create an function ?
22. Enlist various built-in functions.
23. How to create user defined functions ?
24. Describe the term control array.

University Question & Answers

April 2010

1. What do you mean my variable ? Explain scope of variable. [4 M]
Ans. Please refer to Section 2.3 & 2.3.5.

2. Explain if-then-else statement is VB with syntax and example. [4 M]
Ans. Please refer to Section 2.5.2.

3. Write a VB Program to find Fibonacci series. [4 M]
Ans. Please refer to Section 2.6.

4. Write a VB program to display even numbers from an array. [4 M]
Ans. Please refer to Section 2.7.3.

5. Write a VB program to calculate x^y without using built-in function. [4 M]
Ans. Please refer to Section 2.6.

6. Write a VB program to display age in year, month and days. [4 M]
Ans. Please refer to Section 2.6.

7. Explain different control structures used in VB with examples. [4 M]
Ans. Please refer to Section 2.5.

8. Write short note on : Control array.
Ans. Please refer to Sections 2.7.3.

October 2010

1. Describe data types used in VB. [4 M]
Ans. Please refer to Section 2.3.

2. Explain If .... Then .... Else statement in visual basic with syntax and example. [4 M]
Ans. Please refer to Section 2.5.2.

3. Write program in VB to find maximum number from an Array. [4 M]
Ans. Please refer to Section 2.7.3.

4. Write program in VB to find factorial of a given number. [4 M]
Ans. Please refer to Section 2.6.

5. Write program in VB to check whether given no. is Armstrong or not. [4 M]
Ans. Please refer to Section 2.6.

6. Explain any two looping structure used in VB with syntax and example. [4 M]
Ans. Please refer to Section 2.6.

April 2011

1. Explain any four built-in data types in VB. [4 M]
Ans. Please refer to Section 2.2.

2. Explain Do While .... Loop statement in brief. [4 M]
Ans. Please refer to Section 2.6.

3. Write a program in VB to print fibbonacci series. [4 M]
Ans. Please refer to Section 2.6.
4. Write a program in VB to find greatest number among three numbers. [4 M]
Ans. Please refer to Section 2.6.
5. Write program in VB to find all the even numbers from an array. [4 M]
Ans. Please refer to Section 2.7.3.

October 2011

1. What are arrays in visual basic. [4 M]
Ans. Please refer to Section 2.7
2. Explain if-then-else statement in visual basic with syntax and example. [4 M]
Ans. Please refer to Section 2.5.2
3. Write a program in VB to calculate sum of digits of a given number. [4 M]
Ans. Please refer to Section 2.6
4. Write a VB program to find the prime number. [4 M]
Ans. Please refer to Section 2.6.
5. Write a VB program to display odd numbers from an array. [4 M]
Ans. Please refer to Section 2.7.3.
6. What are procedures and functions in Visual Basic? Explain with syntax and example. [8 M]
Ans. Please refer to Section 2.8.
7. What are control arrays? Explain with the help of a suitable example. [8 M]
Ans. Please refer to Section 2.7.3.

April 2012

1. Describe data types used in VB. [4 M]
Ans. Please refer to Section 2.2.
2. What are control arrays ? Explain with suitable example. [4 M]
Ans. Please refer to Section 2.7.3.
3. Write a VB program to display even numbers from an array. [4 M]
Ans. Please refer to Section 2.6.
4. Write a VB program to concatenate two strings. [4 M]
Ans. Please refer to Section 2.6.
5. Write a VB program to find the factorial of number. [4 M]
Ans. Please refer to Section 2.6.
6. Write VB program to display age in year, math and days. [4 M]
Ans. Please refer to Section 2.6.
7. Explain any two looping structure used in VB with syntax and example. [4 M]
Ans. Please refer to Section 2.6.

October 2012

1. Explain constants with an example. [4 M]
Ans. Please refer to Section 2.1.
2. Explain any two looping structures used in VB with syntax and example. [4 M]
Ans. Please refer to Section 2.6.

April 2013

1. What are Control Arrays? Explain with the help of a suitable example. [4 M]
Ans. Please refer to Section 2.7.3.
2. Explain data types in VB. [4 M]
Ans. Please refer to Section 2.2.
3. What are procedures and functions in Visual Basic? Explain with syntax and example.
Ans. Please refer to Section 2.8.

October 2013

1. Explain user defined data types with syntax. [4 M]
Ans. Please refer to Section 2.2.5.
2. Explain any two iteration loop in VB. [4 M]
Ans. Please refer to Section 2.6.
3. Explain any four string functions with example. [4 M]
Ans. Please refer to Section 2.2.1.
4. Attempt the following. [4 M]
   i) Control array
Ans. Please refer to Section 2.7.3.
   ii) Operators
Ans. Please refer to Section 2.4.

April 2014

1. Explain logical operator with suitable example. [4 M]
Ans. Please refer to Section 2.4.
2. Explain While .... Wend statement with suitable example. [4 M]
Ans. Please refer to Section 2.6.6.
3. What is variable? Explain variable declaration in VB with suitable examples.
Ans. Please refer to Section 2.3.

Chapter 3...

Working with Control

Contents ...

This chapter includes

3.1 ADDING CONTROLS ON FORM
3.2 WORKING WITH PROPERTIES AND METHODS OF EACH CONTROLS
    3.2.1   Label
    3.2.2   Text Box
    3.2.3   Command Button
    3.2.4   Option Button
    3.2.5   Check Box
    3.2.6   Frame Control
    3.2.7   List Box
    3.2.8   Combo Box
    3.2.9   Image
    3.2.10 Picture Box
    3.2.11 Timer
    3.2.12 Scroll Bar
    3.2.13 Drive List
    3.2.14 Directory List Box
    3.2.15 File List Box
    3.2.16 Adding other Controls to the Toolbox
3.3 CREATING AN APPLICATION
    3.3.1   Common Properties of the form
    3.3.2   Creating your First Application
3.4 CREATING MDI APPLICATIONS
    3.4.1   Working with Multiple Forms
    3.4.2   Loading, Showing and Hiding Forms
    3.4.3   Setting the Startup form
    3.4.3   Using the MDI
    3.4.5   Arranging MDI Child Window
    3.4.6   Opening New MDI Child Window

3.4.7   Creating Properties in a form
3.4.8   Creating a method in a form
*   Practice Questions
*   University Question & Answers

3.1 ADDING CONTROLS ON FORM

- Controls are the building blocks of a Visual Basic application.
- Controls in VB allow your form to do more than just sit empty on a screen.
- Some controls in VB, (labels or list boxes etc.) give users feedback, while others, (command buttons and text boxes) elicit responses.
- Controls are simple and easy to use and when used properly, can add significant functionality to your programs.
- To add a control to a form you simply double-click the control you want to add, or you can draw the control on a form by clicking the control and then dragging the mouse around the area on the form where you want the control to be.
- After you add some control in your VB application, you can set most of their properties in the Properties window. You simple click the control to make it active and change the appropriate properties in the Properties window.
- Toolbox in VB is the containing window that holds the custom controls for your applications shown in Fig. 3.1.

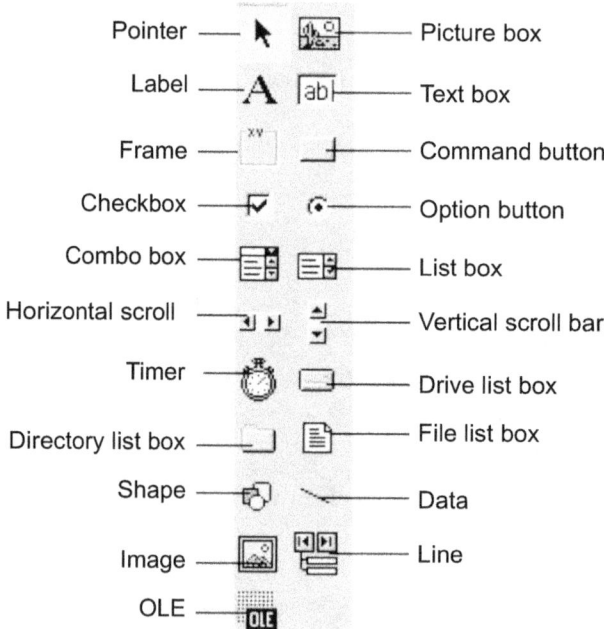

Fig. 3.1 : Visual Basic Toolbox

- There are also several advanced control that come with Visual Basic 6. Some controls work with multimedia, (Multimedia control) and others (Winsock and Internet Transfer Controls) utilize the Internet.
- There are also several new data-aware controls that help you work with databases. You can develop your own ActiveX custom controls and add them to your Toolbox.

3.2 WORKING WITH PROPERTIES AND METHODS OF EACH CONTROLS

- In VB many properties and methods are associated with each control tool which decide controls appearance and behaviour.
- Properties displayed in property window. If user are setting properties through property window means design time setting.
- When user are changing properties through coding is known as run-time setting.
- The syntax for set the property of control is given below.

        Control.Property
    where, Control   : It is the name of control and
           Property : Name of the property user wants to use.

3.2.1 Label

- A label control in VB is similar to a text box control in that both display text. Label control displays read-only text as far as the user is concerned, though you can alter the caption as a run-time property.
- Fig. 3.2 shows label control tool.

Fig. 3.2

Properties of Label Control :

Alignment	DataSource	Height	Parent
Appearance	DragIcon	Index	RightToLeft
AutoSize	DragMode	Left	**TabIndex**
BackColor	Enabled	LinkItem	Tag
BackStyle	**Font**	LinkMode	ToolTipText
BorderStyle	FontBold	LinkNotify	Top
Caption	FontItalic	LinkTimeout	**UseMnemonic**
Container	FontName	LinkTopic	Visible
DataChanged	FontSize	MouseIcon	WhatsThisHelpID
DataField	FontStrikethru	MousePointer	Width
DataFormat	FontUnderline	**Name**	**WordWrap**
DataMember	ForeColor	**OLEDropMode**	

- The most important property of label control is the Name, (prefix of label control is lbl). The Caption property of label control determines the text show in the label. The Caption property, only to find it's too big to fit within the label control.
- BorderStyle property is not related to the form property of the same name- there are only two choices. But by setting BorderStyle to 1 – fixed Single and the BackColor to white the label looks exactly like a text box, except that it's read-only.

Methods of Label Control :

Drag	**LinkRequest**	OLEDrag	ZOrder
LinkExecute	LinkSend	Refresh	
LinkPoke	Move	ShowWhatsThis	

- Link-Request method of label control is sometimes used to update a nonautomatic DDE link.

3.2.2 Text Box

- Every Visual Basic project or application involves at least one text box control.
- Text boxes are commonly used for accepting user input.
- Fig. 3.3 shows text box control.

Fig. 3.3

Properties of Text Box Control :

Alignment	Font	LinkItem	**RightToLeft**
Appearance	FontBold	LinkMode	**ScrollBars**
BackColor	FontItalic	LinkTimeout	**SelLength**
BorderStyle	FontName	LinkTopic	**SelStart**
CausesValidation	FontSize	**Locked**	**SelText**
Container	FontStrikethru	**MaxLength**	**TabIndex**
DataChanged	FontUnderline	MouseIcon	TabStop
DataField	ForeColor	MousePointer	Tag
DataFormat	Height	**MultiLine**	**Text**
DataMember	HelpContextID	**Name**	ToolTipText
DataSource	HideSelection	OLEDragMode	Top
DragIcon	**hWnd**	OLEDropMode	Visible
Dragmode	Index	Parent	WhatsThisHelpID
Enabled	Left	**PasswordChar**	Width

- The property you set first of textbox control is the Name property (prefix is txt). The MaxLegnth property is used for limiting the user to a specified number of characters. This is often used the PasswordChar property.
- MaxLength and PasswordChar properties of textbox control are often employed for a text box on a logon form.
- The MultiLine property of textbox control lets the user more than one line of text into the text box. The SelLength, SelfStart, and SelText properties of this control are useful for dealing with text appropriately.

Methods of Text Box Control :

Drag	**LinkRequest**	OLEDrag	ShowWhatsThis
LinkExecute	**LinkSend**	Refresh	ZOrder
LinkPoke	Move	**SetFocus**	

- The SetFocus method of textbox control, though, is a boon in data-entry applications. Above **boldface** methods are commonly used in VB application.

3.2.3 Command Button

- A command button control is one of the most common and important control in VB. You can use a command button to elicit simple responses from the user or to invoke special functions on forms.

Fig. 3.4

Properties of Command Button Control :

Appearance	**Enabled**	hWnd	**Style**
BackColor	Font	Index	**TabIndex**
Cancel	FontBold	Left	**TabStop**
Caption	FontItalic	MaskColor	Tag
CausesValidation	FontName	MouseIcon	ToolTipText
Container	FontSize	MousePointer	Top
Default	FontStrikethru	**Name**	UseMaskColor
DisabledPicture	FontUnderline	OLEDropMode	Value
DownPicture	ForeColor	Parent	Visible
DragIcon	Height	**Picture**	WhatsThisHelpID
DragMode	HelpContextID	RightToLeft	Width

- Name and Caption are two most important properties of command buttons. The Name property in command button control used to give the control its own identity. The Caption property determines the text which appears on the command button.
- Two other useful properties of command button control are Cancel and Default. When setting the Default property to True means the user can simulate a click on the button by pressing Enter. If setting Cancle to True means the user can close a form by pressing Esc.
- Enabled and Visible properties can stop the user from accessing a command button. By setting the Style property of command button control, you can make the button contain text only or you can add a picture to the button, you can specify the picture's filename in the picture property. You can also place other graphics on the button by setting them using the DisabledPicture and   Down Picture properties.

Methods of Command Button Control :

Drag	OLEDrag	**SetFocus**	ZOrder
Move	Refresh	ShowWhatsThis	

- Sometimes, SetFocus method is used to place the focus on a particular button.

3.2.4 Option Button   (April 12)

- Option button controls, also known as radio buttons.
- Option buttons are used to allow the user to select one, and only one, option from a group of option buttons.
- Basically, option button are grouped together within a frame control, but they can also be grouped on a plain form, if there is be only one group of option buttons.
- Fig. 3.5 shows option button control.

Fig. 3.5

Properties of Option Button Control :

Alignment	FontSize	Picture
Appearance	FontStikethru	RightToLeft
BackColor	FontUnderline	**Style**
Caption	ForeColor	TabIndex
CausesValidation	Height	TabStop
Container	HelpContextID	Tag
DisabledPicture	hWnd	TollTipText
DownPicture	Index	Top
DragIcon	Left	UseMaskColor
DragMode	MaskColor	**Value**
Enabled	MouseIcon	Visible

Font	MousePointer		WhatsThisHelpID
FontBold	**Name**		Width
FontItalic	OLEDropMode		
FontName	Parent		

- The Name property of this control is the one to set first, option buttons have an opt prefix by convention. The Caption property helps you determine the purpose of an option button. The other popular property is Value. Value property is invaluable at both design time and run time.
- A new property added in VB 6 is the Style property. The default setting of style property is 0. Standard property property will draw a normal option button.

Methods of Option Button Control :

Drag	OLEDrag	SetFocus	ZOrder
Move	Refresh	showWhatsThis	

3.2.5 Check Box

- A check box control is rather similar to an option button.
- Both i.e. option button and check box often partake in groups and the Value property is tested to see if a check box is ON or OFF.
- Check boxes are valid as single controls. Check boxes are not mutually exclusive.

Fig. 3.6

Properties of Check Box Control :

Alignment	DownPicture	Height	RightToLeft
Appearance	DragIcon	HelpContextID	Style
BackColor	DragMode	hWnd	**TabIndex**
Caption	**Enabled**	Index	**TabStop**
CausesValidation	**Font**	Left	Tag
Container	FontBold	MaskColor	ToolTipText
DataChanged	FontItalic	MouseIcon	Top
DataField	FontName	MousePointer	UseMaskColor
DataFormat	FontSize	**Name**	**Value**
DataMember	FontStrikethru	OLEDragMode	Visible
DataSource	FontUnderline	Patent	WhatsThisHelpID
DisabledPicture	ForeColor	Picture	Width

- **Methods of Check Box Control :** The methods of check box control are similar to those for the option button control :

Drag	OLEDrag	SetFocus	ZOrder
Move	Refresh	ShowWhatsThis	

3.2.6 Frame Control

- The frame control is not particular useful in Visual Basic project. The controls normally placed in a frame are option buttons and check boxes.

Fig. 3.7

- **Properties of Frame Control :** The frame control has several properties, some of them are listed below :

Appearance	**Enabled**	Height	Parent
BackColor	Font	HelpContextID	RightToLeft
BorderStyle	FontBold	hWnd	TabIndex
Caption	FontItalic	Index	Tag
Container	FontName	Left	ToolTipText
ClipControls	FontSize	MouseIcon	Top
Container	FontStrikethru	MousePointer	Visible
DragIcon	FontUnderline	Name	WhatsThisHelpID
DragMode	ForeColor	OLEDropMode	Width

- After the Name property, perhaps the single most important property is Caption in frame control.
- **Methods of Frame Control :** A frame control supports only a few methods are given below :

Drag	OLEDrag	ShowWhatsThis
Move	Refresh	ZOrder

3.2.7 List Box

- A list box control is an ideal way of presenting users with a list of data. You can browse the data in the list box or select one or more items as the basis for further processing.

Fig. 3.8

Properties of List Box Control : Properties of listbox control are given below :

Appearance	FontBold	**List**	Style
BackColor	FontItalic	**ListCount**	TabIndex
CausesValidation	FontName	**ListIndex**	TabStop
Columns	FontSize	MouseIcon	Tag
Container	FontStrikethru	MousePointer	Text
Datachanged	FontUnderline	**MultiSelect**	ToolTipText
DataField	ForeColor	**Name**	Top
DataFormat	Height	**NewIndex**	TopIndex
DataMember	HelpContextID	OLEDragMode	Visible
DataSource	hWnd	Parent	WhatsThisHelpID
DragIcon	Index	RightToLeft	Width
DragMode	IntergralHeight	SelCount	
Enabled	ItemData	**Selected**	
Font	Left	**Sorted**	

- The Columns property of List Box lets you create a multicolumn list box. The MultiSelect property determines whether the user can select one item or whether they can select more than one.
- The Selected property is a Boolean property and is a run-time property only. A Boolean property is one that can take only a True or False setting.
- Sorted property, is one of those properties that you can set only design time.
- **Methods of List Box Control :** The list box control has many of its own methods, as well as some common to the other methods are given below :

AddItem	Move	SetFocus
Clear	Refresh	ShowWhatsThis
Drag	**RoverItem**	ZOrder

- There are three methods AddItem, Clear and RemoveItem. AddItem property is used for adding items to a list box control. The RemoveItem method, removes items from a list box. To remove all the items use the Clear method.

3.2.8 Combo Box (Oct. 11)

- The basic idea is that a combo box combines the features of both a text box and a list box.
- Fig. 3.9 shows combo box control.

Fig. 3.9

Properties of Combo Box Control :

Appearance	FontItalic	**ListCount**	**Style**
BackColor	FontName	**ListIndex**	TabIndex
CauseValidation	FontSize	Locked	TabStop
Container	FontStrikethru	MouseIcon	Tag
DataChanged	FontUnderline	MousePointer	Text
DataField	ForeColor	**Name**	ToolTipText
DataFormat	Height	**NewIndex**	Top
DataMember	HelpContextID	OLEDragMode	TopIndex
DataSource	hWnd	Parent	Visible
DragIcon	Index	RightToLeft	WhatsThisHelpID
DragMode	IntegralHeight	SelLength	Width
Enabled	ItemData	**SelStart**	
Font	Left	**SelText**	
FontBold	**List**	Sorted	

- The List, ListCount, ListIndex, NewIndex, and Sorted properties are identical to those for a list box.

Methods of Combo Box Control :

AddItem	Move	**RemoveItem**	ZOrder
Clear	OLEDrag	SetFocus	
Drag	Refresh	ShowWhatsThis	

- The important methods of this control are AddItem, Clear, and RemoveItem. With a list box control, it's common practice to populate a combo box with a series of AddItem methods in the Load event of a form.

3.2.9 Image

- The image control is a equivalent of the picture box control.
- Fig. 3.10 shows a image control.

Fig. 3.10

Properties of Image Control :

Appearance	DragIcon	MousePointer	Tag
BorderStyle	DragMode	**Name**	Top
Container	Enabled	OLEDragMode	Visible
DataField	Height	OLEDropMode	WhatsThisHelpID
DataFormat	Index	Parent	Width
DataMember	Left	**Picture**	
DataSource	MouseIcon	**Stretch**	

- You add the graphic by setting the Picture property. The most interesting property here is Stretch. Stretch is a Boolean property and takes the value True or False.

Methods of Image Control :

Drag	OLEDrag	ShowWhatsThis
Move	Refresh	ZOrder

3.2.10 Picture Box

- Picture boxes often display graphics such as bitmaps, icons, JPEGs and GIFs.
- Picture boxes and images have slightly different properties and therefore behave differently.

Fig. 3.11

- **Properties of Picture Box :**

Align	FillStyle	MousePointer	
Appearance	Font	**Name**	
AutoRedraw	FontBold	OLEDragMode	
AutoSize	FontItalic	OLEDropMode	
BackColor	FontName	Parent	
BorderStyle	FontSize	**Picture**	
CausesValidation	FontStrikethru	RightToLeft	
ClipContorls	FontTrasnparent	ScaleHeight	
Container	FontUnderline	ScaleLeft	
CurrentY	ForeColor	ScaleMode	
Currently	HasDC	ScaleTop	
DataChanged	hDC	ScaleWidth	
DataField	Height	TabIndex	
DataFormat	HelpContextID	TabStop	

DataMember	hWnd	Tag
DataSource	**Image**	ToolTipText
DragIcon	Index	Top
DragMode	Left	Visible
DrawMode	LinkItem	WhatsThisHelpID
DrawStyle	LinkMode	Width
DrawWidth	LinkTimeout	
Enabled	LinkTopic	
FillColor	MouseIcon	

- **Methods of Picture Box Control :** The picture box control supports more methods than image box control. The most important methods of picture box control are :

Circle	LinkRequest	**PSet**	TextHeight
Cls	LinkSend	Refresh	TextWidth
Drag	Move	ScaleX	**ZOrder**
Line	OLEDrag	ScaleY	
LinkExecute	**PaintPicture**	SetFocus	
LinkPoke	Point	ShowWhatsThis	

- The Circle, Cls, Line, PaintPicture, and PSet methods are all used when drawing graphics or text in the picture box at run time. Cls is actually used to erase entries. A circle drawn with the Circle method is on the bottom layer.

3.2.11 Timer

- The timer control is one of the few controls always hidden at run time.
- The timer basically checks the system clock and acts accordingly.
- Fig. 3.12 shows timer control.

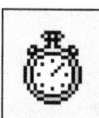

Fig. 3.12

- **Properties of Timer Control:** The timer control does not have many properties.

Enabled	Left	Tag
Index	**Name**	Top
Interval	Parent	

- Apart from the Name property, there control – the Enabled property and the Interval property are two important properties for this control. The Interval property is measured in milliseconds.

3.2.12 Scroll Bar

- A scroll bar control on a form is not to be confused with a scroll bar on a large list box or text box.
- Fig. 3.13 shows control bar control.

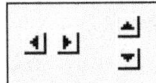

Fig. 3.13

- The scroll bar controls of VB are completely independent objects which exist without reference to any other control.
- The horizontal scroll bar and the vertical scroll bar are identical except for their orientation.

Properties of Scroll Bar Control :

CauseValidation	hWnd	MousePointer	Tag
Container	Index	**Name**	Top
DragIcon	**LargeChange**	Parent	**Value**
DragMode	Left	RightToLeft	Visible
Enabled	**Max**	**SmallChange**	WhatsThisHelpID
Height	**Min**	TabIndex	Width
HelpContextID	MouseIcon	TabStop	

- The most and common useful a scroll bar properties are the Max, Min, LargeChange, and SmallChange properties. The Min and Max properties of scroll bar determine the limits for the Value property of the scroll bar.
- **Methods of Scroll Bar Control :**

Drag	Refresh	ShowWhatsThis
Move	SetFocus	ZOrder

3.2.13 Drive List

- The drive list box control is normally used in conjunction with the directly list and the file list controls.
- Fig. 3.14 shows drive list control.

Fig. 3.14

- **Properties of Drive List Box Control :**

Appearance	FontItalic	List	Tag
BackColor	FontName	ListCount	ToolTipText

CausesValidation	FontSize	ListIndex	Top
Container	FontUnderline	MouseIcon	TopIndex
DragIcon	ForeColor	MousePointer	Visible
DragMode	Height	**Name**	WhatsThisHelpID
Drive	HelpContextID	OLEDropMode	Width
Enabled	hWnd	Parent	
Font	Index	TabIndex	
FontBold	Left	TabStop	

- For the Name property a drv prefix is normally used. The single most important property is Drive. This drive property is run-time property only, which is used to return the drive the user has selected in the drive control.

- **Methods of Drive List Box Control :**

Drag	OLEDrag	SetFocus	ZOrder
Move	Refresh	ShowWhatsThis	

3.2.14 Directory list Box

- The directory list box control, is used in conjunction with the drive control, and file control.
- Fig. 3.15 shows directory list box control. The user can select a directory on the current drive form the directory list.

Fig. 3.15

- **Properties of Directory List Box Control :**

Appearance	FontName	List	TabIndex
BackColor	FontSize	ListCount	TabStop
CausesValidation	FontStrikethru	ListIndex	Tag
Container	FountUnderline	MouseIcon	ToolTipText
DragIcon	ForeColor	MousePointer	Top
DragMode	Height	**Name**	TopIndex
Enabled	HelpContextID	OLEDragMode	Visible
Font	hWnd	OLEDropMode	WhatsThisHelpID
FontBold	Index	Parent	Width
FontItalic	Left	**Path**	

- The most important property of a directory list box control is Name property with a dir prefix.
- The Path property of this control is a run-time property which sets or returns the path to the directory in the directory list.

- **Methods of Directory List Box Control :**

    Drag   OLEDrag   SetFocus   ZOrder
    Move   Refresh   ShowWhatsThis

3.2.15 File List Box

- The File List Box control comes at the end of the drive directory file chain. Fig. 3.16 shows file list box control.
- File List Box control is used to list the actual filenames that are in the directory specified by the Path property.

Fig. 3.16

Properties of File List Box Control :

Appearance	FontName	ListCount	ReadOnly
Archive	FontSize	ListIndex	**Selected**
BackColor	FontStrikethru	MouseIcon	**System**
CausesValidation	FontUnderline	MousePointer	TabIndex
Container	ForeColor	MultiSelect	TabStop
DragIcon	Height	**Name**	Tag
DragMode	HelpContextID	**Normal**	ToolTipText
Enabled	**Hidden**	OLEDragMode	Top
FileName	hWnd	OLEDropMode	TopIndex
Font	Index	Parent	Visible
FontBold	Left	**Path**	WhatsThisHelpID
FontItalic	List	**Pattern**	Width

- The Path property is important and it's run-time property and is often both set and returned.
- The Pattern property can be set at design time and it can also be changed at run time.
- The Archive, Hidden, Normal, ReadOnly, and System properties can all be used to further narrow or expand the list of files. Hidden and System properties are False by default.

- **Methods of File List Box Control :**

Drag	OLEDrag	SetFocus	ZOrder
Move	Refresh	ShowWhatsThis	

3.2.16 Adding other Controls to the Toolbox

- There are many other controls included with Visual Basic. Follow the following simple steps for adding other controls for your application.
1. Add a tab to the Toolbox to keep it neat.
2. Select the controls to add.
3. Move them to the appropriate tab if necessary.
   (a) Right-click the Toolbox to display its pop-up menu.
   (b) Select Add Tab from the pop-up menu.
   (c) When prompted for the tab name, type in Common Controls and click the OK button.
   (d) Now that the Common Controls tab has been added to the Toolbox, click it to make it the active tab.
   (e) Right-click the Toolbox and Select Components from the pop-up menu.
   (f) From the Controls tab on Components dialog box, click the check box next to Microsoft Windows Common Controls 6.0, as show in Fig. 3.17.
   (g) Click the OK button to add the controls to the tab.

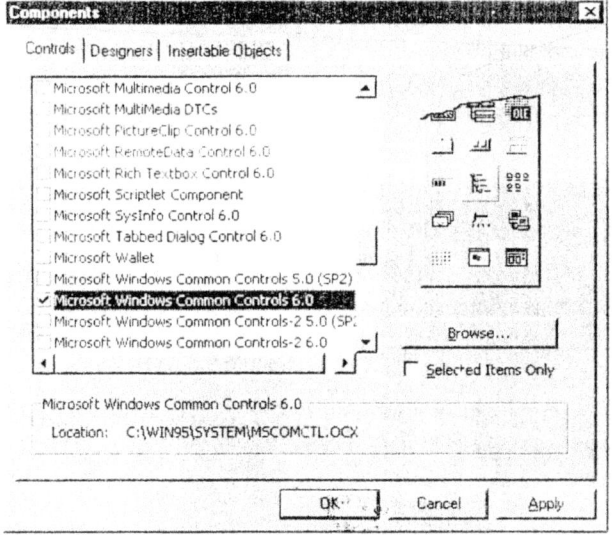

Fig. 3.17 : Adding new controls to the Toolbox

3.2.16.1 Tree View Control

- The Tree View control provides a hierarchical view of folders which can be neatly categorized in a tree style layout.

- Fig. 3.18 shows tree view control.

Fig. 3.18

- **Properties of Tree View Control :**

Appearance	Height	MouseIcon	SingleSel
BorderStyle	HelpContextID	MousePointer	Sorted
CausesValidation	HideSelection	**Name**	**Style**
CheckBoxes	**HotTracking**	Nodes	TabIndex
Container	hWnd	Object	TabStop
DragIcon	**ImageList**	OLEDragMode	Tag
DragMode	**Indentation**	OLEDropMode	ToolTipText
DropHighlight	Index	Parent	Top
Enabled	**LabelEdit**	**PathSeparator**	Visible
Font	Left	**Scroll**	WhatsThisHelpID
FullRowSelect	**LineStyle**	SelectedItem	Width

- The Name property is the first property you should set when working with TreeView control. The standard naming convention prefix is tvw.
- **Methods of Tree View Control :**

Drag	Move	SetFocus	**StartLabelEdit**
GetVisibleCount	OLEDrag	ShowWhatsThis	ZOrder
HitTest	Refresh		

  1. **GetVisibleCount :** This method is used to retrieve the number of nodes that can be viewed in the Tree View at one time.
  2. **HitTest :** This method is used to determine if a node is available as a drop target.
  3. **OLEDrag :** This method is called to initiate an OLE drag operation.
  3. **StartLabelEdit :** This method is used when you want to force a node into label edit mode.

3.2.16.2 List View

- The List View control is often used in conjunction with the Tree View control.
- Fig. 3.19 show list view control.

Fig. 3.19

- **Properties of List View Control :**

AllowColumnReorder	Height	Parent
Appearance	HelpContextID	Picture
Arrange	HideColumnHeaders	PictureAlignment
BackColor	HideSelection	**SelectedItem**
BorderStyle	**HotTracking**	**SmallIcons**
CausesValidation	HoverSelection	**Sorted**
Checkboxes	hWnd	**SortKey**
ColumnHeaderIcon	**Icons**	**SortOrder**
ColumnHeaders	Index	TabIndex
Container	**LableEdit**	TabStop
DragIcon	**LabelWrap**	Tag
DragMode	Left	TextBackground
DropHighlight	**ListItems**	ToolTipText
Enabled	MouseIcon	Top
FlatScrollBar	MousePointer	Visible
Font	**MultiSelect**	WhatsThisHelpID
ForeColor	**Name**	Width
FontName	Object	View
FullRowSelect	OLEDragMode	
GridLines	OLEDropMode	

- The first property you should set it the control's Name property. You can use a prefix like lvw.

- **Methods of List View Control :**

Drag	**HitTest**	Refresh	**StartLabelEdit**
FindItem	Move	SetFocus	ZOrder
GetFirstVisible	**OLEDrag**	ShowWhatsThis	

  1. **FindItem** method is used find a ListItem within the control.
  2. **HitTest** method is used to determine if a ListItem is available a drop target.
  3. **OLEDrag** method is called to initiate an OLE drag operation.
  3. **StartLabelEdit** method is used when you want to fouce a node into label edit mode.

3.2.16.3 Image List

- The Image List control does not actually appear on a form at run time. Image List control serves as a container for icons that are accessed by other controls such as List View, Tree View and Toolbar controls. Fig. 3.20 shows a image list control. User may have Image Lists on a form at a time.

Fig. 3.20

- **Properties of Image List Control :**

BackColor	ImageWidth	MaskColor	Parent
HimageList	Index	Name	Tag
ImageHeight	ListImages	Object	UseMaskColor

- The first property to set is the Name property, prefix is iml. The ImageHeight property is used to set the height of all the images within the Image List. ImageWidth is set to the width of all images in the list.
- MaskColor property is set to the correct color, you can set the UseMaskColor property to True.
- **Image List Control Methods:** The Image List has only one method is Overlay. User can use the Overlay method if he/she want combine two images within an Image List.

3.2.16.4 Status Bar

- The Status Bar control is the important control of the Windows Common Controls collections.
- Fig. 3.21 shows status bar control.
- Status bar control is used to report various bits of information to the user.

Fig. 3.21

- **Properties of Status Bar Control :**

Align	hWnd	OLEDropMode	Tag
Container	Index	Panels	ToolTipText
DragIcon	Left	Parent	Top
DragMode	MouseIcon	ShowTips	Visible
Enabled	MousePointer	SimpleText	WhatsThisHelpID
Font	Name	Style	Width
Height	Object	TabIndex	

- The Name property of status bar should be set first, prefixt sts prefer to name the status bar stsStatus.
- The Panels property returns a reference to the collection of panel objects contained in the Status Bar control. The Style propery determines how the status bar is displayed. The allowed values are 0 (SbrNormal) and 1 (SbrSimple).
- **Methods of Status Bar Control :**

Drag	OLEDrag	SetFocus	ZOrder
Move	Refresh	ShowWhatsThis	

3.2.16.5 TabStrip Control

- The **TabStrip** control is part of a group of custom controls that are found in the MSCOMCTL.OCX file.
- A **TabStrip** control is like the dividers in a notebook or the labels on a group of file folders.
- By using a **TabStrip** control, you can define multiple pages for the same area of a window or dialog box in your application.

Fig. 3.22

- The control consists of one or more **Tab** objects in a **Tabs** collection. At both design time and run time, you can affect the **Tab** object's appearance by setting properties.
- You can also add and remove tabs using the Properties Page of the **TabStrip** control at design time, or add and remove **Tab** objects at run time using methods.
- The **Style** property determines whether the **TabStrip** control looks like push buttons (Buttons) or notebook tabs (Tabs). At design time when you put a **TabStrip** control on a form, it has one notebook tab.
- If the **Style** property is set to **tabTabs**, then there will be a border around the **TabStrip** control's internal area.
- When the **Style** property is set to **tabButtons**, no border is displayed around the internal area of the control, however, that area still exists.
- To set the overall size of the **TabStrip** control, use its drag handles and/or set the **Top**, **Left**, **Height**, and **Width** properties.
- Based on the control's overall size at run time, Visual Basic automatically determines the size and position of the internal area and returns the Client-coordinate properties – **ClientLeft**, **ClientTop**, **ClientHeight**, and **ClientWidth**.
- The **MultiRow** property determines whether the control can have more than one row of tabs, the **TabWidthStyle** property determines the appearance of each row, and, if

TabWidthStyle is set to **tabFixed**, you can use the **TabFixedHeight** and **TabFixedWidth** properties to set the same height and width for all tabs in the **TabStrip** control.

- The TabStrip control is not a container. To contain the actual pages and their objects, you must use Frame controls or other containers that match the size of the internal area which is shared by all Tab objects in the control. If you use a control array for the container, you can associate each item in the array with a specific Tab object, as in the following example :

```
Option Explicit
Private mintCurFrame As Integer' Current Frame visible

Private Sub Tabstrip1_Click()
   If Tabstrip1.SelectedItem.Index = mintCurFrame _
      Then Exit Sub ' No need to change frame.
   ' Otherwise, hide old frame, show new.
   Frame1(Tabstrip1.SelectedItem.Index).Visible = True
   Frame1(mintCurFrame).Visible = False
   ' Set mintCurFrame to new value.
   mintCurFrame = Tabstrip1.SelectedItem.Index
End Sub
```

3.2.16.6 MSChart

- To get this control, select it from component i.e. MSCHRT20.OCX.

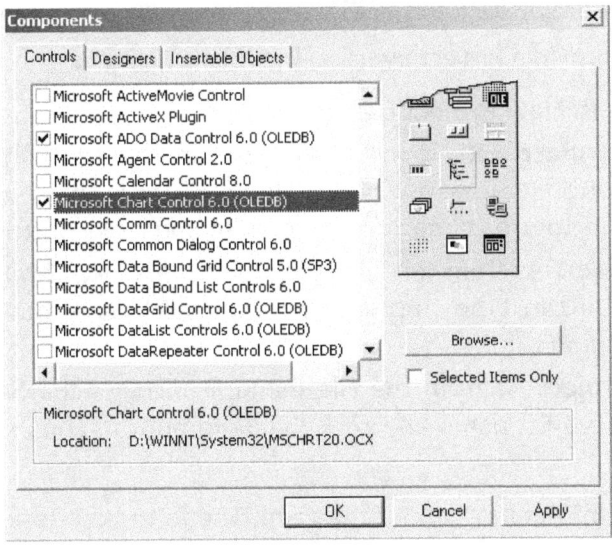

Fig. 3.23 (a)

- From the toolbox, select MSChart control as,

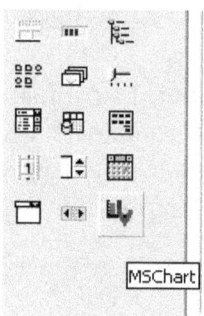

Fig. 3.23 (b)

- A chart that graphically displays data. The **MSChart** control supports the following features:
    1. True three-dimensional representation.
    2. Support for all major chart types.
    3. Data grid population via random data and data arrays.
- The **MSChart** control is associated with a data grid (**DataGrid** object). This data grid is a table that holds the data being charted.
- The data grid can also include labels used to identify series and categories on the chart.
- The person who designs your chart application fills the data grid with information by inserting data or by importing data from a spreadsheet or array.

3.3 CREATING AN APPLICATION

- You can create a Form in a Project by using the following steps :
    1. Start Visual Basic. **New Project** dialog box.
    2. Select the **Standard EXE** icon that appear in the **New Project** dialog box and click the **OK** button. We see a window. This is a blank form with caption Form1. Each form window has maximize, minimize and close button.
    3. Select **Save Form1** As from the File menu of Visual Basic. It will display **Save File As** dialog box. You can type the file name and click **Save** button. This form file has **.FRM** file extension.
    4. Select **Save Project As** from the File menu. It displays the **Save Project As** dialog box. Enter the project name and click the **Save** button. The project file has the **.VBP** file extension.
- The form contains information about the form. The form you design will have the same features at design time and at runtime unless you specify otherwise in the form's properties.

3.3.1 Commomn Properties of the form

1. **Name :** This property is used only in code. It gives the name that you want to use to refer to the Form. The default value is "Form1."
2. **Appearance :** Determines whether the form will have a three-dimensional look. If you leave it at the default value of 1, the form will look three-dimensional. Change it to 0, and the form will appear flat.
3. **BorderStyle :** Drop down the list and you can see the value and a description. You can choose among five values from this property. The default value is 2 which sizable allows the user to size and shape the form.

Value	Description
0	None
1	Fixed Single
2	Sizable
3	Fixed Double
4	Fixed Tool Window
5	Sizable Tool Window

3. **Caption:** As you already know, the caption property sets the title of the form. The caption is also the title that a Microsoft window uses for the application icon when the user minimizes the application.
5. **Enabled :** Set Enabled to False, and the form cannot respond to any events. Usually, you toggle this property back and forth in response to some event.
6. **Font :** You make changes to the font used for information displayed on the form.
7. **Height, Width :** You make changes to the height and width of the form.
8. **Icon :** This property determines the icon your application will display when it is minimized on the toolbar or turned into a stand - alone application on the Window desktop.
9. **Left, Top :** Determines the distance between the left or top of the form and the screen. Set the value of the Top property to 0, and the form you are designing is flush with the top. Set the value of the Left property to 0, and it will be flush with the left side of the screen. Using the Form Layout window is, of course, another way to control these properties. These settings work in much the same way as the Height and Width properties.
10. **Visible :** Set the value of this property to False, and the form will no longer be visible. You usually will want to make a form invisible only when you are designing an application with multiple forms. Then you will often want to hide one or more of the forms by using the visible property. Often, you will reset this property by using code and not at the time you design the application.
11. **Window State :** Determines how the form will look at run time. A setting of 1 reduces the form to an icon, and a setting of 2 maximizes the form. A setting of 0 is the normal default setting. This property is most often changed in code.

3.3.2 Creating Your First Application

- The Welcome to Visual Basic program is historically the first application when one learns a new programming language.
- While very simple, it gives you tangible results with a minimal amount of coding, and it will give you a feel for working with Visual Basic and using the IDE environment.
- To create the Welcome to Visual Basic application, follow the following steps :
    1. Click File → New Project.
    2. If it is not already visible, open the Form Layout window by selecting View → Form Layout Window.
    3. Right-click the form in the Form Layout window. Select Startup Position → Center Screen from the pop-up menu.
    4. Resize the form by dragging its borders until it's about 4 inches wide and 2 inches high.
    5. Double-click the Command Button control in the toolbox to create a command button of default size in the center of the form. Drag the button near the bottom center of the form.
    6. Double-click the Label control in the toolbox to create a label on the form. Drag the label so is sits just below the top of the form. Resize the label so it is roughly the height of one line of text and wide enough to contain the text "Welcome to Visual Basic".

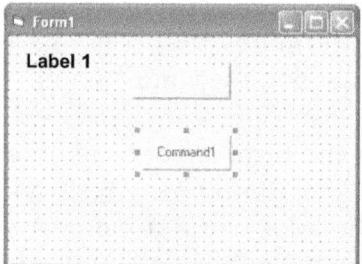

Fig. 3.24

    7. Now, click the form once to select it. you can tell that the form is selected because its properties are listed in the Properties window. If you cannot see the Properties window, press F3.
    8. Set the following two properties for the form by typing in the text under the Setting column in the appropriate property field.

Property	Setting
Caption	My First VB Application!
Name	frm Welcome to Visual Basic

The Caption property setting appears in the title bar of the form, the Name property is a very important one and is used to refer to the form in program code.

9. Now, click the label and set the next two properties:

Property	Setting
Name	lbl Welcome to Visual Basic
Text	Welcome to Visual Basic

10. Click the Command button and set its properties as follows:

Property	Setting
Name	cmdOK
Caption	&OK

    This time the Caption property shows as the text on the button. The ampersand character (&) before the first letter adds an underline to the letter O; this provides a quick keyboard alternative to a mouse-click to activate the button (here it's Alt+O).

11. Now double-click the cmdOK button. Double-clicking a control opens the Code window at the default event for the control. The default event for a command button is the Click event. You should be looking at a procedure template or stub for cmdOK_Click, as shown in Fig. 3.25. You can afford to ignore the private Sub prefix for now, the important point is the name of the procedure: cmdOK_Click. This means that any code entered in the procedure will be executed when the user clicks the cmdOK button.

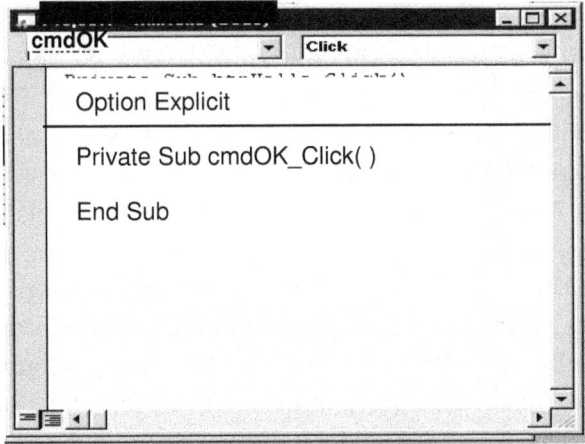

Fig. 3.25 : The procedure in the Code window

12. Type the following line of code between the Private Sub. And End Sub lines :

    ```
    Unload Me
    Set frmWelcome to Visual Basic = Nothing
    ```

13. Click File → Save project. Enter **frmVB.frm** as the name of the form and **Welcome to Visual Basic.vbp** as the name of the project. Before a project as a whole is saved, all the individual component files are saved.
13. Click Run → Start. If you have followed the directions correctly, you should see a form, similar to the one in Fig. 3.26 that simply says "Welcome to Visual Basic."
14. Click the OK button to end. If things go wrong, check through the previous steps to find you mistake.

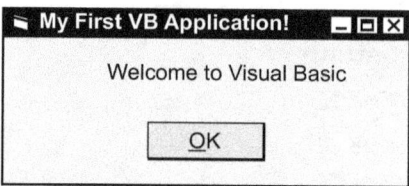

Fig. 3.26 : Your fist application the Welcome to Visual Basic applet

3.4 CREATING MDI APPLICATIONS (Oct. 11)

3.4.1 Working with Multiple Forms

- A Visual Basic project can have only one MDI form.
- An MDI form contains several documents, controls, each with its own window.
- The MDI form is the container for all the individual child forms which are Single Document Interface (SDI).
- To create MDI application, use the following steps :
    1. For creating a new project, select New Project from File menu. Select Standard.EXE. Click OK button. We get a Forml. Save the project by selecting Save Project As from File menu. Enter Images as project name and click Save button. Select Save Form1 As from File menu. Type Imagel as form name and click Save button. So the Images.VBP project file and Imagel.FRM form file was created.
    2. Select Add MDI Form from the Project menu. Click the MDI Form icon in the Add MDI Form dialog box. Then click the Open button. We see a blank form with the default name MDIForm1. If you double-click the MDIForm icon, you will notice that this form has a shorter list of properties than a standard form. You can observe the icon of the Imagel.frm and MDI Forml.frm by selecting Project Explorer from View menu. Select Save MDIForml As from File menu. Save it by name Images. In your Project there is one parent form (Images.frm) and a simple form (Imagel.frm).
    3. Click the View Object icon at the top of the Project window. Click Imagel.frm, so that it becomes active. Then go to the property window of the form, change the MDIChild property of Imagel.frm to True. You can observe the icon of the Imagel.frm which is a child form and icon of the Images.frm which is a parent form. In the parent form, large form is dark and in child form, the little form is dark.

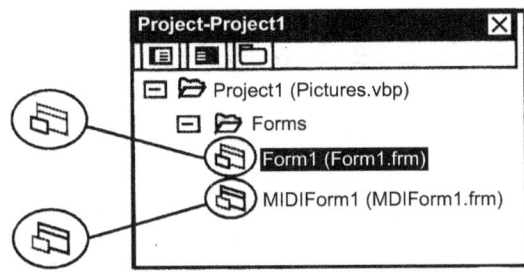

Fig. 3.27

4. Add the more child forms. Select AddForm from Project menu. Select the Form icon and then click the Open button. Change the MDIChild property of Form2.frm to True. Save it with name Image2.frm.
5. Click on the Images.frm in the Project Explorer, so that it becomes active.

The properties table of the parent form Images.frm.

Object	Property	Setting
Form (MDIForm)	Name	FrmImages
	Caption	The Parent Window

The menu table of the parent form Images.frm.

Caption	Name
&File	mnuFile
---- E&xit	mnuExit
&Show Images	mnuImages
---- Show Image&1	mnuShowImage1
---- Show Image&2	mnuShowImage2

6. The properties table of the Image1.frm (child form) :

Object	Property	Setting
Form	Name	frmImage1
	Caption	Picture1 child
	MDI Child	True
Image	Name	imgBell
	Picture	BELL.BMP
	Stretch	False
Command Button	Name	cmdClose
	Caption	&Close

7. The properties table of the Image2.frm (child form) :

Object	Property	Setting
Form	Name	frmImage2
	Caption	Picture2Child
	MDI Child	True
Image	Name	imgCup
	Picture	CUP.BMP
	Stretch	False
Command Button	Name	cmdClose
	Caption	&Close

After completing the form designing, we will write the code in the parent form. Double click on the Images.frm.

1. The code in the general declaration section of the Images.frm :

    ```
    'Each variable must be declared
    Option Explicit.
    ```

2. Enter the following code in the MDIForm_Load ( ) procedure of the frmImages form :

    ```
    Private Sub MDIForm_Load ( )
        'show the child forms
        frmImage1.show
        frmImage2.show
    End Sub
    ```

3. Enter the following code in the mnuExit_Click ( ) procedure of the frmImages form :

    ```
    Private Sub mnuExit_Click ( )
        'terminate the program End
    End Sub
    ```

4. Enter the following code in the minuShowImage1.Click( ) procedure of the frmImages form :

    ```
    Private Sub mnuShowImage1_Click ( )
        frmImage1.show
    End Sub
    ```

5. Enter the following code in the miuShowImagel-Click ( ) procedure of the frmImages form :
```
Private Sub mnuShowImage2_Click ( )
    frmImage2.show
End Sub
```

Enter the code of the frmImagel form :
1. Enter the following code in the general declarations section of the frmImagel form :
```
'Each variable must be declared.
Option Explicit
```
2. Enter the following code in the cmdClose_Click ( ) procedure of the frmImagel form :
```
Private Sub cmdClose_Click ( )
    Unload frmImagel
End Sub
```

Enter the code of the frmImage2 form :
1. Enter the following code in the general declarations section of the frmImage2 form :
```
'Each variable must be declared
Option Explicit
```
2. Enter the following code in the cmdClose_Click ( ) procedure of the frmImage2 form :
```
Private Sub cmdClose_Click ( )
    Unload frmImage2
End Sub
```
Save the project. Run the application by pressing F5.

Procedure for creating MDI form :
1. Select project → Add MDI form
2. Create Menu from Tools → Menu Editor.

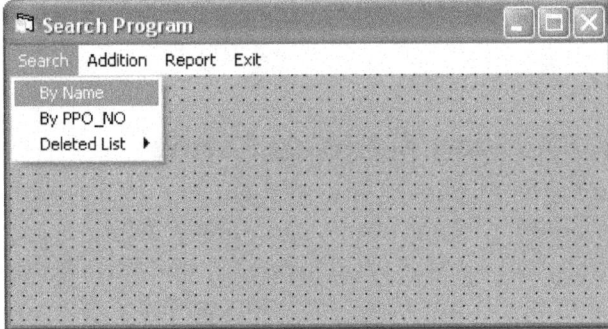

Fig. 3.28

3. Add Form from Project menu.

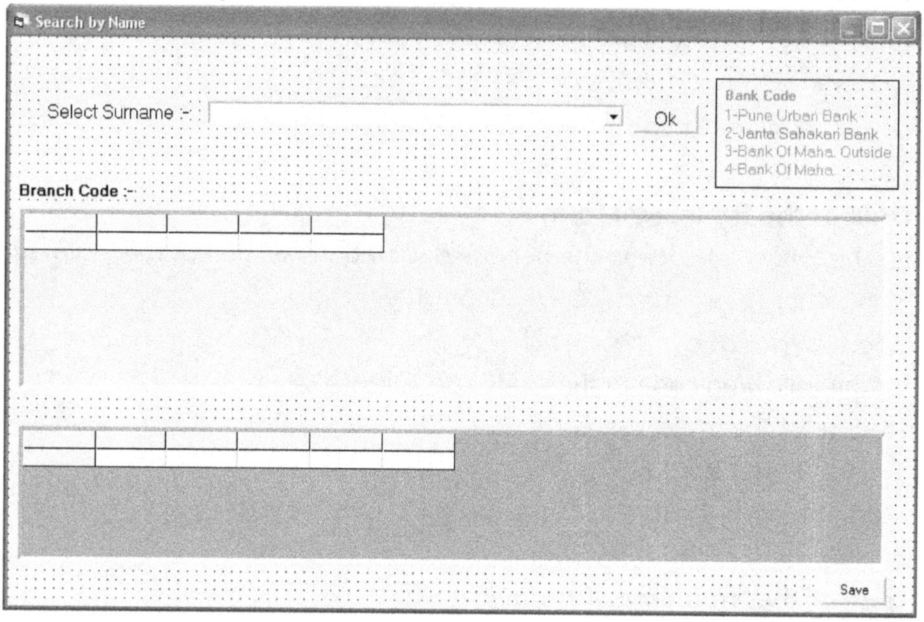

Fig. 3.29

Tool bar control	Properties	Description
Form1	Name	frmname
Label1	Caption	Select Surname
Combo Box	Name	cmbnm
MSFlexGrid1	Name	msflxbr
MSFlexGrid1	Name	msflxrpt
Command Button1	Name	cmdok

write following code on **By Name** menu as :

```
Private Sub mnuname_Click()
Me.MousePointer = 11
fname.Show
End Sub
```

3.4.2 Loading, Showing & Hiding Forms

- Having multiple forms as part of your Visual Basic .NET program may be nice, but when your Visual Basic .NET program runs, it normally displays one form. To make the other forms of your program appear (or disappear), you have to use BASIC code to tell your program, "Okay, now put this particular form on the screen and hide this other form out of sight."

Opening a form
- Before you can open (or close) a form, you need to know the specific name of the form you want to open or close. The Solution Explorer window lists the names of all the forms that make up your Visual Basic .NET program, such as a form named frmMain.vb.
- After you know the name of the form that you want to display, you need to use BASIC command to open the form, such as the following:
    ```
    Dim oForm As FormName
    oForm = New FormName()
    oForm.Show()
    oForm = Nothing
    ```

Hiding (and showing) a form
- If you want to temporarily make a form disappear, you can use the magic Hide command, such as:
    ```
    FormName.Hide()
    ```
- After you've hidden a form, you'll eventually want to make it visible again by using the Show command, such as:
    ```
    FormName.Show()
    ```

Closing a form
- Hiding a form just tucks it out of sight, but the form is still loaded in the computer's memory. To clear a form out of memory, you need to use the Close command, such as:
    ```
    FormName.Close()
    ```
- To make your program end, you have to shut down all your forms. At least one form of your program needs to have an exit command such as an Exit button or a File --> Exit command available from a pull-down menu. The BASIC code to close the last form of your program looks like this:
    ```
    Me.Close()
    ```
- If you look at the BASIC code that Visual Basic .NET automatically creates for each form, you'll see a command that looks like this:
    ```
    Form1 = Me
    ```
- This command just tells Visual Basic .NET, "The word Me represents the current form. So instead of having to type the form's complete name, such as frmMainWindow, you can just type Me instead."

3.4.3 Setting the Startup form
- The Startup object or Startup form property for a project defines the entry point to be called when the application loads. Generally you set this either to the main form in your application or to the Sub Main procedure that should run when the application starts.
- You can set the Startup object or Startup form property in the Application page of the Project Designer.

- The Startup form/Startup object option in the Project Designer depends on the project type. For example, a Console Application has a Startup Object option, which can be Sub Main or Module1. A Windows Application has a Startup Form option, which can be Form1 or Sub Main (see following note). Because class libraries do not have an entry point, their only option for this property is (None).
- The Enable application framework option specifies whether a project will use the application framework. This setting affects the options available in Startup form/Startup object:
    - If Enable application framework is selected (the default), the option is Startup form, and shows only forms because the application framework only supports startup forms, not objects.
    - If Enable application framework is cleared, this option becomes Startup object and shows forms and classes, or modules with a Sub Main. When you disable the application framework, your application uses a custom Sub Main procedure that you have created, and you must add code in the Sub Main procedure for the form.
    - When using a custom Sub Main procedure as the Startup object, code in the application events (Startup, Shutdown, StartupNextInstance, and UnhandledException) is not executed.

To change the startup object or startup form
1. With a project selected in Solution Explorer, on the Project menu, click Properties.
2. Click the Application tab.
3. Select a Startup object from the Startup object or Startup form drop-down list.

To set the startup object for a Windows Application to Sub Main
1. With a project selected in Solution Explorer, on the Project menu, click Properties.
2. Click the Application tab.
3. Clear the Enable application framework check box.
4. Select Sub Main from the Startup object drop-down list.

3.4.3 Using the MDI

Example:
- A new standard EXE project is opened. An MDI form is inserted by selecting Add MDI Form from the project menu. The project now contains a standard form and an MDI Form. The project is saved as mdifirst.vbp. the form is save as childmdi.frm and the mdi form as parent.frm.

Object	Properties	Settings
MDIForm1	Caption	ParentForm
	Caption	ChildForm
Form1	Caption	ChildForm
	MDIChild	True

- Menu items are added to the MDI form as per the specifications shown in following table.

Caption	Name
&File	Mnufile
...&New	submnuNew
...Exit	submnuExit
&Window	mnuWindow
...&Cascade	submnuCascade
...&Tile	submnuTile

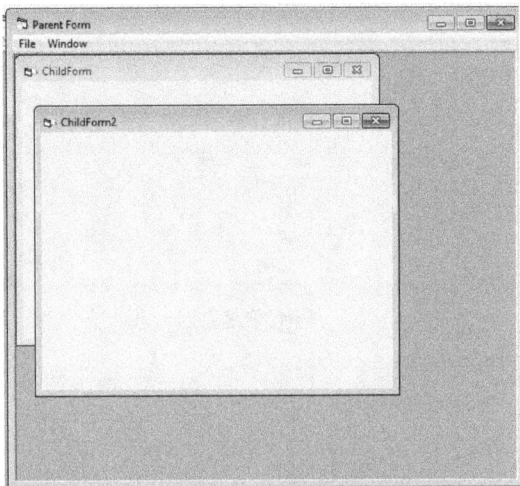

Fig. 3.30 : Adding child form in MDI

- The following code is entered in the mnuNew_click() procedure of MDI Form.
  ```
  Private sub mnuNew_click()
  Dim newform1 as new form1
  Dim newform2 as new form2
  Newform1.show
  Newform2.show
  End sub
  ```

- The first statement in the above procedure declares a variable called newform1 and newform2 as copy of the child form form1 and form2. This implies that, for all purpose, the newform1 and newform2 can be used as an instance of the form1,form2. With the same properties that form1 has at the time of design. The second statement in the procedure causes the newly crated form to pop up. Every time when the menu item is clicked in the MDI Form, a new form pops up.

```
Private sub submnuTile_click()
MDIForm1.arrange vbTileHorizontal
End sub
```

- The code in the mnuTile_click() procedure uses the Arrange method with vbTileHorizontal as the argument to the Tile the child forms.

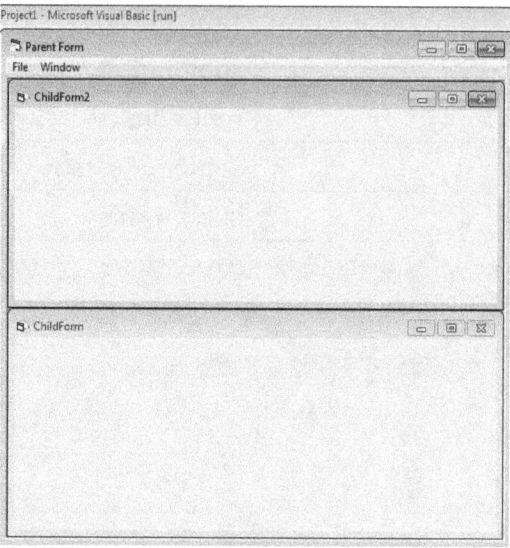

Fig. 3.31

```
Private sub submnuCascase_click()
MDIForm1.arrange vbcascade
End sub
```

- The code in the submnucascade_click() procedure uses the arrange method with vbcascade as the argument to cascade the child forms. Following fig. represents cascaded forms.

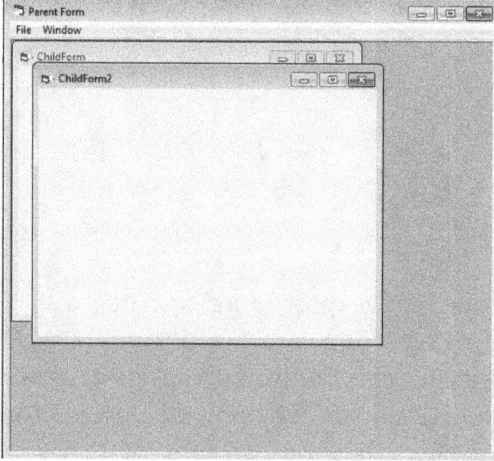

Fig. 3.32

- The following code is entered in the mnuexit_click() to exit the procedure.
  ```
  Private submnuexit_click()
  End
  End sub
  ```

3.4.5 Arranging MDI Child Window

- As mentioned earlier, some applications list actions such as Tile, Cascade, and Arrange Icons on a menu, along with the list of open child forms. Use the Arrange method to rearrange child forms in the MDI form. You can display child forms as cascading, as horizontally tiled, or as child form icons arranged along the lower portion of the MDI form. The following example shows the Click event procedures for the Cascade, Tile, and Arrange Icons menu controls.
  ```
  Private Sub mnuWCascade_Click ()
      ' Cascade child forms.
      frmMDI.Arrange vbCascade
  End Sub
  Private Sub mnuWTile_Click ()
      ' Tile child forms (horizontal).
      frmMDI.Arrange vbTileHorizontal
  End Sub

  Private Sub mnuWArrange_Click ()
      ' Arrange all child form icons.
      frmMDI.Arrange vbArrangeIcons
  End Sub
  ```

3.4.6 Opening New MDI Child Window

- MDI Form cannot contain objects other than child Forms, but MDI Forms can have their own menus. However, because most of the operations of the application have meaning only if there is at least one child Form open, there's a peculiarity about the MDI Forms. The MDI Form usually has a menu with two commands to load a new child Form and to quit the application. The child Form can have any number of commands in its menu, according to the application. When the child Form is loaded, the child Form's menu replaces the original menu on the MDI Form
- Following example illustrates the above explanation.
  * Open a new Project and name the Form as Menu.frm and save the Project as Menu.vbp
  * Design a menu that has the following structure.
    <> MDIMenu Menu caption
      o MDIOpen opens a new child Form
      o MDIExit terminates the application

* Then design the following menu for the child Form
  < > ChildMenu Menu caption
    o Child Open opens a new child Form
    o Child Save saves the document in the active child Form
    o Child Close Closes the active child Form

At design time double click on MDI Open and add the following code in the click event of the open menu.

```
Form1.Show
```

And so double click on MDI Exit and add the following code in the click event

```
End
```

Double click on Child Close and enter the following code in the click event

```
Unload Me
```

Before run the application in the project properties set MDI Form as the start-up Form. Save and run the application. Following output will be displayed.

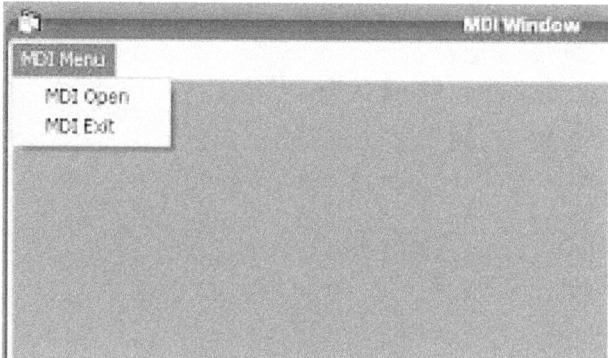

Fig. 3.33 : Output

- And as soon as you click MDI Open you can notice that the main menu of the MDI Form is replaced with the Menu of the Child Form. The reason for this behavior should be obvious. The operation available through the MDI Form are quite different from the operations of the child window. Moreover, each child Form shouldn't have it's own menu.

3.4.7 Creating Properties in a form

- Properties in VB of a form describe the characteristics of an object. Properties can be used to manipulate the identity of an object, its appearance or even its behavior.
- Every and each Visual Basic object has at least one property, but most have many more.
- The properties for a form objects are given below :

ActiveControl	DrawWidth	HelpContextID	NegotiateMenus
ActiveForm	Enabled	hWnd	Picture
Appearance	FillColor	Icon	ScaleHeight

AutoRedraw	FillStyle	Image	ScaleLeft
BackColor	Font	KeyPreview	**ScaleMode**
BorderStyle	FontBold	**Left**	ScaleTop
Caption	FontItalic	LinkMode	ScaleWidth
ClipControls	FontName	LinkTopic	**ShowInTaskbar**
ControlBox	FontSize	**MaxButton**	Tag
Controls	FontStrikethru	MDIChild	Top
Count	FontTransparent	**MinButton**	Visible
CurrentX	FontUnderline	MouseIcon	WhatsThisButton
CurrentY	**ForeColor**	MousePointer	WhatsThisHelp
DrawMode	HDC	Moveable	**Width**
DrawStyle	**Height**	**Name**	**WindwoState**

1. **BackColor property :**

   This property sets the background color of the form. When you double-click BackColor in the properties window or click the drop-down arrow next to the color selection, the properties window will display a dialog box containing a color palette and a system color palette.

2. **BorderStyle :**

   This property of a form determines how the border of a form behaves. A form can have fixed borders that cannot be stretched or sizeable borders that can be stretched by dragging them with the mouse. Procedure for set BorderStyle property are given below :
   (i) In the Form Designer, click the form once to make it the active control.
   (ii) Because the Welcome to Visual Basic form acts more as a dialog box than a useful form, set its BorderStyle property to 3 – Fixed Dialog.
   (iii) Run your modified Welcome to Visual Basic program by selecting Run → Start.

3. **Caption :**

   A caption property is the text that appears on the title bar of the form.

4. **ControlBox Property :**

   The True are False setting determine whether the Control menu is visible.
   Stop your Welcome to Visual Basic application if you have not already done so. In design mode, do the following procedure :
   (i) Make the form the active control by clicking it.
   (ii) In the Properties window, set the ControlBox property to False.
   (iii) Run the program again (Run → Start).

5. **ForeColor Property :**

    This property does not affect the color of objects you place on a form, though it does affect the color of text you print to a form.

    Let's try adding a command button to a form and changing the color of the text and the form itself.

    1. Start a new project by Selecting File → New Project.
    2. Add a command button to Form 1 by double-clicking the command button control in the Toolbox.
    3. Once, the button is ON the form, double-click it to open the button's Click( ) event.
    4. In the Click event procedure for the command button, enter the following line :

        Print "Welcome to Visual Basic"

    Now changing the BackColor and ForeColor properties at design time using the Properties window.

    ```
    BackColor = ForeColor
    ```

6. **Height Property :**

    Use this property to change the height of a form. You can also set the height by dragging the form's borders in design view. The default units for measuring the Height property are twips.

    Using your form from the previous example.

    1. In the Properties window, set the Width property to 4200.
    2. Set the Height property to 4200.

7. **Icon Property :**

    This property select an icon by double-clicking this property. The Icon property determines the icon to display on the Taskbar when the form is minimized at run time.

8. **Left Property :**

    The functions of Left property much like the Height and Width properties. The difference is this property determines the distance of the form from the left to the screen. This property is commonly used in conjunction with the form's Top property, which sets the vertical spacing of the form.

    1. Stop the previous program if you have not already done so.
    2. Double-click the form to get back to the form's Resize event.
    3. Add these two lines of code to the Resize event, below the Width = Height statement.

        ```
        Left = (Screen.Width - Width) / 2
        Top = (Screen.Height - Height) / 2
        ```
    4. Run the program using F5.

9. MaxButton Property :

The setting MaxButton property to True, you form will show the standard Maximize button on the right side of the title bar. If you do not want your users to maximize the form, set this property to False.

10. MinButton Property :

By setting MinButton property to True, your form will show the standard Minimize button on the right side of the title bar. If you do not want your users to minimize the form, set this property to False.

11. Name :

This property is the single most important property in Visual Basic. This is the name of a control that Visual Basic refers to when the program runs.

12. ScaleMode Property :

If you wanted to set the size and position of a command button using the more familiar system of pixels, then set the ScaleMode property for the form to 3 – Pixel.

13. Width Property :

This property specifies the width of the form in twips.

14. WindowState :

This property is responsible for how the form starts up. There are three options.

	Option	Effect
0	Normal	The form will open in its normal state.
1	Minimized	The form will open, but it will be minimized.
2	Maximized	The form will be maximized when it opens.

3.4.8 Creating a method in a form

A form contain following methods :

```
Circle          Move            Pset            TextHeight
Cls             PaintPicture    Refresh         TextWidth
Hide            Point           Scale           Unload
Item            Print           SetFoucs        ZOrder
Line            PrintForm       Show
```

Show, Hide and Unload are the three most popular methods of apply to a form.

Practice Questions

1. What is meant by form control ?
2. Describe procedure for adding a control to a form.
3. Describe following VB controls with their properties and methods.
   - (i) Label
   - (ii) Textbox
   - (iii) Command button
   - (iv) Checkbox
   - (v) Radio buttons
   - (vi) Picture box
4. How to create a VB application?
5. How to create a property in form?
6. What is MDI form?
7. How to display forms in a program?
8. Write procedure for creating a method for a form.
9. Explain the term : coding events for control.
10. How to manipulate a form using variables.
11. What are the event occurring when form is unloaded?

University Question & Answers

April 2010

1. Property used to enable Textbox Control.
Ans. Please refer to Section 3.2.2.

2. Property used to display all *.doc extension file in Filelistbox.
Ans. Please refer to Section 3.2.15

3. Property used to resize picture to fit in the Image Control.
Ans. Please refer to Section 3.2.9.

4. Property to set tab order for the control of the form.
Ans. Please refer to Section 3.2.16.5.

5. Property used to display a read only combo box.
Ans. Please refer to Section 3.2.8

6. Property used to set timer control.
Ans. Please refer to Section 3.2.11.

7. Property used to display text on a label control.
Ans. Please refer to Section 3.2.1.

Programming in Visual Basic (BCA : IV)   3.41   Working with Controls

8. Property used to set special password character of textbox control.
Ans. Please refer to Section 3.2.2.

9. Property used to count number of item in the listbox control.
Ans. Please refer to Section 3.2.7.

10. Property used to place a picture on a command button.
Ans. Please refer to Section 3.2.3.

11. Write short notes on : MDI.   **[4 M]**
Ans. Please refer to Section 3.4.

October 2010

1. Property to place a picture on the command button.
Ans. Please refer to Section 3.2.3.

2. Property to set maximum number of characters to be input using textbox.
Ans. Please refer to Section 3.2.2.

3. Property to set control items alphabetically in a combo box.
Ans. Please refer to Section 3.2.8.

4. Property used to set value of check boxes.
Ans. Please refer to Section 3.2.5.

5. Property used to disable label control.
Ans. Please refer to Section 3.2.1.

6. Property used to remove an item from a list.
Ans. Please refer to Section 3.2.7.

7. Property to set path property of DirList Box.
Ans. Please refer to Section 3.2.14.

8. Property to set tab order for the controls on the form.
Ans. Please refer to Section 3.2.16.5.

9. Explain briefly MDI from. How it different from single form.   **[4 M]**
Ans. Please refer to Section 3.4.

April 2011

1. Property to display picture at run time.
Ans. Please refer to Section 3.2.10.

2. Property to set value of check box.
Ans. Please refer to Section 3.2.5.

3. Property to set items alphabetically in the list.
Ans. Please refer to Section 3.2.7.

4. Property to display text in multiple lines.
Ans. Please refer to Section 3.2.2.

5. Property to add horizontal scroll bar to a text box.
Ans. Please refer to Section 3.2.2.

6. Property to disable text box control.
Ans. Please refer to Section 3.2.2.

7. Property to set caption of a label.
Ans. Please refer to Section 3.2.1.

8. Property to hide image at run time.
Ans. Please refer to Section 3.2.9.

9. Explain ImageList control in detail. [4 M]
Ans. Please refer to Section 3.2.16.3.

10. Differentiate between simple form and MDI form. [4 M]
Ans. Please refer to Sections 3.4.

11. Write short note on tabstrip control. [4 M]
Ans. Please refer to Section 3.2.16.5.

October 2011

1. Property used to type multiline text in a textbox.
Ans. Please refer to Section 3.2.2.

2. Property used to enable textbox control.
Ans. Please refer to Section 3.2.2

3. Property used to display the form as full screen at run time.
Ans. Please refer to Section 3.2.16.

4. Property used to display text in a textbox at centre.
Ans. Please refer to Section 3.2.2.

5. Property used to display picture on the command button.
Ans. Please refer to Section 3.2.3

6. Property display colour on the command button.
Ans. Please refer to Section 3.2.3

7. Property used to count the number of item in the list box control.
Ans. Please refer to Section 3.2.7.

8. Property used to set the timer control.
Ans. Please refer to Section 3.2.11.

9. Property used to set the special password character of textbox control. [2 M]
Ans. Please refer to Section 3.2.2

Programming in Visual Basic (BCA : IV) — 3.43 — Working with Controls

10. State the difference between combobox and list box. **[4 M]**
Ans. Please refer to Sections 3.2.8 and 3.2.7.

11. Explain the structure of MDI.
Ans. Please refer to Sections 3.4.

April 2012

1. Property to set path property of DIR List box.
Ans. Please refer to Section 3.2.14.

2. To status bar for your program.
Ans. Please refer to Section 3.2.16.4.

3. Property used to set value of check box.
Ans. Please refer to Section 3.2.5.

4. Property used to set special password character of text box.
Ans. Please refer to Section 3.2.2.

5. Property used to set timer control.
Ans. Please refer to Section 3.2.11.

6. Property used to place a picture on a command button.
Ans. Please refer to Section 3.2.3.

7. To resize image control.
Ans. Please refer to Section 3.2.9.

8. Write short note on : option button or radio button. **[2 M]**
Ans. Please refer to Section 3.2.4.

October 2012

1. Property used to make the background of the label transparent.
Ans. Please refer to Section 3.2.1.

2. Property used to display information on the command button.
Ans. Please refer to Section 3.2.3.

3. Property used to display information in text box control.
Ans. Please refer to Section 3.2.2.

4. Property used to set the value of check boxes.
Ans. Please refer to Section 3.2.5.

5. Property used to resize picture dynamically to fit the dimensions of the picture box control.
Ans. Please refer to Section 3.2.10.

6. Property to sort the items in a combo box.
Ans. Please refer to Section 3.2.8.

7. Property used to remove items from and list box.
Ans. Please refer to Section 3.2.7.

8. Property used to select *.doc files from a file list box control.
Ans. Please refer to Section 3.2.7.

9. Property used to specify the high end range of the scroll bar control.
Ans. Please refer to Section 3.2.12.

10. Short notes :
    i) MDI.
Ans. Please refer to Section 3.4.

    ii) List View Control.
Ans. Please refer to Section 3.2.7.

    iii) Input Box
Ans. Please refer to Section 3.2.2.

April 2013

1. Property used to Disable Label Control.
Ans. Please refer to Section 3.2.1.

2. Property to set maximum number of characters to be input using textbox.
Ans. Please refer to Section 3.2.2.

3. Property used to display a read only combo box.
Ans. Please refer to Section 3.2.8.

4. Property used to Set Timer Control.
Ans. Please refer to Section 3.2.11.

5. Property used to Set Special Password Character.
Ans. Please refer to Section 3.2.2.

6. Property used to Set Value of Check Boxes.
Ans. Please refer to Section 3.2.5.

7. To resize Image Control.
Ans. Please refer to Section 3.2.9.

8. Property used to count number of item in the listbox control.
Ans. Please refer to Section 3.2.7.

9. Property used to place a picture on a command batton.
Ans. Please refer to Section 3.2.3.

10. Short notes :
    i) Picture Box.
Ans. Please refer to Section 3.4.
    ii) MDI.
Ans. Please refer to Section 3.4.
    iii) Input Box
Ans. Please refer to Section 3.2.2.

October 2013

1. Property used to specify the colour of text to be displayed in the control.
Ans. Please refer to Section 3.2.2.
2. Property used to set timer control.
Ans. Please refer to Section 3.2.11.
3. Property used to resize image control.
Ans. Please refer to Section 3.2.9.
4. Property used to specify the style of the Combo Box appearance.
Ans. Please refer to Section 3.2.8.
5. Property used to set special password character of Text Box.
Ans. Please refer to Section 3.2.2.
6. Property used to type multiline text in a text box.
Ans. Please refer to Section 3.2.2.
7. Short notes :
    i) Combo box control
Ans. Please refer to Section 3.2.8.
    ii) Scroll Bars
Ans. Please refer to Section 3.2.12.

April 2014

1. Property used to stretch the image control to fit the picture.
Ans. Please refer to Section 3.2.9.
2. Property set the shape of the mouse pointer when pointer over a text box.
Ans. Please refer to Section 3.2.2.
3. Property used to specify mask character to be display in the text box.
Ans. Please refer to Section 3.2.2.
4. Property used to type multiline text in a text box.
Ans. Please refer to Section 3.2.2.

5. Property used to remove items from a list box

Ans. Please refer to Section 3.2.7.

6. Compare combo box and list box.

Ans. Please refer to Section 3.2.8 and 3.2.7.

10. Short notes :

　　i) MDI.

Ans. Please refer to Section 3.4.

　　ii) Radio Button

Ans. Please refer to Section 3.2.4.

　　iii) Timer Control.

Ans. Please refer to Section 3.2.11.

　　iv) Input Box

Ans. Please refer to Section 3.2.2.

Chapter 4...

Working with ActiveX Controls

Contents ...

This chapter gives concepts of ActiveX Controls in Visual Basic such as:

4.1 INTRODUCTION
    4.1.1 Need for ActiveX Control
    4.1.2 How to Create ActiveX Control?

4.2 CREATING STATUS BAR FOR YOUR PROGRAM
    4.2.1 Use of StatusBar Control
    4.2.2 Adding a Status Bar to a Program
    4.2.3 Adding Panels to a Status Bar
    4.2.4 Creating Simple Status Bar
    4.2.5 Displaying Images in a Status Bar

4.3 WORKING WITH PROGRESS BAR
    4.3.1 Adding Progress Bar to a Form
    4.3.2 Using a Program Bar

4.4 WORKING WITH TOOLBAR
    4.4.1 Adding a Toolbar to a Form
    4.4.2 Adding Buttons to a Toolbar
    4.4.3 Adding Separators to a Toolbar
    4.4.4 Adding Images to Toolbar Buttons
    4.4.5 Writing Code for Toolbars

4.5 SETTING UP THE IMAGE LIST CONTROLS
    4.5.1 Adding and Deleting Images with Code
    4.5.2 Study of Different Dialog Boxes

4.6 MENU
    4.6.1 Designing Menus
    4.6.2 Creating the Menu with Menu Editor
    4.6.3 Adding Shortcut and Access Keys to Menu Item
    4.6.4 Adding Code to Menus

4.7 POP-UP MENU
    4.7.1 Creating Pop-up Menu
    4.7.2 Activating Pop-up Menu
4.8 ADDING MENU ITEMS AT RUN-TIME
4.9 ADDING MENU ITEMS FOR MDI CHILD FORM
    * Practice Questions
    * University Question & Answers

4.1 INTRODUCTION

- Visual Basic's ActiveX controls are based on the Visual Basic's UserControl object. When we create an ActiveX control, we create a control class file with the extension ctl.
- Visual Basic uses that file to create the actual control, which has the extension **.ocx**. After we register that control with Windows, the control will appear in the Visual Basic Components dialog box, ready for you to add to a program. We can also use these ActiveX controls in Web pages.
- We can add controls to a Visual Basic program like any other control, we also use ActiveX controls on the Internet, embedding them in our web pages, as we will see when we work on creating ActiveX controls.
- ActiveX controls can support properties, events and methods. Our ActiveX control can be built entirely from scratch, it can be built on another control.
- You can combine existing controls, or create your own control from scratch. ActiveX controls created with visual Basic have events, data binding support, licensing support, property pages, Internet features and more.
- ActiveX documents boost your Visual basic application to the Internet and Interanet browser windows. Visual Basic allows you to author full-featured ActiveX controls.
- AcitveX controls, which exist as separate files with a .ocx file name extension. These include controls that are available in all editions of Visual Basic (data-bound grid, combo box, list controls, and so on) and those that are available only in the Professional and Enterprise editions (such as Listview, toolbar, animation, and tabbed dialog). The chapter included explain many of the features of the UserControl object that enable ActiveX control capabilities.

4.1.1 Need for ActiveX Control

- ActiveX controls began as Visual Basic controls that user could add to earlier versions of Visual Basic to expand upon the tool box tools that came with Visual Basic.
- The controls of Visual Basic were not compatible with browser technology, such as, the Internet, and other windows programming tools such as VC++. The Visual Basic controls in the early versions of Visual Basic were important for extending the Visual Basic

progrmmer's ability to write code. The more controls the programmer had, the less work he/she had to do. As a result, an entire programming community and business developed that created Visual basic controls that manipulated graphics, data, grids, multimedia and many more. Due to the popularity of Visual Basic controls, Microsoft was forced to redesign them.

- Between Visual Basic controls and ActiveX controls, Microsoft designed special 32-bit OCX controls. The order VBX controls supported only 16-bit applications. These new Visual Basic controls extended Visual Basic as well as other programming languages, such as Visual C++. OCX controls had an .OCX filename extension.

- The OCX controls, although compatible with Visual C++, did not work easily over the internet, for this reason, Microsoft upgraded them to be ActiveX controls so that Internet browsers, as well as multiple applications and programming languages, work well with them.

4.1.2 How to Create ActiveX Control?

- The following example helps you to create ActiveX control in the program.
    1. Start Visual Basic and then select New Project from File menu.
    2. Select the ActiveX control icon in the New Project window and then click the Open button.
    3. You see Usercontrol window is the active window. Save this project as prjactx and save UserControl as myactx.ctl.

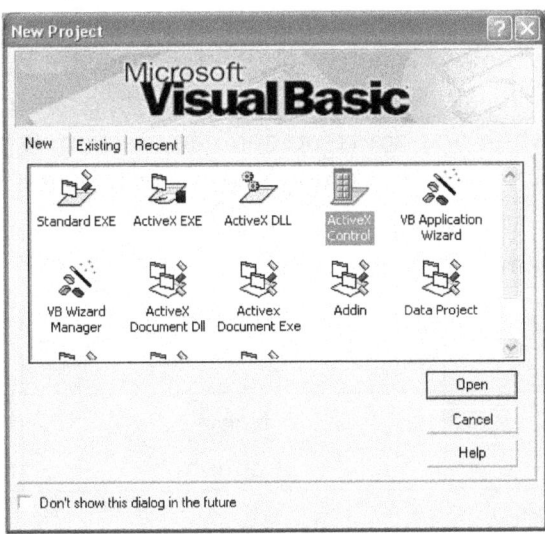

Fig. 4.1

4. Select Project1 Properties from Project menu of Visual Basic. You see Project type as ActiveX Control. Change the Project Name as myactx. Type the Project Description as myactx testing. Click on OK button.

5. Use following toolbox control on the UserControl window.

Toolbar control	Properties	Description
Command button1	Name	Cmdtest
	Caption	Test
Command button2	Name	Cmdclear
	Caption	Clear
Label1	Caption	Empty
	Name	lbltest

Attach the code given below :

```
Private Sub cmdclear_Click( )
lbltest.Caption = ""
End Sub
Private Sub cmdtest_Click( )
lbltest.Caption = "This is my first program to ActiveX"
End Sub
```

6. And save project select Make myactx.ocx from File menu . You cannot run the ActiveX control directly. You can use it in the Form.

7. So select New Project from File menu. Select Standard exe and click on Ok button.

- During the implementation of the Standard EXE project, first to place the myactx OCX ActiveX control in the toolbox window and then to place the myactx control in the form of the Standard EXE project. For this, you select Component in Project menu. Click on activeX component which you are created in early section as myactx. You can see this myactx component in toolbox. You simply select myactx control and drag on the form as other toolbar control you use.

- You add following controls on the Form as :

Toolbar Control	Property	Description
User Control1		
Command button1	Name	Cmdexit
	Caption	Exit

- Write code on Exit button as :

```
Private sub cmdexit_click( )
End
End sub
```

4.2 CREATING STATUS BAR FOR YOUR PROGRAM (Oct. 10, 12)

- Basically, status bars appear at the bottom of windows and hold several panels in which you can display text. Therefore, the status bar is there give feedback to the user on program operation.
- The status bars usually display text in panels, there is a simple status bar style which makes the status bar function as one long panel.
- Status bars are built around the Panels collection. Panel collection which holds the panel in the status bar, up to 16 panel objects can be contained in the collection.
- Each object can display an image and text. We can change the text, images, or widths of any Panel object, using its Text, Picture and Width properties of status bar control.
- To add Panel objects at design time, right-click the status bar and click properties to display the property pages dialog box.
- A status bar is a horizontal window at the bottom of a parent window in which an application can display various kinds of status information.
- The status bar can be divided into parts to display more than one type of information.
- We add the Status Bar Control tool to the toolbox by following the same steps to add the Toolbar Control tool, because the status bar controls is also part of the Microsoft Windows common controls. Click on projects --> components --> microsoft windows common controls.
- The Status Bar Control tool is shown in Fig. 4.2.

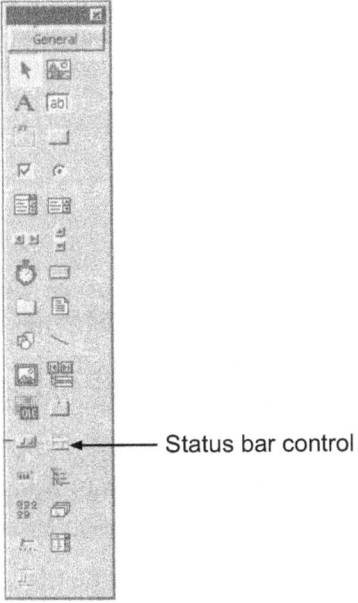

Fig. 4.2 : Status Bar Control tool

- Fig. 4.3 shows the status bar in the Microsoft Windows Paint application.
- The status bar is the area at the bottom of the windows that contains Help text and coordinates information.

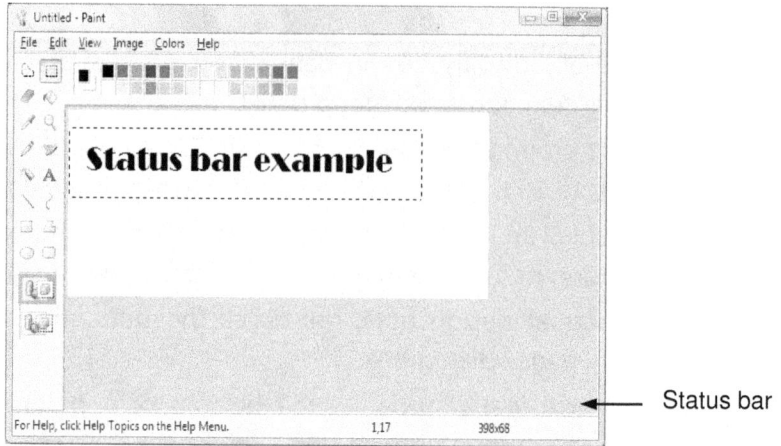

Fig. 4.3

- A StatusBar control is a frame that can consist of several panels which inform the user of the status of an application.
- The control can hold up to sixteen frames. Additionally, the control has a "simple" style, (set with the Style property), which switches from multi-panels to a single panel for special messages.
- The StatusBar control can be placed at the top, bottom, or sides of an application. Optionally, the control can "float" within the application's client area.

4.2.1 Use of StatusBar Control

- Uses of statusBar control are given below :
    1. To inform the user of a database table's metrics, such as number of record and the present position in the database.
    2. To give the user information about a RichTextBox control's text and font status.
    3. To give status about key states, such as the Caps Lock or the Number Lock.
- The StatusBar control is built around the Panels collection. Up to sixteen Panel objects can be contained in the collection. Each object can display an image and text.
- At run time, you can dynamically change the text, images, or widths of any Panel object, using the Text, Picture and Width properties. To add Panel objects at design time, right-click on the control, and click on Properties to display the Property Pages dialog box, as shown in Fig. 4.4.
- Using this dialog box, you can add individual Panel objects and set the various properties for each panel.

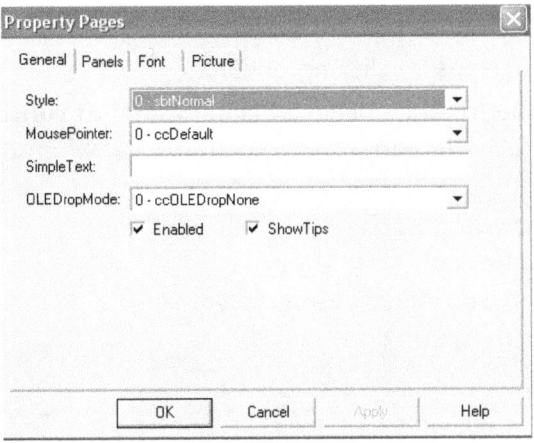

Fig. 4.4 : StatusBar panel

4.2.2 Adding a Status Bar to a Program

- We could design the program with the Visual Basic Application Wizard, which automatically adds a status bar to our program.
- Many programmers will want to add their own status bar to their programs, and you create a status bar by adding a status bar control to a form. Procedure as follows :
  1. Select the Project/Components menu item.
  2. Click the controls tab in the Components dialog box.
  3. Select the Microsoft Windows Common Controls item, and click on OK to close the Components dialog box.
- Above procedure adds the Status Bar Control tool to the Visual Basic toolbox, as shown in Fig. 4.2. To place a status bar in your form, just double-click the Status Bar Control.

Aligning Status Bars in a Form

- We can set the alignment of the status bar with its Align property, which can take following values.
  - vbAlignNone : 0
  - vbAlignTop : 1 (the default)
  - vbAlignBottom : 2
  - vbAlignLeft : 3
  - vbAlignRight : 4

4.2.3 Adding Panels to a Status Bar

- A status bar control has a Panels collection, and you add the panels you want to that collection.
- To do adding panels at **design time**, follow the following steps :
  1. Right-click the status bar and select the Properties item in the menu that opens.
  2. Click the Panels tab in the property pages, as shown in Fig. 4.5

3. Click the Insert Panel button as many times as you want panels in your status bar.
4. Close the property pages by clicking on OK.

- It's also easy and simple to add a new status bar **panel at runtime** — just use the panels collection's **Add** method. We add a panel to status bar when the user clicks a command button :

```
Private Sub Command1_Click( )
    Dim panel7 As Panel
    Set panel7 - StatusBar1.Panels.Add( )
    Pane7.Text - "Status : OK"
End Sub
```

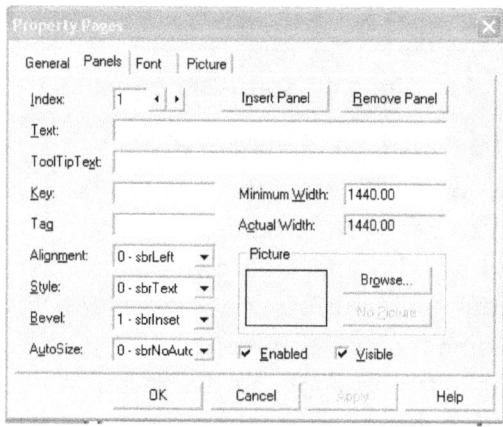

Fig. 4.5

- The text in a status bar is displayed in the status bar's panels. Displaying text in a status bar's panels is very easy and simple, just select the panel you want to work with as the index into the status bar's **Panels** collection and use that panel's **Text** property.
- For example, we will display the program status, "OK", in the first panel of the status bar when the user clicks a command button, **Command1** :

```
Private Sub Command1_Click()
   StatusBar1.Panels(1).Text = "OK"
End Sub
```

Adding New Panels to a Status Bar at Runtime

- It's easy and simple to add a new status bar panel at runtime, you just use the **Panels** collection's **Add** method.
- For example, we add a panel to a status bar when the user clicks a command button :

```
Private Sub Command1_Click ()
    Dim panel7 As Panel
    Set panel7 = StatusBar1.Panels.Add()
    Panel7.Text = "Status : OK"
  End Sub
```

4.2.4 Creating Simple Status Bar

- There is a way of using a status bar without using panels by making the status bars simple status bar.
- Simplestatus bars have only one panel and you set the text in that panel with the **SimpleText** property.
- For example, we just display the message "Status : OK" in the simple status bar when the user clicks a button.

```
Private Sub Command_Click()
   SubstusBar1.SimpleText = "Status : OK"
End Sub
```

Output:

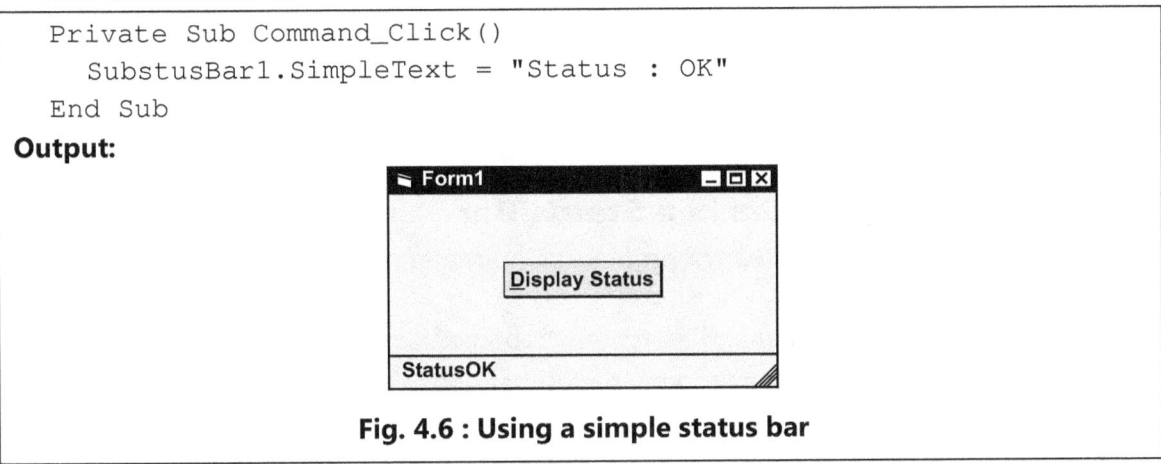

Fig. 4.6 : Using a simple status bar

Displaying Time, Dates, and Key States in a Status Bar

- The status bar controls are already set up to display common status such as key states and dates.
- To display one of those items, just right-click the status bar, select the properties item in the menu that appears, click the Panels tab, select the panel you want to work with and set the **Style** property in the box labeled Style to one of the following :
  - **sbrText (0) :** (the default) : text a bitmap. This property displays text in the **Text** property.
  - **sbrCaps (1) :** Caps Lock key : This displays the letters "CAPS" in bold when Caps Lock is enabled and dimmed when disabled.
  - **sbrNum (2) :** Num Lock key : Which displays the letters "NUM" in bold when the Num Lock key is enabled and dimmed when disabled.
  - **sbrIns (3) :** Insert key : Which displays the letters "INS" in bold when the Insert key is enabled and dimmed when disabled.
  - **sbrScrl (4) :** Scroll Lock key : Which displays the letters "SCRL" in bold when Scroll Lock is enabled and dimmed when disabled.
  - **sbrTime (5) :** time : Which displays the current time in the system format.
  - **sbrDate (6) :** date : Which displays the current date in the system format.

- **sbrKana (7) :** Kana lock. : Which displays the letters "KANA" in bold when kana lock is enabled and dimmed when disabled

  Fig. 4.7 shows a status bar with time.

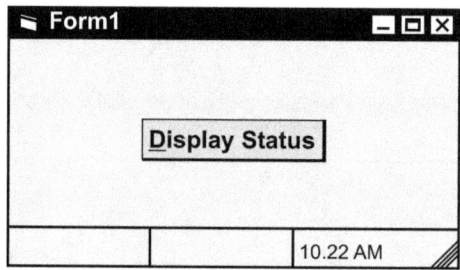

Fig. 4.7 : Displaying time in a status bar

4.2.5 Displaying Images in a Status Bar

- Status bar panels have **a Picture** property. To place an image in a status bar panel at design time, follow the following steps :
  1. Right-click the status bar and Select the Properties item in the menu that appears.
  2. Click the Panels tab in the property pages that open.
  3. Select the panel you want to work with.
  4. Set the panel's **Picture** property by clicking the Browse button in the box labeled Picture. You can set this property with an image file on disk.
  4. Close the property pages by clicking on OK.
- We can also set status bar panel's image at run-time.

  For example : Write the following code :
  ```
  Private sub command1_click ( )
  StatusBar1.Panels (1) Picture = Picture2. Picture
       End sub
  ```

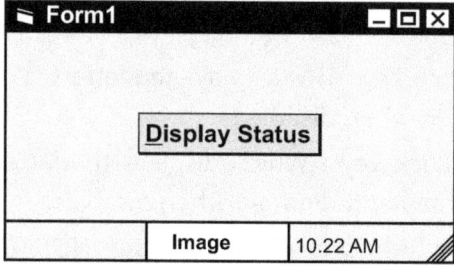

Fig. 4.8 : Displaying images in a status bar

- **Example 1 :** Add Statusbar in the program. Use the set statement with the Add Method to Create Panels at Run Time.
- To add statusBar in the program use the following steps :

  1. Select New Project from File menu. SelectStandard exe and click on Ok button.

2. Right click on toolbar panel, select Components..., click on Microsoft Windows Common Controls6.0(sp6). Click on Ok button.
3. You see some additional tools in toolbox. You click on the Statubar Control. And drag it into the Form. It always come at the bottom of the form. Change its Name property as sbrDB

- To add Panel objects at run time, use the Set statement with the Add method. First declare an object variable of type Panel, then set the object variable to a Panel created with the Add method, as shown in the code below:

```
' The StatusBar control is named "sbrDB."
Dim pnlX As Panel
Set pnlX = sbrDB.Panels.Add()
```

- Once, you have created a Panel object and set the object variable to reference the new object, you can set the various properties of the Panel:

```
pnlX.Text = Drive1.Drive
pnlX.Picture = LoadPicture("mapnet.bmp")
pnlX.Key = "drive"
```

- If you plan to have the control respond when the user clicks on a particular Panel object, be sure to set the Key property. Because the Key property must be unique, you can use it to identify particular panels.
- Use the Select Case Statement in the PanelClick Event to Determine the Clicked Panel. To program the StatusBar control to respond to user clicks, use the Select Case statement within the PanelClick event. The event contains an argument (the *panel* argument) which passes a reference to the clicked Panel object.
- Using this reference, you can determine the Key property of the clicked panel, and program accordingly, as shown in the code below :

```
Private Sub sbrDB_PanelClick(ByVal Panel As Panel)
  Select Case Panel.Key
  Case "drive"
     Panel.Text = Drive1.Drive
  Case "openDB"
     Panel.Text = rsOpenDB.Name
  Case Else
   ' Handle other cases.
  End Select
End Sub
```

- The code below creates eight Panel objects and assigns one of the eight styles to each :

```
Private Sub MakeEight()
  ' Delete the first Panel object, which is
```

```
' created automatically.
StatusBar1.Panels.Remove 1
Dim i As Integer
' The fourth argument of the Add method
' sets the Style property.
For i = 0 To 7
    StatusBar1.Panels.Add , , , i
Next i
' Put some text into the first panel.
StatusBar1.Panels(1).Text = "Text Style"
End Sub
```

- For example, if you are performing a database operation, the Simple style may be used to notify the user of the current state of the transaction, as seen in the code below :

```
Private Sub GetRecords(State)
    ' The query finds all records which match
    ' the parameter State. While the query
    ' is creating the recordset, show the
    ' SimpleText on the StatusBar control.
    sbrDB.SimpleText = "Getting records …"
    sbrDB.Style = sbrSimple ' Simple style.
    sbrDB.Refresh   ' You must refresh to see the
                    ' Simple text.
    Set  rsNames = mDbBiblio.OpenRecordset _ ("select * from Names
                                             Where State= " & _State)
End sub
```

Properties of StatusBar

- Properties of StatusBar are given below :

1. The Style Property : Automatic Status Functions

One feature of the StatusBar control is its ability to display key states, time, and date with a minimum of code. By simply setting the Style property, any Panel object can display one of the following :

Constant	Value	Description
sbrText	0	(Default). Text and/or a bitmap. Set text with the Text property.
sbrCaps	1	Caps Lock key. Displays the letters CAPS in bold when Caps Lock is enabled, and dimmed when disabled.
sbrNum	2	Number Lock. Displays the letters NUM in bold when the number lock key is enabled, and dimmed when disabled.

sbrIns	3	Insert key. Displays the letters INS in bold when the insert key is enabled, and dimmed when disabled.
sbrScrl	4	Scroll Lock key. Displays the letters SCRL in bold when scroll lock is enabled, and dimmed when disabled.
sbrTime	5	Time. Displays the current time in the system format.
sbrDate	6	Date. Displays the current date in the system format.
sbrKana	7	Kana displays the letters KANA in bold when kana lock is enabled, and dimmed when disabled. (enabled on Japanese operating systems only)

2. **Bevel, AutoSize, and Alignment Properties : Program Appearance**

   Using the Bevel, AutoSize, and Alignment properties, you can precisely control the appearance of each Panel object. The Bevel property specifies whether the Panel object will have an inset bevel (the default), raised, or none at all. Settings for the Bevel property are :

Constant	Value	Description
sbrNoBevel	0	The Panel displays no bevel, and text looks like it is displayed right on the status bar.
sbrInset	1	The Panel appears to be sunk into the status bar.
sbrRaised	2	The Panel appears to be raised above the status bar.

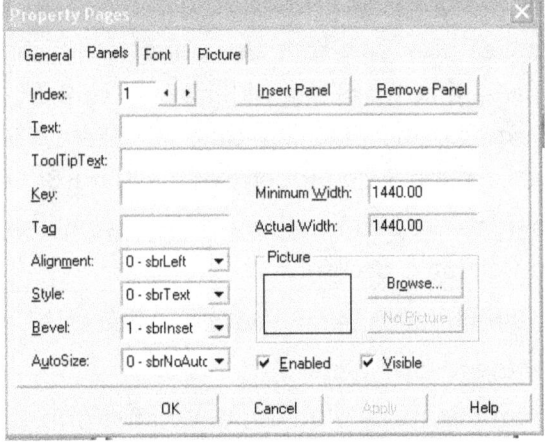

Fig. 4.9

The AutoSize property determines how a Panel object will size itself when the parent container, (either a Form or a container control) is resized by the user. When the *container,* (the Form on which the StatusBar control is placed) of the control is resized, notice that the first panel retains its width, the second "springs" to fill the extra space, and the third sizes according to its contents (and therefore retains its width). Settings for the AutoSize property are :

Constant	Value	Description
sbrNoAutoSize	0	None. No autosizing occurs. The width of the panel is always and exactly that specified by the Width property.
sbrSpring	1	Spring. When the parent form resizes and there is extra space available, all panels with this setting divide the space and grow accordingly. However, the panels' width never falls below that specified by the MinWidth property.
sbrContents	2	Content. The panel is resized to fit its contents.

Set the AutoSize property to Content (2) when you want to assure that the contents of a particular panel are always visible. The Alignment property specifies how the text in a panel will align relative to the panel itself as well as any image in the panel. As with a word processor, the text can be aligned left, center, or right. Settings for the Alignment property are:

Constant	Value	Description
sbrLeft	0	Text appears left-justified and to right of bitmap.
sbrCenter	1	Text appears centered and to right of bitmap.
sbrRight	2	Text appears right-justified but to the left of any bitmap.

3. **Style Property and the SimpleText Property:**

   The StatusBar control features a secondary mode in which the multiple panels are replaced by a single panel that spans the width of the control. This single panel has one property, the SimpleText property which specifies what text is displayed on the panel. To display this single panel, set the Style property of the StatusBar to sbrSimple (1).

   One reason for switching to the Simple style and displaying a single panel is to notify the user that a lengthy transaction is occurring.

- **Example 2 :** To create simplestatus bar in your application.

   For this you can follow the following steps :

1. Select **New Project** from **File** menu. You can get blank Form. Change properties of form as given in the table.

Property Name	Value
Name	Frmsbr
Caption	Test program of StatusBar control
WindowState	2-Maximized

2. Select **Microsoft Windows Common controls 6.0(SP6)** from **Component** of **Project** menu. You see some additional control in toolbar.
3. Select **Statusbar** control and drag it into bottom of the **Form.**

Toolbar control	Property	Value
Option1	Caption	Option1
Option2	Caption	Option2
Option3	Caption	Option3
StatusBar	Caption	StatusBar1

4. Write the following code :

```
Option Explicit
    Private Sub Option1_Click(Index As Integer)
        StatusBar1.Panels(1).Text = "Choice: " & Format$(Index)
    End Sub
```

5. Run the program by pressing F5. As you select Option1 it show in the status bar.

4.3 WORKING WITH PROGRESS BAR (April 10, 12, 13)

- The Progress Bar control shows the progress of a lengthy operation by filling a rectangle with chunks from left to right.
- The ProgressBar control monitors an operation's progress toward completion.
- Progress bar control tool give the user some visual feedback on what is happening during a time-consuming operation. You can use a progress bar when an operation will take some time to finish.
- A ProgressBar control has a range and a current position. The range represents the entire duration of the operation.
- The current position represents the progress the application has made toward completing the operation. The Max and Min properties set the limits of the range.
- The Value property specifies the current position within that range. Because chunks are used to fill in the control, the amount filled in only approximates the Value property's current setting. Based on the control's size, the Value property determines when to display the next chunk.
- User add the progress Bar Control tool to the toolbox by following the same steps to add the statusbar tool, because the progress bar control is also part of the Microsoft Windows common controls.

- The Progress Bar Control tool is shown in Fig. 4.10.

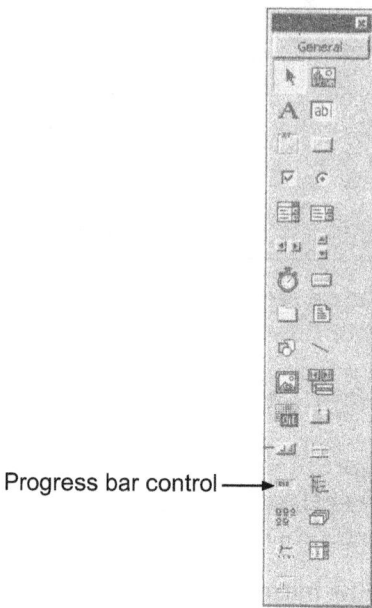

Progress bar control

Fig. 4.10 : The progress bar control tool

- The ProgressBar control's Height and Width properties determine the number and size of the chunks that fill the control.
- The more chunks, the more accurately the control portrays an operation's progress. To increase the number of chunks displayed, decrease the control's Height or increase its Width.
- The BorderStyle property setting also affects the number and size of the chunks. To accommodate a border, the chunk size becomes smaller.
- You can use the Align property with the ProgressBar control to automatically position it at the top or bottom of the form.
- To shrink the chunk size until the progress increments most closely match actual progress values, make the ProgressBar control at least 12 times wider than its height.

Note : The ProgressBar control is part of a group of ActiveX controls that are found in the MSCOMCTL.OCX file. To use the ProgressBar control in your application, you must add the MSCOMCTL.OCX file to the project. When distributing your application, install the MSCOMCTL.OCX file in the user's Microsoft Windows System or System32 directory.

4.3.1 Adding Progress Bar to a Form

- To add a progress bar to a form, follow the following steps :
    1. Select the Project/Components menu item.
    2. Click the Controls tab in the Components dialog box.

3. Select the Microsoft Windows Common Controls item and click on OK to close the Components dialog box. This adds the Progress Bar Control tool to the Visual Basic toolbox, as shown in Fig. 4.10.
4. To place a progress bar in your form, just add it as you would any control, using the Progress Bar Control tool.
5. Set the progress bar's Min (default 0) and Max (default 100) properties as desired to match the range of the operation you are reporting on.

4.3.2 Using a Program Bar

- How to use progress bar in your application, Follow the following steps for adding a progress bar to your form or VB application.

Example 1 :

1. select New Project from File menu. You can get blank Form. Change properties of form as given in the table.

Property Name	Value
Name	Frmpbr
Caption	Test program of ProgressBar control
WindowState	2-Maximized

2. Select Microsoft Windows Common controls 6.0 (SP6) from Component of Project menu. You see some additional control in toolbar.

Toolbar control	Property Name	Value
ProgressBar	Name	prgtest
Command Button	Name	Cmdtest
	Caption	&Start
Check box	Name	Chksmooth
	Caption	S&mooth
Frame	Name	Fraborder
	caption	&Border
Option Button1	Name	Optborder
	Caption	&None
	Index	0
Option Button2	Name	Optborder
	Caption	&Single
		1
Option Button3	Name	Optborder
	Caption	3&D
	Index	2

Your form looks given below :

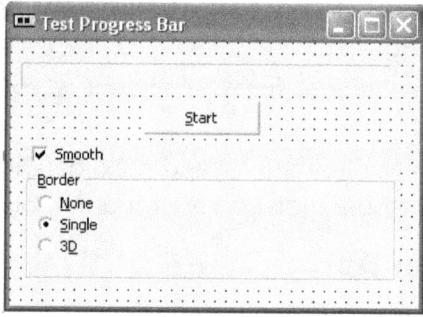

Fig. 4.11

3. Add class module in the project. Give **Name** property as cPropPick. Write the following code :

```
Option Explicit
Private m_picPicture As StdPicture
Public Property Set Picture(ByVal picPicture As StdPicture)
                            Set m_picPicture = picPicture
End Property
Public Property Get Picture() As StdPicture
    Set Picture = m_picPicture
End Property
```

4. Write the code on form as :

```
Option Explicit
Private m_bIn As Boolean
Private Declare Sub Sleep Lib "kernel32" (ByVal dwMilliseconds As Long)
Private Type GUID
    Data1 As Long
    Data2 As Integer
    Data3 As Integer
    Data4(7) As Byte
End Type
Private Declare Function GetSystemDefaultLCID Lib "kernel32" () As Long
Private Declare Function OleCreatePropertyFrame Lib "oleaut32.dll"
_(ByVal hwndOwner As Long, _ ByVal X As Long, _ ByVal Y As Long, _ByVal lpszCaption As Long, _ ByVal cObjects As Long,_ ByRef ppUnk As Long, _ ByVal cPages As Long, _ ByRef pPageClsID As GUID, _ ByVal lcid As Long, _ ByVal dwReserved As Long, _ ByVal pvReserved As Long) As Long
```

```vb
Public Enum PropertyPickerPages
    ppickColor = 1
    ppickPicture = 2
    ppickColorPicture = 3
    ppickPictureColor = 4
End Enum
Public Sub ShowPicker(ByVal hwndOwner As Long, ByVal Caption As String, ByVal PropObject As Object, ByVal Pages As PropertyPickerPages)
    Dim rclsid(1) As GUID
    Dim lObjects(0) As Long
    Dim clsidColor As GUID
    Dim clsidPicture As GUID
    Dim lPageCount As Long
    Dim lRet As Long
    If Not PropObject Is Nothing Then
        lObjects(0) = ObjPtr(PropObject)
        'Guid of CStockColorPage
        '0x7ebdaae1, 0x8120, 0x11cf, 0x89, 0x9f, 0x0, 0xaa,
                                            0x0, 0x68, 0x8b, 0x10
        With clsidColor
            .Data1 = &H7EBDAAE1
            .Data2 = &H8120
            .Data3 = &H11CF
            .Data4(0) = &H89
            .Data4(1) = &H9F
            .Data4(2) = &H0
            .Data4(3) = &HAA
            .Data4(4) = &H0
            .Data4(5) = &H68
            .Data4(6) = &H8B
            .Data4(7) = &H10
        End With
        'Guid of CStockPicturePage
        '0x7ebdaae2, 0x8120, 0x11cf, 0x89, 0x9f, 0x0, 0xaa,
                                            0x0, 0x68, 0x8b, 0x10
        With clsidPicture
            .Data1 = &H7EBDAAE2
            .Data2 = &H8120
            .Data3 = &H11CF
            .Data4(0) = &H89
            .Data4(1) = &H9F
            .Data4(2) = &H0
            .Data4(3) = &HAA
            .Data4(4) = &H0
```

```vb
                .Data4(5) = &H68
                .Data4(6) = &H8B
                .Data4(7) = &H10
            End With
            Select Case Pages
                Case ppickColor
                    rclsid(0) = clsidColor
                    lPageCount = 1
                Case ppickColorPicture
                    rclsid(0) = clsidColor
                    rclsid(1) = clsidPicture
                    lPageCount = 2
                Case ppickPicture
                    rclsid(0) = clsidPicture
                    lPageCount = 1
                Case ppickPictureColor
                    rclsid(0) = clsidPicture
                    rclsid(1) = clsidColor
                    lPageCount = 2
            End Select
lRet     =      OleCreatePropertyFrame(hwndOwner,   0,    0,
StrPtr(Caption),   1,   lObjects(0),   lPageCount,   rclsid(0),
GetSystemDefaultLCID, 0&, 0&)
            If lRet <> 0 Then Err.Raise lRet
        End If
End Sub
Private Sub pProgress()
Static iPos As Long
Static iDir As Integer
    If (iDir = 0) Then iDir = 1
    Do While (m_bIn)
        iPos = iPos + iDir
        If (iPos = 100) Then iDir = -1
        If (iPos = 0) Then iDir = 1
        prgTest.Position = iPos
        Sleep 50
        DoEvents
    Loop
End Sub
Private Sub chkSmooth_Click()
    prgTest.Smooth = chkSmooth.Value * -1
End Sub
Private Sub cmdTest_Click()
    If (cmdTest.Caption = "&Start") Then
        cmdTest.Caption = "&Stop"
```

```
            m_bIn = True
            pProgress
        Else
            cmdTest.Caption = "&Start"
            m_bIn = False
        End If
End Sub
Private Sub Form_QueryUnload(Cancel As Integer, UnloadMode _
                                                    As Integer)
    m_bIn = False
End Sub
Private Sub optBorder_Click(Index As Integer)
    prgTest.BorderStyle = Index
End Sub
```

5. Run the project by pressing F5.

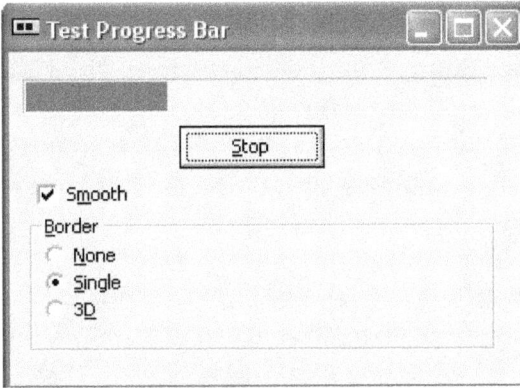

Fig. 4.12

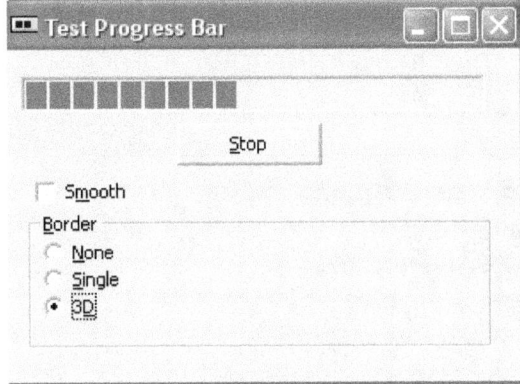

Fig. 4.13

- **Example 2 :** How to create a progress Bar without using progress bar control?
1. Select **New Project** from **File** menu. You can get blank Form. Change properties of form as given in the table.

Property Name	Value
Name	Frmpbr
Caption	Test program of ProgressBar control
WindowState	0-Normal

2. Add following button in the **Form**.

Toolbar control	Property Name	Value
Picture	Name	Picture1
Command button	Name	Command1
	Caption	Start

3. Write the following code :

```
Dim tenth As Long
#If Win32 Then

Private Declare Function BitBlt Lib "gdi32"_(ByVal hDestDC As
Long, ByVal x As Long, ByVal y As Long,_ByVal nWidth As Long,
ByVal nHeight As Long,_ByVal hSrcDC As Long, ByVal xSrc As Long,
ByVal ySrc As Long,_ByVal dwRop As Long) As Long
#Else

Private Declare Function BitBlt Lib "GDI" (ByVal hDestDC As _
Integer, ByVal x As Integer, ByVal y As Integer, ByVal nWidth _
As Integer, ByVal nHeight As Integer, ByVal hSrcDC As Integer,
_ByVal xSrc As Integer, ByVal ySrc As Integer, ByVal dwRop As
_Long) As Integer
#End If
   Sub UpdateStatus(FileBytes As Long)
'-----------------------------------------------------------
' Update the Picture1 status bar
'-----------------------------------------------------------
    Static progress As Long
    Dim r As Long
    Const SRCCOPY = &HCC0020
    Dim Txt$
    progress = progress + FileBytes
    If progress > Picture1.ScaleWidth Then
        progress = Picture1.ScaleWidth
    End If
    Txt$ = Format$(CLng((progress / Picture1.ScaleWidth) *
100))+ "%"
```

```
        Picture1.Cls
Picture1.CurrentX=_(Picture1.ScaleWidth_Picture1.TextWidth
                                                    (Txt$)) \ 2
        Picture1.CurrentY=_(Picture1.ScaleHeight_Picture1.TextHeight
                                                    (Txt$)) \ 2
        Picture1.Print Txt$
      Picture1.Line (0, 0)-(progress, Picture1.ScaleHeight),_
        Picture1.ForeColor, BF
        r = BitBlt(Picture1.hDC, 0, 0, Picture1.ScaleWidth,_
                  Picture1.ScaleHeight, Picture1.hDC, 0, 0, SRCCOPY)
End Sub
Private Sub Command1_Click()
    Picture1.ScaleWidth = 109
    tenth = 10
    For i = 1 To 11
        Call UpdateStatus(tenth)
        x = Timer
        While Timer < x + 0.75
            DoEvents
        Wend
    Next
    Command1.Caption = "Completed"
End Sub
Private Sub Form_Load()
    Picture1.FontBold = True
    Picture1.AutoRedraw = True
    Picture1.BackColor = vbWhite
    Picture1.DrawMode = 10
    Picture1.FillStyle = 0
    Picture1.ForeColor = vbBlue
End Sub
```

- Run the program by pressing F5.

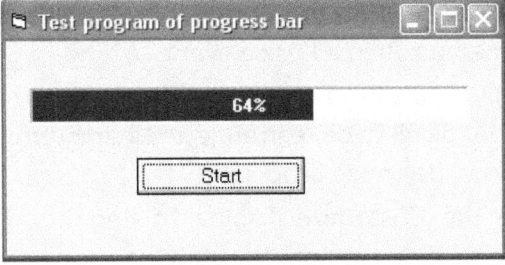

Fig. 4.14

4.4 WORKING WITH TOOLBAR (Oct. 11)

- A toolbar contains buttons that correspond to items in an application's menu, providing an easy interface for the user to reach frequently used functions and commands.
- The user can also customize toolbars by applying the following procedure. Double-clicking a toolbar at runtime opens the Customize Toolbar dialog box, which allows the user to hide, display or rearrange toolbar buttons.
- The toolbar also called a ribbon or control bar. It has become a standard feature in many Windows-based applications.
- A toolbar provides quick access to the most frequently used menu commands in an application.
- Creating a toolbar is easy and convenient using the toolbar control, which is available with the Professional and Enterprise editions of Visual Basic.
- Fig. 4.15 shows a toolbar control of VB.
- A Toolbar control contains a collection of Button objects used to create a toolbar you can associate with an application.
- Typically, a toolbar contains buttons that correspond to items in an application's menu, providing a graphic interface for the user to access an application's most frequently used functions and commands.
- The Toolbar control can also contain other controls, such as ComboBox or TextBox controls.
- To create a toolbar, you must add Button objects to a Buttons collection; each Button object can have optional text and/or an image, supplied by an associated ImageList control.
- Set text with the Caption property, and an image with the Image property for each Button object. At design time, you can add Button objects to the control with the Toolbar Property Pages dialog box.
- At run time, you can add or remove buttons from the Buttons collection using Add and Remove methods.
- To add other controls at design time, simply draw the desired controls on the toolbar. Alternatively, you can create a Button object with a Placeholder style and position the desired control over the button in a Resize event.
- Double-clicking a toolbar at run time invokes the Customize Toolbar dialog box, which allows the user to hide, display, or rearrange toolbar buttons. To enable or disable the dialog box, set the AllowCustomize property.
- You can also invoke the Customize Toolbar dialog box by invoking the Customize method. If you wish to save and restore the state of a toolbar, or allow the end user to do so, use the SaveToolbar and RestoreToolbar methods.

- **Uses of toolbar :**
  1. Provide a consistent interface between applications with matching toolbars.
  2. Place commonly used functions, such as File operations, in an easy to access place.
  3. Provide a graphical, intuitive interface for your application.
- Fig. 4.15 shows a toolbar control.
- For adding buttons to a toolbar, you add Button objects to its **Buttons** collection, usually by working with the toolbar's property pages.
- Each button can have test and/or an image. Set text with the **Caption** property and an image with the **Image** property for each Button object.
- At runtime, you can add or remove buttons from the **Buttons** collection using **Add** and **Remove** methods.

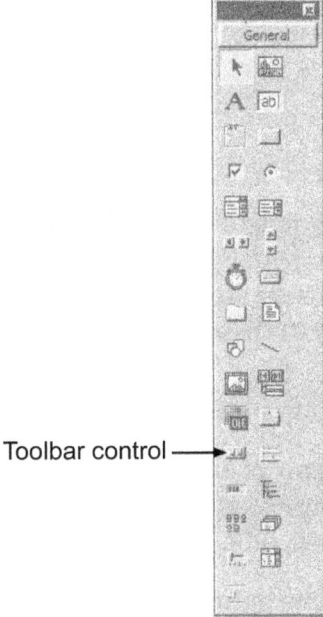

Toolbar control

Fig. 4.15 : The toolbar control tool

- If you are using the Learning Edition of Visual Basic, you can create toolbars manually. The following example demonstrates creating a toolbar for an MDI application; the procedure for creating a toolbar on a standard form is basically the same.
- **To manually create a toolbar :**
  1. Place a picture box on the MDI form. The width of the picture box automatically stretches to fill the width of the MDI form's workspace. The workspace is the area inside a form's borders, not including the title bar, menu bar, or any toolbars, status bars, or scroll bars that may be on the form. You can place only those controls that support the Align property directly on an MDI form, (the picture box is the only standard control that supports this property).

2. Inside the picture box, place any controls (Command Button) you want to display on the toolbar. Typically, you create buttons for the toolbar using command buttons or image controls. To add a control inside a picture box, click the control button in the toolbox, and then draw it inside the picture box. When an MDI form contains a picture box, the internal area of the MDI form does not include the area of the picture box. For example, the ScaleHeight property of the MDI form returns the internal height of the MDI form, which does not include the height of the picture box. You can create buttons for the toolbar using image controls.
- You can change **Style** the property of **Command Button** as **1-Garphical** and **Picture** as add bmp to that button, remove whatever **Caption** is there.

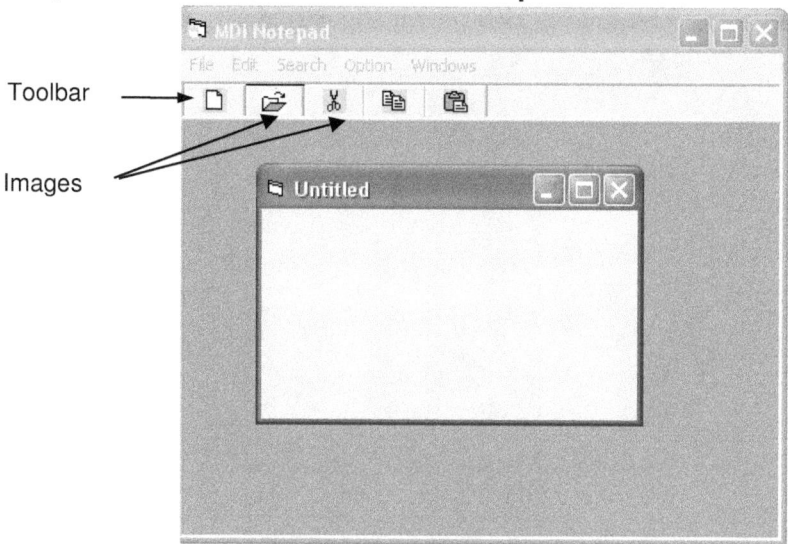

Fig. 4.16

3. Set design-time properties. One advantage of using a toolbar is that you can present the user with a graphical representation of a command. The image control is a good choice as a toolbar button because you can use it to display a bitmap. Set its Picture property at design time to display a bitmap; this provides the user with a visual cue of the command performed when the button is clicked.

   You can also use *ToolTips*, which display the name of the toolbar button when a user rests the mouse pointer over a button, by setting the ToolTipText property for the button.

4. Write code on each command button. Because toolbar buttons are frequently used to provide easy access to other commands, most of the time you call other procedures, such as a corresponding menu command, from within each button's Click event.

4.4.1 Adding a Toolbar to a Form

- Probably the easiest and simplest way to add a toolbar to a program is to design that program with the Visual Basic Application Wizard.

- By using the Application Wizard to create a program, that program gets a toolbar automatically.
- User can arrange and configure the toolbar with the Application Wizard Customize Toolbar dialog box, shown in Fig. 4.17, which appears when user's create a program with the Application Wizard.
- When you run the program it generates, you see a fully functional toolbar in that program, as shown in Fig. 4.18.

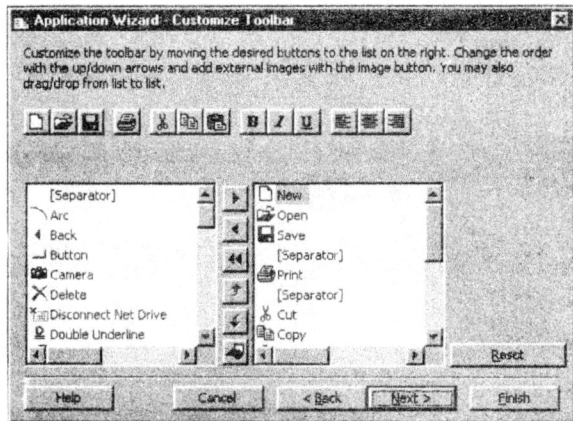

Fig. 4.17 : Application Wizard customize toolbar dialog box

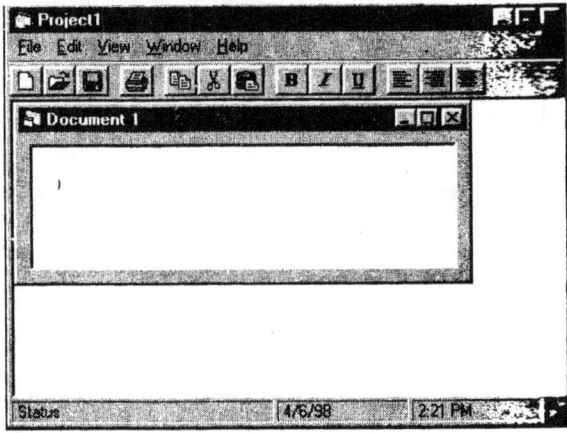

Fig. 4.18 : An application Wizard program with toolbar

- Many software programmers will want to add their own toolbars to their programs and you create a toolbar by adding a toolbar control to a form.
- For creating a toolbar follow the following steps :
    1. Select the Project/Components menu item.
    2. Click the Controls tab in the Components dialog box.
    3. Select the Microsoft Windows Common Controls item.
    4. Click on OK to close the Components dialog box.

- Above procedure adds the Toolbar Control tool to the Visual Basic toolbar as shown in Fig. 4.18. To place a toolbar in your form, just double-click the Toolbar Control tool.

Aligning Toolbars in a Form

- User can set the alignment of the toolbar with its Align property, which can take the following values :
  1. vbAlignNone : 0
  2. vbAlignTop : 1 (the default)
  3. vbAlignBottom : 2
  4. vbAlignLeft : 3
  5. vbAlignRight : 4

4.4.2 Adding Buttons to a Toolbar

- User can add buttons to a toolbar control at design time by right-clicking the control and clicking the properties item in the menu that appears.
- When the toolbar's property pages open, click the Buttons tab, as shown in Fig. 4.19.
- User can insert new buttons by clicking the Insert Button button method. When user add a new button to a toolbar, he/she can associate a picture or caption with it.
- For example, to give a button a caption, just fill in the Caption box in Fig. 4.19.
- Each button of toolbar gets a new Index value, which will be passed to the Click event handler.
- User can also give each button a Key value, which is a string that he/she can use to identify the button. When user are done, click on the OK button to close the toolbar's property pages.

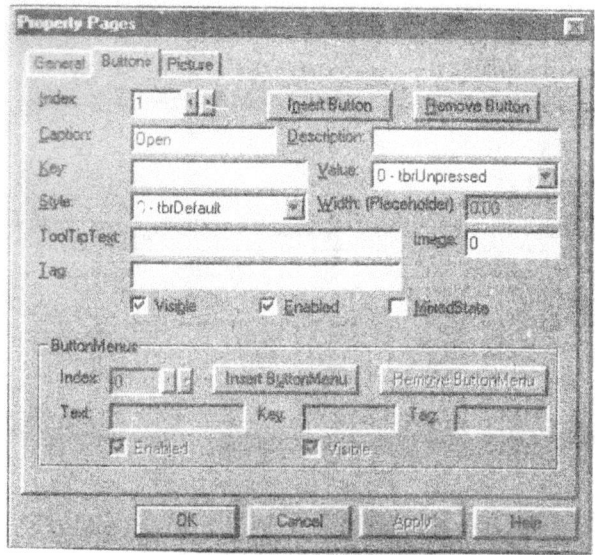

Fig. 4.19 : Adding new buttons to a toolbar

4.4.3 Adding Separators to a Toolbar

- In toolbars, separators just appears as blank spaces, setting groups of buttons apart.

  For example : Insert a new button into a toolbar and set its **Style** property to **tbrSeparatror**, as shown in Fig. 4.20 (a).

- Now add other buttons and click on OK to close the toolbar's property pages. When user do, he/she will see that the separator puts some distance between the buttons, as shown in Fig. 4.20 (b).

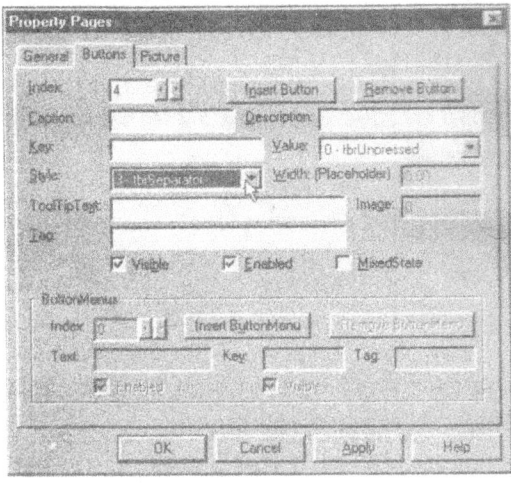
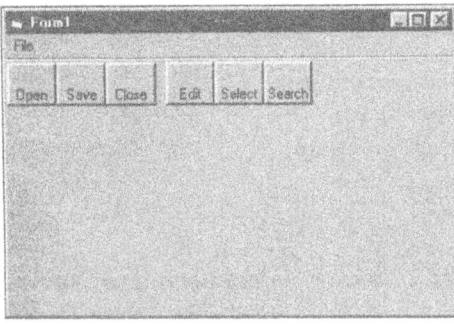

(a)   (b)

Fig. 4.20 : Adding a separator to a toolbar

4.4.4 Adding Images to Toolbar Buttons

- User can give toolbar buttons if he/she place those images into an image list control. Image lists are Windows common controls just as toolbars are, so add an image list to a program now.

- To place the images you want in the buttons in the image list, following the following steps :

  1. Right-click the image list control.
  2. Select the Properties menu item.
  3. Click the Images tab in the image control's property pages.
  4. Click the Insert Picture button to insert the first image.
  5. Keep going until all the images have been added to the image control,
  6. Click on OK to close the property pages.

- Now user need to associate the image control with the toolbar and he/she do that in the toolbar's property pages; just follow the following steps :

  1. Right-click toolbar and select the Properties item to open the toolbar's property pages, (Refer Fig. 4.21).
  2. Next, click the Buttons tab in the property pages, (Refer Fig. 4.22).

3. Enter the index of the image in the image control you want to connect to the first button in the box labeled Image.
4. Keep going for the other buttons, entering the image control indices of the images you want to connect to those buttons.
5. Click on OK to close the property pages.

- When user run the program, the images appear in the toolbar.

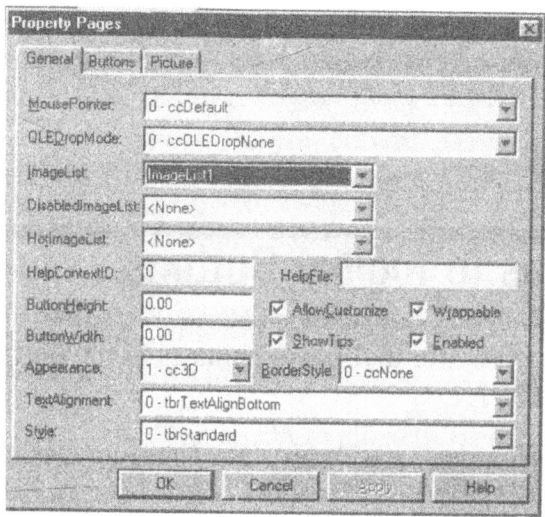

Fig. 4.21 : Adding images from an image control to a toolbar control

- User can also connect an image control to a toolbar at runtime, using the toolbar's **ImageList** property :

```
Private Sub Command1_Click()
    tbr1.ImageList = ImageList1
End Sub
```

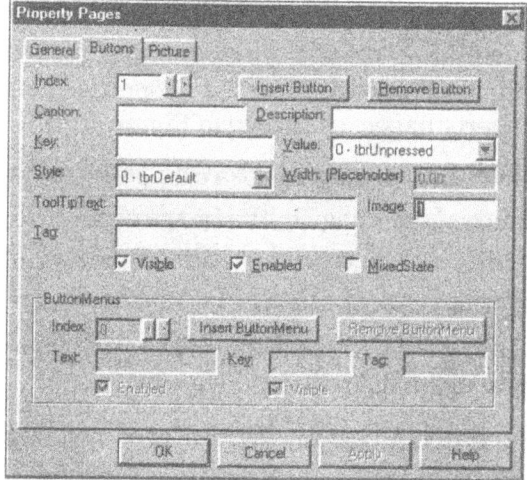

Fig. 4.22 : Connecting images from an image control to toolbar buttons

4.4.5 Writing Code for Toolbars

- Toolbars are used to provide the user with a quick way to access some of the application's commands.
- For example, the first button on the toolbar in Fig. 4.16 is a shortcut for the File New command.
- There are now three places in the MDI NotePad sample application where the user can request a new file :
    - On the MDI form, (New on the MDI form File menu)
    - On the child form, (New on the child form File menu)
    - On the toolbar, (File New button)
- Rather than duplicate this code three times, you can take the original code from the child form's mnuFileNew_Click event and place it in a public procedure in the child form. You can call this procedure from any of the preceding event procedures.

```
' This routine is in a public procedure.
Public Sub FileNew ()
    Dim frmNewPad As New frmNotePad
    frmNewPad.Show
End Sub
' The user chooses New on the child form File menu.
Private Sub mnuchildFileNew_Click ()
    FileNew
End Sub
' The user chooses New on the MDI form File menu.
Private Sub mnumdiFileNew_Click ()
    frmNotePad.FileNew
End Sub
' The user clicks the File New button on the toolbar.
Private Sub btnFileNew_Click ()
    frmNotePad.FileNew
    End Sub
```

Create Buttons at Design Time or Run Time

- To create Button objects at design time follow the following steps :
    1. Select New Project from File menu. You can get blank Form.
    2. Select Microsoft Windows Common controls 6.0(SP6) from Component of Project menu. You see some additional control in toolbar.

3. Right-click on the Toolbar control and click Properties to display the Toolbar Property Pages.
4. Click the Buttons tab to display the dialog box shown in Fig. 4.23.
5. Click Insert Button to insert a new Button object.
6. Set appropriate properties, such as Key, Caption, Image, and ToolTipText.
7. Set the Button object's Style property by clicking the Style box and selecting a style.

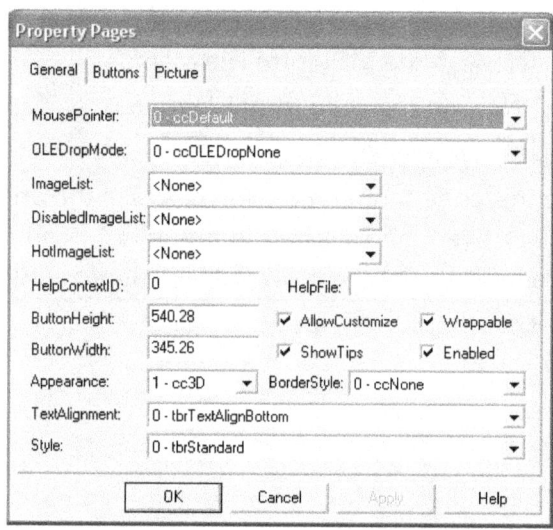

Fig. 4.23 : Toolbar control property pages

- **To create a collection of Button objects at run time :**
  1. Declare an object variable of type Button. As you add each Button object, the variable will contain the reference to the newly created object. Use this reference to set various properties of the new Button object.
  2. Using the Set statement with the Add method, set the object variable to the new Button object.
  3. Using the object variable, set the properties of the new Button object.
- The code below uses the Form object's Load event to create one Button object, then sets the Key, Caption, ToolTipText, and Style properties of the new Button object.

```
Private Sub Form_Load()
    ' Declare a variable, then set using the Set
    ' statement with the Add method, create a new
    ' Button object, and set the object variable to
    ' the new Button. Use the reference to set
    ' properties.
    Dim myButton As Button
    Set myButton = tlbTools.Buttons.Add()
    myButton.Key = "left"
```

```
    myButton.Caption = "Align Left"
    myButton.ToolTipText = "Align Left"
    myButton.Style = tbrSeparator
End Sub
```

Note : Using the arguments of the Button collection's Add method is more efficient than setting the properties with the object variable. In this case, the code above could be rewritten as :

```
    tlbTools.Buttons.Add , "left", "Align Left", _tbrSeparator
        Properties of Toolbar control
```

Properties of Toobar

1. **Button Style Property; Determines Button Behavior :**

   An important property of the Button object is the Style property. The Style property determines how a button behaves and the function assigned to the button can have a bearing on which style is applied to it. The five button styles are listed below, with their possible uses :

Constant	Value	Possible Use
tbrDefault	0	Use the Default button style when the function it represents has no dependence on other functions. For example, a Save File operation can be performed at any time. Further, when the button is depressed, it springs back again when the function is finished.
tbrCheck	1	The Check style should be used when the function it represents is a toggle of some kind. For example, when using a RichTextBox control, selected text can be either bold or not. Thus, when the button is depressed, it stays depressed until it is pressed again.
tbrButtonGroup	2	Use the ButtonGroup style when a group of functions are mutually exclusive. That is, only one of the functions represented by the group of buttons can be on at a time. For example, text in a RichTextBox control can only be left-aligned, center-aligned, or right-aligned — it cannot be more than one style at a time. Note: although only one button at a time can be depressed, all buttons in the group can be unpressed.
tbrSeparator	3	The separator style has no function except to create a button that is eight pixels wide. Use the separator style to create a button that separates one button from another. Or use it to enclose the group of buttons with the ButtonGroup style.

tbrPlaceholder	4	The placeholder style functions as a "dummy" button: use this button to create a space on the Toolbar control where you want to have another control (such as a ComboBox or ListBox control) appear.

Placing Controls on the Toolbar

- You can easily place other controls, such as the ComboBox, TextBox or OptionButton control, on the Toolbar control at design time.

1. **To place other controls on the Toolbar control at design time**
    (i) Create Button objects and assign appropriate properties.
    (ii) Create a space on the toolbar where you want the other control to appear, then add a button with the Placeholder style and set the Width property to an appropriate value.
    (iii) Draw the other control in the space occupied by the placeholder button.

2. **Reposition Other Controls in the Resize Event :**

- If the Wrappable property is set to True, the Toolbar control wraps automatically when the end user resizes the form. While Button objects wrap automatically, controls placed on them do not. To enable controls to wrap, first create a Button object with the Placeholder style, and draw the control in the space created by the button. Then reposition the control over the button using the Move method in the Form object's Resize event, as shown below :

```
Private Sub Form_Resize()
    ' The Toolbar is named "tlbRTF"
    ' The Button object's Key is "btnFonts"
    ' The Combobox is named "cmbFonts"
    ' The ComboBox is placed over the position of the
    ' Button object using the Move method.
    With tlbRTF.Buttons("btnFonts")
        cmbFonts.Move .Left, .Top, .Width
        cmbFonts.ZOrder 0
    End With
End Sub
```

3. **Use the Select Case Statement in the ButtonClick Event to Program Button Functionality :**

    The ButtonClick event occurs whenever a button, (except buttons with the placeholder or separator style) is clicked. You can identify the button that was clicked by its Index property or its Key property. Using either of these properties, use the Select Case statement to program the button's function, as shown in the example code below :

```
Private Sub tlbRTF_Click(ByVal Button As Button)
   Select Case Button.Key
   Case "OpenFile"
      ' Call a user-defined function to open a file.
      OpenFile
   Case "Bold"
      ' Call a user-defined function to bold text.
      BoldText
   Case Else
      ' Handle other cases.
   End Select
End Sub
```

4. **Use the MixedState Property to Signify Indeterminate States :**

   In some cases, a function of your application may return an indeterminate state a state that is a combination of two or more states. For example, if the user selects text in a RichTextBox, and some of the text is italicized, the button that represents italicized text cannot be either checked or unchecked; the text in the selection is both. To signify this indeterminate state, set the MixedState property to True. This dithers the image on the button to create a third state of the button's image.

5. **Set ToolTip Text with the ToolTipText Property :**

   A *ToolTip* is the text that appears above a button whenever the cursor hovers (without clicking) over a Button object. You can add a ToolTip to any button at design time by typing the text you want to appear in the ToolTipText box of the Toolbar control's Property Pages.

   At run time, you can dynamically change the ToolTip by setting the ToolTipText property for the Button object. The following code occurs in a CommandButton control that changes the Key and ToolTipText property of one button :

```
Private Sub cmdChangeButton_Click()
   ' The name of the toolbar is "tlbFunctions"
   ' Reset the Key and ToolTipText properties of
   ' a button with Key property value "1 funct"
   tlbfuncts.Buttons("1 funct"). _
   ToolTipText = "Function 7"
   tlbfuncts.Buttons("1 funct").Key = "7 funct"
End Sub
```

4.5 SETTING UP THE IMAGE LIST CONTROLS

- An ImageList control contains a collection of images that can be used by other Windows Common Controls specifically, the ListView, TreeView, TabStrip, and Toolbar controls.

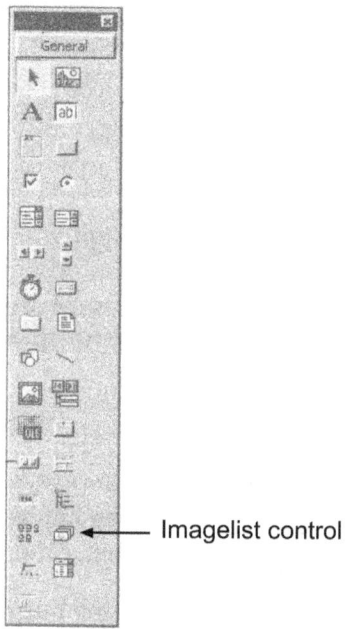

Fig. 4.24 : The Image List control tool

- For example, the ImageList control can store all the images that appear on a Toolbar control's buttons.

- Image list controls are invisible controls that serve are important purpose to hold images that are used by other controls. In general you add image list control at design time, using the Insert Picture button in the control's property pages. You can also add images to an image list at runtime, using the Add method of its internal image collection, ListImages.

- The Image List Control tool appears in the Visual Basic toolbar shown in Fig. 4.24.

- The ImageList control can also be used with controls that assign a Picture object to a Picture property, such as the PictureBox, Image, and CommandButton controls.

- Using the ImageList control as a single repository saves you development time by allowing you to write code that refers to a single, consistent catalog of images. Instead of writing code that loads bitmaps or icons (using the LoadPicture function), you can populate the ImageList once, assign Key values if you wish, and write code that uses the Key or Index properties to refer to images.

- The control uses bitmap (.bmp), cursor (.cur), icon (.ico), JPEG (.jpg), or GIF (.gif) files in a collection of ListImage objects. You can add and remove images at design time or run time.
- The ListImage object has the standard collection object properties : Key and Index. It also has standard methods, such as Add, Remove, and Clear.

Uses of ImageList Control
- To store the images that represent open folders, closed folders, and documents. These images can then be dynamically assigned to the TreeView control's Node object to represent its different states as it expands or collapses, or whether or not it is a document or a folder.
- To store images that represent common computer operations, such as saving, opening and printing files. These images can then be assigned to Button objects on a Toolbar control used by your application.
- To store images for drag-and-drop operations, such as MousePointer icons and DragIcons.

Working with Design Environment
- To add an image to at design time, use the ImageList control's Property Pages dialog box.
- To add ListImage objects at design time :
    1. Right-click the ImageList control and click Properties.
    2. Click the Images tab to display the ImageList control's Property Pages, as shown below.

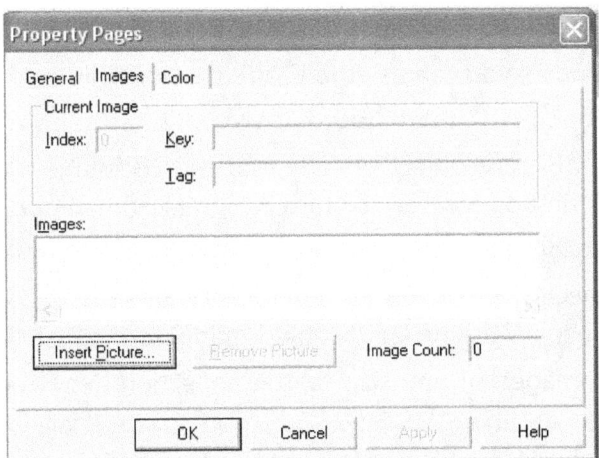

Fig. 4.25 : ImageList control Property Pages dialog box

3. Click Insert Picture to display the Select Picture dialog box.
4. Use the dialog box to find either bitmap or icon files, and click Open.

Note : You can select multiple bitmap or icon files.

5. Assign a unique Key property setting by clicking in the Key box and typing a string.
6. Optional. Assign a Tag property setting by clicking in the Tag box and typing a string. The Tag property doesn't have to be unique.
7. Repeat steps 3 through 6 until you have populated the control with the desired images.

4.5.1 Adding and Deleting Images with Code

1. **Add Method** : Adds a ListImage object to a ListImages collection.

    Syntax :

    ```
    object.Add(index, key, picture)
    ```

    The Add method syntax has these parts :

Part	Description
object	Required. An object expression that evaluates to an object in the Applies to list.
index	Optional. An integer specifying the position where you want to insert the ListImage. If no *index* is specified, the ListImage is added to the end of the ListImages collection.
key	Optional. A unique string that identifies the ListImage object. Use this value to retrieve a specific ListImage object. An error occurs if the key is not unique.
picture	Required. Specifies the picture to be added to the collection.

- The ListImages collection is a 1-based collection. You can load either bitmaps or icons into a ListImage object.
- To load a bitmap or icon, you can use the LoadPicture function, as follows :

    ```
    Set imgX = ImageList1.ListImages.Add(,,LoadPicture("file name"))
    ```

- You can also load a Picture object directly into the ListImage object. For example, this example loads a PictureBox control's picture into the ListImage object :

    ```
    Set imgX = ImageList1.ListImages.Add(,,Picture1.Picture)
    ```

- If no ListImage objects have been added to a ListImages collection, you can set the ImageHeight and ImageWidth properties before adding the first ListImage object.
- You can then add images of any size to the collection. However, when the ImageList control is bound to another Windows Common Control, all images you add to the collection will be displayed (in the bound Windows Common Control) at the size specified by the ImageHeight and ImageWidth properties.
- Once a ListImage object has been added to the collection, the ImageHeight and ImageWidth properties become read-only properties.

> **Note :** You can the use the ImageList control with any control by setting the **Picture** property of the second control to the Picture object of any image contained by the ImageList control. However, the size of the displayed image will not be affected by the ImageHeight and ImageWidth properties. In other words, the second control will display the image at its original size.

- You should use the Key property to reference a ListImage object if you expect the value of the Index property to change.
- For example, if you allow users to add and delete their own images to the collection, the value of the Index property may change. When a ListImage object is added to the collection, a reference to the newly created object is returned. You can use the reference to set other properties of the ListImage, as follows :

```
Dim imgX As ListImage
Dim I As Integer
    Set imgX = ImageList1.ListImages. _
    Add(,,LoadPicture("icons\comm\net01.ico"))
    imgX.Key = "net connect" ' Use the new reference to assign
    Key.
```

- You can use the Add method of the ListImages Collection to add images to the ImageList at runtime. The syntax for Add is as follows :
    ```
    ImageList1.ListImages.Add([index], [key], picture)
    ```
- Here, ImageList1 is the name of the ImageList control on your form. Index and Key are optional **parameters**. If Index is specified, it will be the location at which the image is loaded into the ListImages Collection.
- If Index is omitted, the new image will be inserted at the end of the collection.
- Key is a string value that you can use to refer to an image in the list without knowing its index value. For example if an image were added as follows :
    ```
    imageList1.ListImages.Add(, "folder icon",LoadPicture("folder.ico"))
    ```
- You might not know the index value of the new image, but you could still refer to it in this way :
    ```
    Picture1.Picture  =  ImageList1.ListImages("folder icon").Picture
    ```
- Using the **ListImages** key makes your code more readable than if you refer to images with the Index property. You can remove a ListImage from the ListImages Collection with the Remove method. You can use Remove either by specifying the index of the image:
    ```
    ImageList1.ListImages.Remove 1
    ```
              OR
  by providing the image's key value :
    ```
    ImageList1.ListImages.Remove "key value
    ```

- **ListImage Object, ListImages Collection :**

    A ListImage object is a bitmap of any size that can be used in other controls. A ListImages collection is a collection of ListImage objects. All the images contained in the ImageList control are stored in the ListImages Collection. Each icon and bitmap in the collection is a separate ListImage object.

    You can refer to each image in the list by its index :

    ```
    ImageList1.ListImages(1).Picture
    ```

    or,

    if a key (for example, "Smiley") were assigned to a particular ListImage object, you could refer to it by its key value :

    ```
    ImageList1.ListImages("Smiley").Picture
    ```

    You can use the ListImages Collection to loop through all the images in the list. If you wanted to display all the stored images in a PictureBox, one after another.

- **Looping through the images in an imagelist control :**

    ```
    Dim picImage as ListImage
    For Each picImage in ImageList
    ImageList1.ListImages
    Picture1.Picture = picImage.Picture
    Next
    ```

    If you knew the image you wanted to move to a PictureBox, you could just code this :

    ```
    Picture1.Picture = ImageList1.ListImages(3).Picture
    ```

    OR

    ```
    Picture1.Picture = ImageList1.ListImages("Smiley").Picture
    ```

    In the first example, the third image in the ImageList control would be loaded into PictureBox Picture1, and in the second example, the image whose key is FirstImage would be loaded.

    Syntax :

    ```
    imagelist.ListImages
    imagelist.ListImages(index)
    ```

    The syntax lines above refer to the collection and to individual elements in the collection, respectively, according to standard collection syntax.

    The ListImage Object, ListImages Collection syntaxes have these parts :

Part	Description
Imagelist	Required. An object expression that evaluates to an object in the Applies To list.
Index	An integer or string that uniquely identifies the object in the collection. The integer is the value of the Index property; the string is the value of the Key property.

The **ListImages** collection is a 1-based collection. You can add and remove a **ListImage** at design time using the General tab of the ImageList Control Properties page or at run time using the **Add** method for **ListImage** objects. Each item in the collection can be accessed by its index or unique key. For example, to get a reference to the third **ListImage** object in a collection, use the following syntax :

```
Dim imgX As ListImage
    ' Reference by index number.
Set imgX = ImageList.ListImages(3)
    ' Or reference by unique key.
Set imgX = ImageList1.ListImages("third")' Assuming Key is "third."
    ' Or use Item method.
   Set imgX = ImageList1.ListImages.Item(3)
```

- Each ListImage object has a corresponding mask that is generated automatically using the MaskColor property. This mask is not used directly, but is applied to the original bitmap in graphical operations such as the Overlay and Draw methods.

Managing ListImage Objects and ListImages Collections

- The ImageList control contains the ListImages collection of ListImage objects, each of which can be referred to by its Index or Key property value.
- You can add or remove images to the control at design time or run time.

Adding ListImage Objects at Run Time

- To add an image at run time, use the Add method for the ListImages collection in conjunction with the **LoadPicture function**. The following example occurs in a form's Load event; an ImageList control named "imlImages" is loaded with a single bitmap :

```
Private Sub Form_Load()
    ' Assuming the path is correct, the open.bmp
    ' picture will be added to the ListImages
    ' collection. The Key property will also be
    ' assigned the value "open"
    imlImages.ListImages. _
    Add ,"open", LoadPicture("c:\bitmaps\open.bmp")
End Sub
```

- Assigning a unique Key property value to the ListImage object allows you to create code that is easier to read. When assigning the image to a property, you can use its Key value instead of its Index value.
- Thus, assigning an image to a property might result in code like the following :

```
' Assign an image to a TreeView control Node object.
' The unique key of the image is "open".
TreeView1.Nodes.Add , , ,"Folder1","open"
```

Determining Image Sizes

- You can insert any size image into the ImageList control. However, the size of the image displayed by the second control depends on one factor: whether or not the second control is also a Windows Common control bound to the ImageList control.
- When the ImageList control is bound to another Windows Common Control, images of different sizes can be added to the control, however the size of the image displayed in the associated Windows Common Control will be constrained to the size of the first image added to the ImageList.
- For example, if you add an image that is 16 by 16 pixels to an ImageList control, then bind the ImageList to a TreeView control (to be displayed with Node objects), all images stored in the ImageList control will be displayed at 16 by 16 pixels, even if they are much larger or smaller.
- On the other hand, if you display images using the Picture object, any image stored in the ImageList control will be displayed at its original size, no matter how small or large.

Note : An exception is when you use an image from the ImageList control with the Image control. Setting the Image control's Stretch property to True will cause the image to resize to fit the control.

- At design time, you can specify the height and width, in pixels, of images in the control by choosing a size from the General tab of the ImageList control's Property Pages dialog box.
- You can choose a predetermined size, or click Custom and set the image size by typing the size you desire in the Height and Width boxes.
- This can only be done when the ImageList contains no images. Attempting to change the size after the control contains images will result in an error.

Methods that allow you to create Composite Images

- You can use the ImageList control to create a composite image (a picture object) from two images by using the Overlay method in conjunction with the MaskColor property.
- For example, if you have an "international no" image (a circle with a diagonal bar inside it), you can lay that image over any other image.
- The syntax for the Overlay method requires two arguments. The first argument specifies the underlying image; the second argument specifies the image that overlays the first.
- Both arguments can be either the Index or the Key property of a ListImage object.
- Thus the code to achieve the effect above is as follows :

```
' The composite image appears in a PictureBox
' control named "picOver". The Index value of
' the cigarette image is 2; the index value of the
```

```
' "no" symbol is 1.
ImageList1.MaskColor = vbGreen
Set picOver.Picture = ImageList1.Overlay(2, 1)
```

- You could also use the Key property of the images, resulting in this code :

```
    ' Assuming the first image's Key is "smokes", and the
' second is "no".
    Set picOver.Picture = ImageList1.Overlay("smokes","no")
```

- The code example above also illustrates how the MaskColor property works. In brief, the MaskColor property specifies the color which will become transparent when an image is overlaid over another.
- The "no" image has a green background color. Thus, when the code specifies that the MaskColor will be vbGreen (an intrinsic constant), the green in the image becomes transparent in the composite image.

Limitation of ImagList Control

- Each image that is displayed in a TreeView or ListView control must first be placed in an ImageList control. If many items are placed in the control, it will run out of memory (error 7).
- To avoid this, reuse ImageList items whenever possible. For example, if you are representing percentages, draw 100 items, each representing a percentage, in the ImageList and reuse them.
- To avert memory problems when you use the ImageList control, draw the percentage item only when it is required.

4.5.2 Study of Different Dialog Boxes   (April 10, 12, 13)

- In Visual Basic common dialog control is used for access various dialog boxes provided by windows.

    For example : File save As dialogBox is used to save the file without designing programmer. User can directly use it using common dialogBox.

- The common dialog Box control is contained in cmbBlg 32. ocx. OCX file wraps up the function call to commdlg.dll that in the windows system directory on the computer. For opening or closing a file user must first write the logic.
- By default common dialog box control is not available in ToolBox. To add this control user can go components from project window then add it on ToolBox. These dialog Boxes acts as a user interface.
- The Common Dialogs control provides its services to the application, but it does not need to be displayed on the Form at runtime.

- The Common Dialogs control provides the following built-in Windows dialog boxes:
    - **(i)** **Open :** The File Open common dialog box lets users select a file to open.
    - **(ii)** **Save As :** The File Save common dialog box lets users select or specify a filename in which the current document will be saved.
    - **(iii)** **Color :** The Color dialog box lets users select colors or specify custom colors.
    - **(iv)** **Font :** The Font common dialog box lets users select a typeface and style to be applied to the current text selection.
    - **(v)** **Print :** The Print common dialog box lets users select and set up a printer.
    - **(vi)** **Help :** The Help common dialog box displays Help topics.

Method	Value	Action
ShowOpen	1	Displays the Open dialog box
ShowSave	2	Displays the Save As dialog box
ShowColor	3	Displays the Color dialog box
ShowFont	4	Displays the Font dialog box
ShowPrinter	5	Displays the Printer dialog box
ShowHelp	6	Invokes the Windows Help engine

4.5.2.1 Color Common Dialog Box

- The Color common dialog box, is shown in Fig. 4.26.
- It is one of the simplest and easierest dialog boxes color dialog box has a single property, Color, which returns the color selected by the user.
- Before opening the color dialog box with the ShowColor method, you can set a number of flags through its Flags property, whose values are given below :

Constant	Value	Description
cdCCIFullOpen	&H2	Displays the full dialog box, including the Define Custom Colors section.
cdICCHelpButton	&H8	Displays a Help button in the dialog box
cdICCPreventFullOpen	&H4	Hides the Define Custom Colors section
cdICCRGBInit	&H1	Sets the value of the color initially selected when the dialog box is opened.

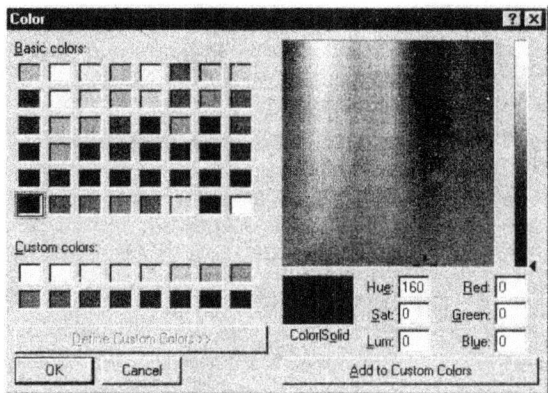

Fig. 4.26 : The color common dialog box

For example :

1. Add Common dialog control in the box and place it on a form.

   Put a common button on a form, set its Caption = Color and name as cmdColor and enter the following code in the cmdColor_Click( ) procedure.

```
Private sub cmdColor_Click()
  CommonDialog1_showColor 'Displays color Selection box.
  Form1.BackColor - commonDialogcolor
End Sub
```

- In above example, showcolor method display color Dialog Box. When you select a particular color from color dialog box, color property of common dialog control contains its value.

4.5.2.2 Font Common Dialog Box

- The Font common dialog box, shown in Fig. 4.27. It lets the user review and select a font and its size and style.
- To open the Font dialog box, set the Action property to 4 or invoke the ShowFont method of the Common Dialogs control.

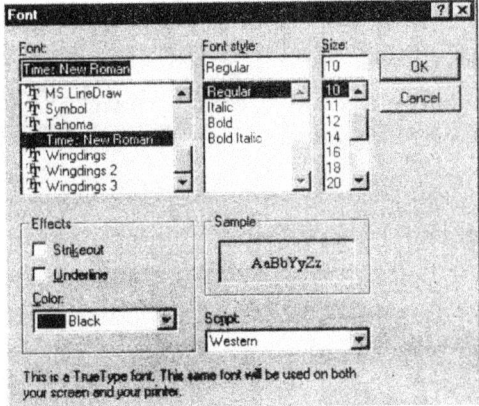

Fig. 4.27 : The font common dialog box

- After the user selects a font, its size and style and possibly some special effects and clicks the OK button, the Common Dialogs control returns the attributes of the selected font through the following properties :
  - **Color** : Color property returns the font's selected color
  - **FontBold** : It is True if the bold attribute is set.
  - **FontItalic** : It is True if the italic attribute is set.
  - **FontStrikethru** : It is True if the strikethrough attribute is set.
  - **FontUnderline** : It is True if the underline attribute is set.
  - **FontName** : This property returns the selected font's name.
  - **FontSize** : This property returns the selected font's size.
- Now we will see the example, which will display font dialog box. Place a label on the form, set its Caption to Hello world. Put a common button, cmdFont, set its caption to Font. Add following code in cmFont_Click( ) procedure.

```
Private Sub cmFont_Click()
    Commondialob1.showFont
    Label1.Font.Name      =   CommonDialog1.FontName
    Label1.Font.Size      =   CommonDialog1.FontSize
    Label1.Font.Bold      =   CommonDialog1.FontBold
    Label1.Font.Italic    =   CommonDialog1.FontItalic
    Label1.Font.Underline =   CommonDialog1.FontUnderline
End sub
```

- Similarly, user can show printer setup and printer selection, we have show Printer and to show help we have show Help method. The procedure to handle these is exactly same, as we have seen for Color, and Font dialog boxes. These are the commonly used dialog boxes created using common dialog control.

4.5.2.3 FileOpen and FileSave Common Dialog Boxes

- FileOpen and FileSave are the two most commonly and widely used common dialog boxes.
- Nearly every application prompts the user for a filename. Windows 95 provides two highly customizable common dialog boxes for this purpose.
- The two dialog boxes are nearly identical and most of their properties are common.

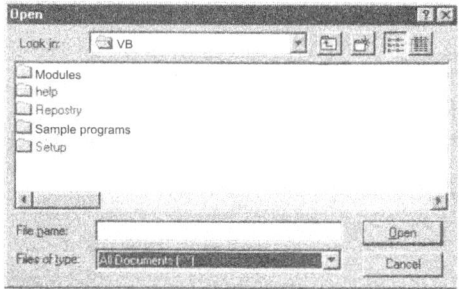

Fig. 4.28

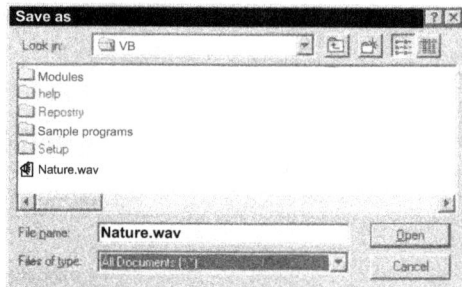

Fig. 4.29

- When a file common dialog box is opened, it rarely displays all the files in any given folder, (Refer Fig. 4.28).

4.5.2.4 Print Common Dialog Box

- The Print common dialog box enables users to select a printer, set certain properties of the printout and set up a specific printer.
- Fig. 4.30 shows print dialog box.

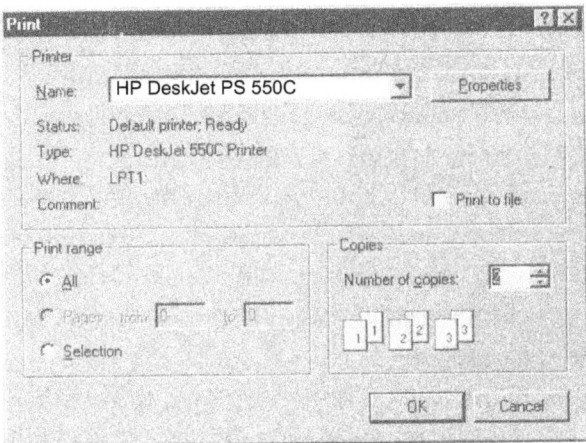

Fig. 4.30 : The print common dialog box

- Print dialog box, sets the Action property of the Common Dialogs control to 5 or invoke the ShowPrinter method of the Common Dialogs control.
- After you selects a printer and clicks OK, the Common Dialogs control returns the printer's device context and the attributes of the desired printout to the calling program through the following properties :
  - **Copies :** Specifies the number of copies to print.
  - **FromPage :** Specific the pages on which to start printing.
  - **ToPage :** Specifies the page on which to stop printing.

4.5.2.5 Help Common Dialog Box

- The Help common dialog box is as simple and easy to use as the other ones, but you must first prepare your Help files.
- Visual Basic's Help file is called VB6. User do not have to specify an extension or a path; WinHelp knows where the Help files are located.
  - **HelpFile :** This property specifies the filename of a Windows Help file that will be used to display online Help.
  - **HelpCommand :** This property sets or returns the type of Help requested.
  - **HelpContextID :** The property sets or returns a context number for an object.
  - **HelpKey :** This property sets or returns the keyword which identifies the requested Help topic.

4.6 MENU (Oct. 10, 11, 13; April 12)

- If you want your application to provide a set of commands to users, menus offer a conventional and consistent way to group commands and an easy way for users to access them.
- Designing the right kind of menus will make your applications much more user-friendly. In this chapter we will learn how to create a menu.
- A menu control displays a custom menu for your application.
- A menu can include commands, sub menus and separator bars.
- Each menu you create can have up to six levels of submenus.
- Windows applications provide groups of related commands in Menus. These commands depends on the application, but some-such as Open and Save are frequently found in applications.
- Menus are intrinsic controls. Menus behave differently from other controls.
- For example, you don't drop menu items on a form from the Toolbox; rather, you design them in the Menu Editor window.
- You invoke this tool from the Menu Editor button on the standard toolbar or by pressing the Ctrl+E shortcut key. There's also a Menu Editor command in the Tools menu, but you probably won't use it often.
- Visual Basic provides an easy way to create menus with the modal Menu Editor dialog.
- Menu Editor window by right clicking on the Form and selecting Menu Editor.

Concept of Menu

- A menu system typically consists of several related elements, some of which are more directly visible than others. Menu systems need not necessarily implement each of the elements.
- The following table describes the menu elements of a typical user interface, such as those used by Microsoft Windows Applications :

No.	Menu Element	Description
1.	Menu Bar	The menu bar is a special toolbar at the top of the screen that contains menus such as **File, Edit,** and **View.** We can customize the menu bar the same way we customize any built-in toolbar, for example we can quickly add and remove buttons and menus on the menu bar, but we can not hide the menu bar.
2.	Menu	The menu contains the list of commands that appear when you click a menu bar item. This list includes the menu little at the top.

Contd...

3.	Menu Item	A menu item, also called a command, refers to one of the choices listed on a menu. According to standard user-interface design guidelines, every menu should contain at least one command.
4.	Submenu	A submenu, or cascading menu, is a menu that branches-off from a menu item. The command from which the cascading menu braches has an arrow next to it to indicate that a new menu will appear when user points to that command.
5.	Pop-up menu	A pop-up menu is a context-sensitive menu that typically appears when we right-click the mouse (or secondary mouse button) in our application. However, this can be controlled through our code. A pop-up menu contains commands that are commonly associated with the object that is clicked. For example, if a selection of text is clicked, the pop-up menu may contain Cut, Copy, Paste and Delete commands.

- In the Fig. 4.31, the symbol ▶ shows that menu item **paste** has sub menu. We can open a submenu by using the standard window conventions : press **Enter** click the item with the mouse, or press **LEFT** arrow.

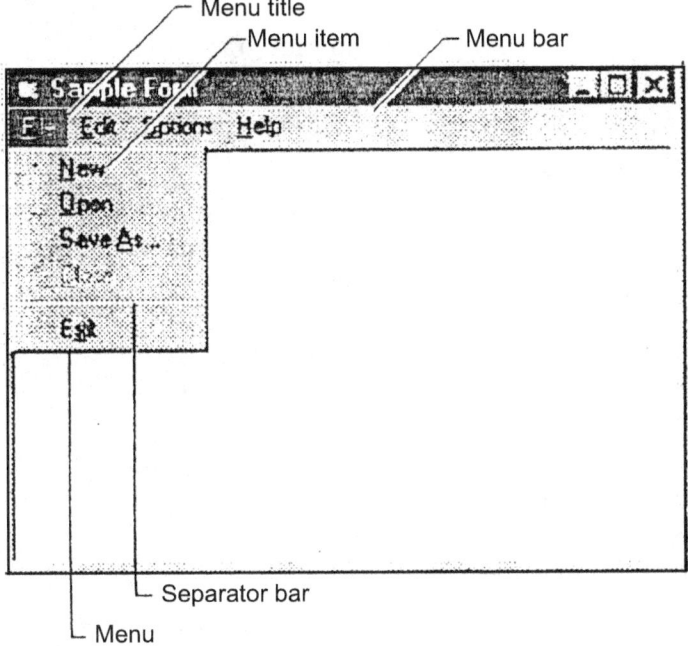

(a)

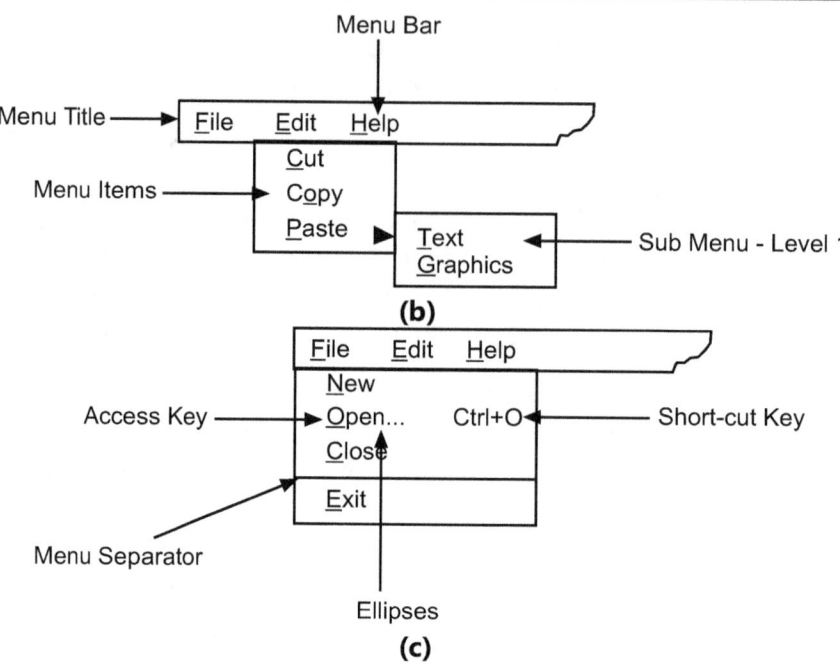

Fig. 4.31 : Menu Elements of a Menu Interface

- Notice that all the menus have one letter underline. Pressing **ALT** and the underlined letter open that menu. Another way to access the menu is to press **ALT** alone to activate the menubar when we do, notice the **file** menu item is highlighted. We can now use the arrow keys to move around the menubar. Press Enter or Down Arrow to open the menu. Once menu is open all you need is a single accelerator key (also called an **access** or **hot key**) to select a menu option.
- For example : If the help menu is open, pressing L brings up the tutorial.

  Note : Accelerator keys are not case sensitive.
- Some menu items have shortcut keys. A shortcut key is usually a combination of keys.
- When you are working with menu following things must know to you :
  1. **Menu Naming Conventions :**
     (a) Item names should be unique within a menu.
     (b) Item names be single, compound, or multiple words.
     (c) Each item (if any) should have a unique mnemonic access character.
     (d) An ellipsis(.....) should follow names of command that require more information.
     (e) Use separator bar to separate one group of menu commands from another from the same menu.
  2. **Menu Control array :**
     (a) By default (if do not set an index property menu items are treated as individual controls.
     (b) A menu control array is a set of menu items on the same menu that share the same name and event procedures.

(c) Index property is used to distinguish between menu items in a menu control array.

(d) When a member of a menu control array recognizes an event. Visual basic passes its index property to the event procedure as an additional argument.

(e) In a Dynamic menu control array :
- A menu can grow at runtime.
- You must use menu control array at run time use Add/Remove a menu item at run time.
- To add/remove menu items at run time use Load/Remove methods.
- Considerations are similar to control arrays.

4.6.1 Designing Menus (April 10, Oct. 10, April 11, Oct. 11)

- Menus are one of the most common and important characteristic elements of the Windows user interface.
- Menus were used to display methodically organized choices and guide the user through an application.
- A menu control displays a custom menu for your application.
- A menu can include commands, submenus and separator bars. Each menu you create can have up to six levels of submenus.
- Menu can be attached only to forms and you design them with the menu editor and to define their properties.
- The Menu Editor, you can add new commands to existing menus, replace existing menu commands with your own commands, create new menus and menu bars, and change and delete existing menus and menu bars.
- The main advantage of the menu Editor is its ease of use. You can customize menus in a complete interactive manner that involves very little programming.

4.6.1.1 Menu Design Considerations

- In general every Windows programmer/developer is familiar with the parts of a menu.
- The menu names in a program appear in the menu bar – usually just under the title bar – and when the user selects a menu, the menu opens, like the File menu is in Fig. 4.32.
- Every menu usually contains items arranged in a vertical list. These menu items are often grouped into functional groups with menu separators, or thin horizontal rules, as shown in Fig. 4.32.
- When the user selects a menu item that item appears highlighted; pressing Enter or releasing the mouse button opens that item.
- Menu items can also be disabled as shown in Fig. 4.32. A disable menu item is not accessible to the user and does nothing if selected.

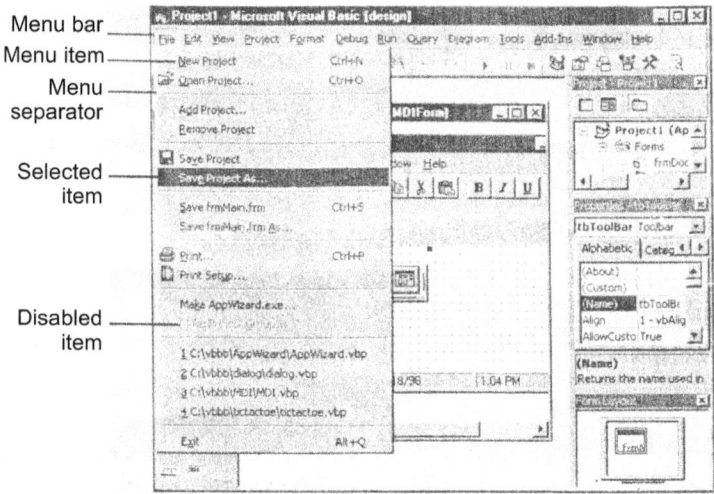

Fig. 4.32 : Visual Basic Menu

4.6.1.2 Designing Your Menus (Oct. 07, 10)

- Windows gives the user a common interface, no matter what program they are using and users have come to expect that.
- Number of programs have a File menu first (at left) in the menu bar, followed by other menus, like a View menu, a Tools menu and many more followed by a Help menu, which usually appears last. Users expect to find certain standard items in particular menus.
- Microsoft recommends that you keep your menu item names short. When you want to release our application internationally, the length of words tends to increase approximately 30 percent in foreign versions, and we many not have enough space to list all of your menu items.

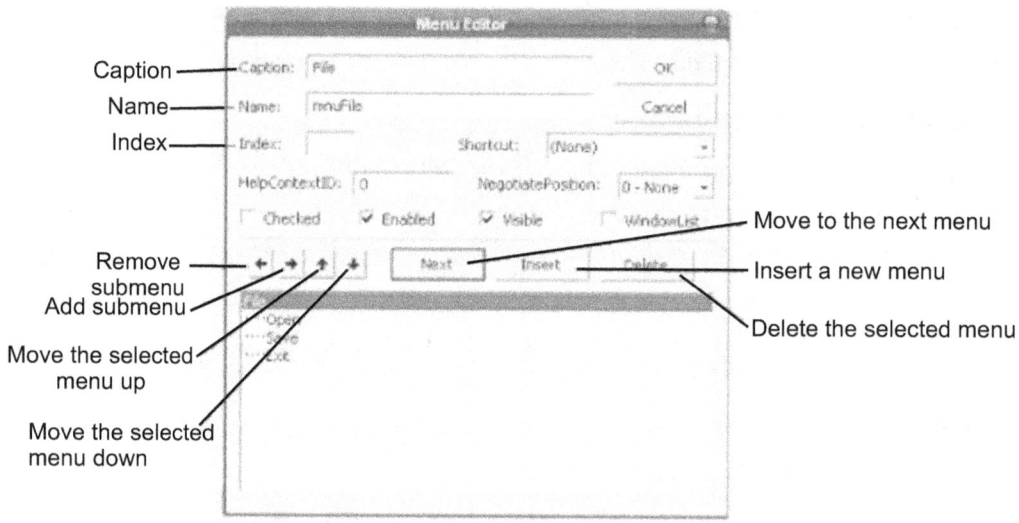

Fig. 4.33

- Microsoft also recommends that we use the **mnu** prefix in code for menus like **munView**, and menu items, like **mnuViewZoom**.
- Building a menu is a simple. We enter the item's Caption and Name, set other properties, (or accept the default values for those properties), and press Enter to move to the next item.
- When we want to create a submenu, you press the Right Arrow button, (or the Alt+R hot key). When we want to return to work on top-level menus-those items that appear in the menu bar when the application runs-we click the Left Arrow button, (or press Alt+L).
- We can move items up and down in the hierarchy by clicking the corresponding buttons or the hot keys Alt+U and Alt+B, respectively.
- We can create up to five levels of submenus (six including the menu bar), which are too many even for the most patient user. If we find ourself working with more than three menu levels, think about trashing our specifications and redesigning our application from the ground up.
- We can insert a separator bar using the hypen (-) character for the Caption property. But even these separator items must be assigned a unique value for the Name property, which is a real nuisance.
- If we forget to enter a menu item's Name, the Menu Editor complains when we decide to close it. The convention used in this book is that all menu names begin with the three letters mnu.

An expanded menu :

- One of the most annoying defects of the Menu Editor tool is that it does not permit us to reuse the menus we have already written in other applications.
- It would be great if we could open another instance of the Visual Basic IDE, copy one or more menu items to the clipboard, and then paste those menu items in the application under development.
- We can do that with controls and with pieces of code, but not with menus ! The best thing we can do in Visual Basic is load the FRM file using an editor such as Notepad, find the portion in the file that corresponds to the menu we are interested in, load the FRM file we are developing (still in Notepad), and paste the code there.
- This is not the easiest operation, and it's also moderately dangerous: If we paste the menu definition in the wrong place, we could make our FRM form completely unreadable. Therefore, always remember to make backup copies of our forms before trying this operation.

An expanded Menu Editor window :

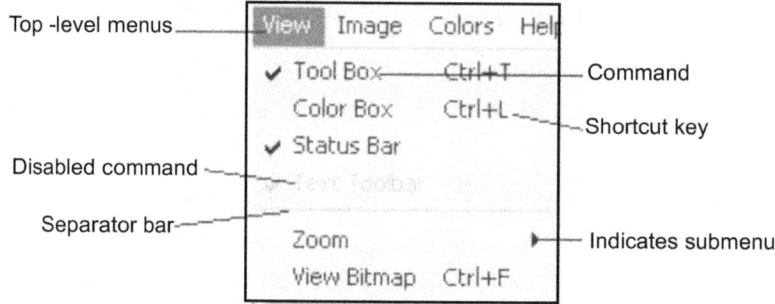

Fig. 4.34

- When we can add a finished menu to a form in our application with just a few mouse clicks. All have to do is activate the of us Add-In Manager from the Add-Ins menu, choose the VB 6 Template Manager, and tick the Loaded/Unloaded check box.
- After doing that, we will find three new commands in the Tools menu : **Add Code Snippet**, **Add Menu**, and **Add Control Set**. Visual Basic 6 comes with a few menu templates, as we can see in the Fig. 4.35, that we might find useful as a starting point for building our own templates.
- To create our menu templates, we only have to create a form with the complete menu and all the related code and then store this form in the \Templates\Menus directory. The complete path, typically c:\Program Files\Microsoft Visual Studio\VB98\Template, can be found in the Environment tab of the Options dialog box on the Tools menu.
- The Template Manager was already available with Visual Basic 5, but it had to be installed manually and relatively few programmers were aware of its existence.

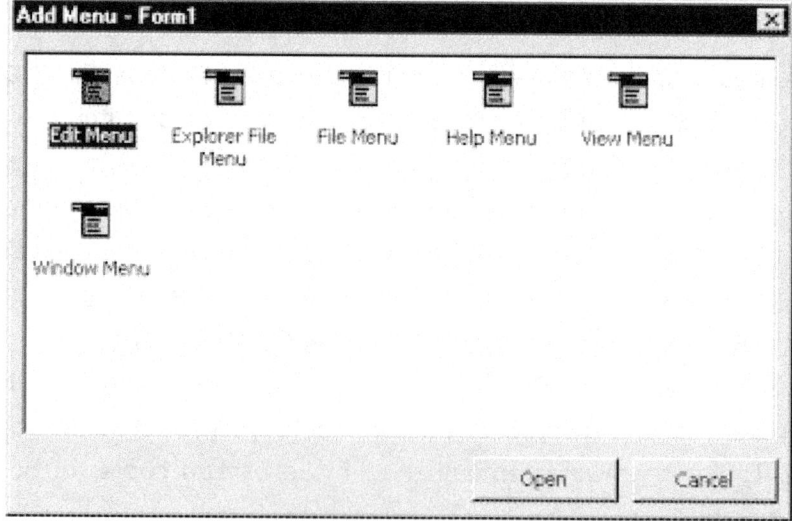

Fig. 4.35 : The Template Manager In Action

- The programmer can create menu control arrays. The Index TextBox specifies the menu's index in the control array. The Menu Editor dialog also provides several CheckBoxes to control the appearance of the Menu.

  Checked : This is unchecked by default and allows the programmer the option of creating a checked menu item (a menu item that act as a toggle and displays a check mark when selected). The following is a Check Menu items.

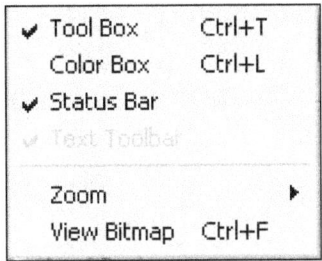

Fig. 4.36

Enabled : Specifies whether a menu is disabled or not. If you see a disabled command in a menu that means that feature is not available. The Visible checkbox specifies whether the menu is visible or not.

- To add commands to the Form's menu bar, enter a caption and a name for each command. As soon as we start typing the command's caption, it also appears in a new line in the list at the bottom of the Menu Editor window. To add more commands click Enter and type the Caption and the Name.

Creating Menus (Oct. 10)

- Open a new Project and save the form as menu.frm and save the project as menu.vbp. Choose **Tools → Menu Editor** and type the menu items as shown below :

Caption	Name
File	mnuFile
Open	mnuOpen
Save	mnuSave
Exit	mnuExit
Edit	mnuEdit
Copy	mnuCopy
Cut	mnuCut
Paste	mnuPaste

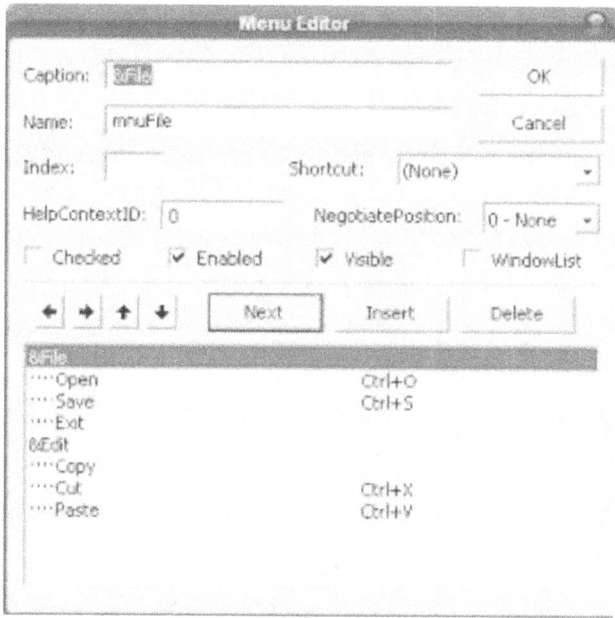

Fig. 4.37

- Run the application by pressing F5. We can see that we can select a menu.

4.6.2 Creating the Menu with Menu Editor (Oct. 12; April 12)

- In this section we learn how to create a menu. We can use the following steps to design menu.
    1. Start a new standard EXE project. The Form1 appears in the design window.
    2. Choose Tools → Menu Editor to open the Menu Editor or we can click on the Menu Editor button in the toolbar.
- In menu editor, different properties of menu are given. According to our program, we can select property of menu with the help of these properties we can create shortcut of menu item and give proper access key to that menu item. The menu Editor consists of :
    1. **Caption :** The string we type in the text box that appears on our menu bar or in our menu. Unlike other Visual Basic controls, menu items do not have default caption. ALT+P is the access key for the caption text box in the Menu Editor window.

        To create a separator bar in our menu, type a single hyphen(-) in the caption property. Separator bar divide menu items into logical groups, and even though they have the structure of regular menu commands, they do not react to the mouse click.

        To give the user keyboard access to the menu item, insert an ampersand (&) before a letter. At runtime, this letter is underlined, and the user can access the menu or command by pressing ALT and the access key.

    2. **Name :** A text box in which we enter a control name for menu item. This property does not appear on the screen, but our code uses it to program the menu command. Each menu item must have a control name. Unless the menu items are part of a

control array, they must have different control names, what we enter in the Name text box becomes the control name that is used by Visual Basic for the client event procedure for menu items. Visual Basic will not let we leave the Menu Editor window until we give each menu item a control name. The access key is ALT+M.

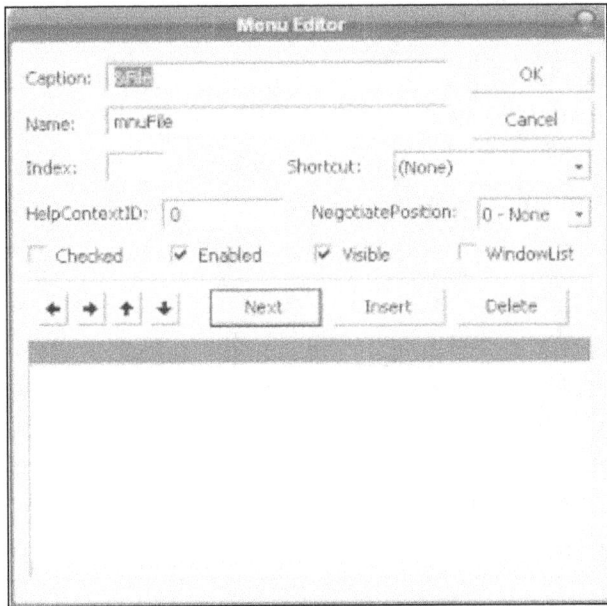

Fig. 4.38 : Data Font Size

3. **Index :** Use the Index box if you want to make a menu item is part of a control array. All the menu commands have the same name and unique index that distinguishes them. The control array; let we add new instances of the control at run time. In the case of menu items, this would let we have the menu enlarge or shrink while the program is running. Once, we have set a menu item to be part of a control array at runtime, we add new menu items with the Load method. Similarly, we remove menu items from a control array by using the Unload method. It is quite common to leave. The caption property blank for the first menu items in a control array.

4. **Shortcut :** Lets we add accelerator keys to our menu items. Recall that accelerator keys are either function key or CTRL + keys combinations that activate a menu item without the user's needing to open the menu at all. If we click the down arrow to the right of the shortcut box, a list box drops down with the choices for accelerator keys. We need only click the key we want.

5. **Help ContextId :** A text-box in which we assign the unique numeric value for the context ID. This value is used to find the appropriate Help topic in the Help file identified by the HelpFile property.

6. **Negotiate Position :** A drop-down list, (box from which we can select the menu's negotiate), Position property. This property determines whether and how the menu appears in a container form.

7. **Checked :** A check box we select if we want a check mark to appear initially at the left of a menu item. This is generally, used to indicate whether a toggle option is turned ON or OFF. The default is OFF.

8. **Enabled :** A check box you select if we want the menu item to respond to events, or clear if we want the item to be unavailable and appear dimmed.

9. **Visible :** A check box we select if we want the menu item to appear on the menu. If a menu item is made invisible, all its submenus are also invisible.

10. **WindowList :** This option is used with MDI (Multiple Document Interface) applications to maintain a list of all open windows.

11. **Buttons :** A set of outlining buttons that enable us to move menu items to a higher or lower level.

    ← → : Use these buttons to change the level of a menu from a higher level to a lower level. Submenus are indicated by the indentation level, (The left and right arrow buttons control the identification level clicking on the right arrow button moves the highlighted item in one level; clicking on the right arrow button moves it one indentation level deeper.

    ↑ ↓ : Clicking on the up arrow button interchanges the highlighted menu item above it, clicking on the down arrow button interchanges the highlighted item with the item below it. The up and down arrows do not change the indentation pattern of an item.

12. **Next :** Clicking this button moves us to the next menu item or inserts a new item if we are at the end of the menu. The indentation of the new item starts out the same as the indentation of the previous item ALT + N is the access key. We can also use the mouse to move among items.

13. **Insert :** Clicking this button inserts a menu item above the currently highlighted menu item. ALT+I is the access key.

14. **Delete :** Clicking the Delete button removes the currently highlighted item. The access key is ALT + T.

Note : We cannot use the DEL key to remove menu items.

15. **Ok and Cancel :** Clicking the OK button when we are finished designing the menu. Click the Cancel button if we decide not be build the menu at all.

Example : A program of Temperature conversion using menu. Designing the program by implementing the form of the program.

1. Start a new Standard EXE project.
2. Save the form of the project as conversion frm and save the project as con.vbp.

- The properties table of the conversion program.

Object	Property	Value
Form	Name	Frm conversion
	Caption	Temperature conversion
Label 1	Name	lblt
	Caption	Enter the temperature
Label 2	Name	lblo
	Caption	(make it empty)
Label 3	Name	lblr
	Caption	(make it empty)
Text 1	Name	txtt
	Text	(make it empty)
Text 2	Name	txtr
	Text	(make it empty)
Command 1	Name	cmdc
	Caption	& Close

3. Creating the Menu of the Temperature Conversion Program.
    (a) Select **Menu Editor** from the **Tools** menu. Visual Basic responds by displaying the menu editor.
    (b) In the **Caption** text box of **Menu Editor**, type and source. In the **Name** text box type menus.

NOTE : The & character in &source causes Visual Basic to underline Source. When we run the program, pressing ALT+S has the same result as clicking the source menu title.

   (c) Now create the menu item of the Source menu.
       (i) Click the **Next** button of the **Menu Editor** window. Visual Basic responds by highlighting the next row in the menu control list. In the **Caption** text box type &centigrade. In the **Name** text box, type mnusc.
       (ii) Again click the **Next** button. In the **Caption** text box type &Farenheit. Type **mnusf** in Name text box.
   (d) Click the left arrow button of the Menu Editor. In **Caption** text box, type &Target. In **Name** text box, type mnut.
       (i) Click the **Next** button. Type &centigrade in the **Caption** text box. Type muntc in the **Name** text box.
       (ii) Click the **Next** button. Type &Farenheit in the **Caption** text box. Type mnutf in the **Name** text box.
   (e) Click the OK button in the Menu Editor.

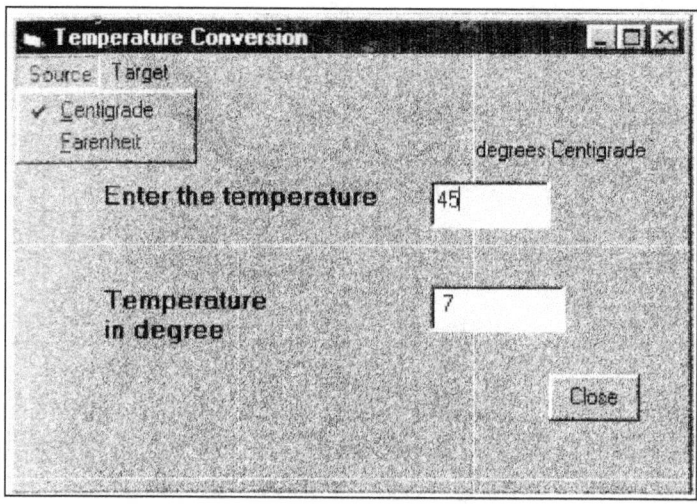

Fig. 4.39

4. Now write the code on the form. Double click on the anywhere in the form. We get form's code window

   (a) Make sure that the General Declarations section of the form has the Option Explicit in it as follows :
   ```
   'All variables must be declared
   Option Explicit
   Dim r As Integer
   ```
   (b) The code for the click procedure on the mnusc as follows :
   ```
   Private Sub mnusc_Click( )
       mnusc.Checked = True
       mnusf.Checked = False
       'change the item on target menu
       mnutc.Enabled = False
       mnutf.Enabled = True
       lblo.Caption = "degrees Centigrade"
   End sub
   ```
   (c) Write the code on mnusf as follows :
   ```
   Private Sub mnusf_Click( )
       mnusc.Checked = False
       mnusf.Checked = True
       'change the item on target menu
       mnutc.Enabled = True
       mnutf.Enabled = False
       lblo.Caption = "degrees Farenheit"
   End sub
   ```
   (d) The following code we write on mnutc as;
   ```
   Private Sub muntc_Click ( )
       lblr.caption = "Temperature in degree Centigrade"
   ```

```
            If mnusf.Checked Then
                r = 1.8 * txtt + 32
                txtr  = Str (r)
            End If
        End Sub
```
(e) The following code we write on munf tf as;
```
        Private Sub muntf_Click ( )
            lblr.caption = "Temperature in degree Farenheit"
            If mnusc.Checked Then
                r = (0.55 * (val (txt) -32))
                txtr  = Str (r)
            End If
        End Sub
```
5. Write code on command button cmdc as :
```
        Private Sub cmdc_Click ( )
            End
        End Sub
```
6. Save the form and project.

    How to run the above application ?

    We can apply the following instructions :
    1. Press F5.
    2. Click on the text box which is infront of the "Enter the temperature".
    3. Enter the value.
    4. Click on the Source menu item and select the any one choice. Of centigrade or Fahrenheit.
    5. We get the result.
    6. We exit from form click on the close button.

Adding a Menu to a Form

- User use the Visual Basic Menu Editor for adding new menu for a form.
- User will get a basic introduction to Menu Editor.
- To add a menu to a from, select that form and open the Menu Editor by selecting the Menu Editor in the Tools menu or we can select its icon in the toolbar ---.
- The Visual Basic Menu Editor appears in Fig. 4.38.

Creating A New Menu

- To create a new menu, user only have to provide two essential items, the caption of the menu and its name.
- The **caption** property of menu editor holds the title of the menu, such as File, and the Name property holds the name we will use for that menu in code, such as **mnuFile.**
- Fill in the **Caption** and **Name** properties for our new menu now.

Creating A New Menu Item

- We can add a new menu item, for example, New, to the File menu we have just created. To do so, click the Next button in the Menu Editor, moving the highlighted bar in the box at the bottom of the Menu Editor down one line.
- If we just entered new **Caption** and **Name** values and left it at that, we would create a new menu, not a new menu item. So click the right-pointing arrow button in the Menu Editor now to indent the next item four spaces in the box at the bottom of the Menu Editor.

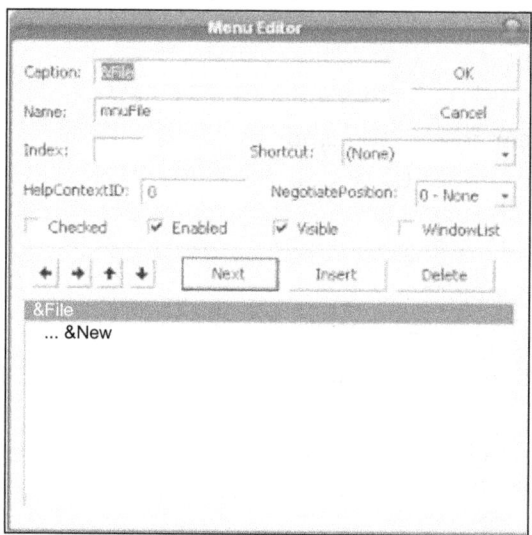

Fig. 4.40 : Visual Basic Menu Editor

- Now enter the **Caption** ("New") and name, ("mnuFileNew") values for the new menu item.
- The menu item we have just created appears in the Menu Editor given below the File menu item and indented.

      File
       ......New

- This means that we now have a File menu with one item in it – New.
    1. Enter the first menu's **Caption** and **Name**.
    2. Click the Next button (or press Enter).
    3. Click the right arrow to indent one level, making this next entry a menu item.
    4. Enter the menu item's **Caption** and **Name.**
    5. Click the Next button (or press Enter).
    6. Repeat Steps 4 and 5 for all the items in the first menu.
    7. Click the Next button (or press Enter).
    8. Click the left arrow to outdent, making this next entry a menu.

9. Enter the next menu's **Caption** and **Name.**
10. Click the right arrow to indent one level, making this next entry a menu item.
11. Repeat Steps 4 and 5 for the items in this new menu.
12. Repeat Steps 7 through 11 for the rest of the menus in the program.
13. Click on OK to close the Menu Editor.
14. Edit the code.

- This opens the menu item's event handler, like this :
    ```
    Private Sub mnuFileNew_Click( )
    End Sub
    ```

Modifying and Deleting Menu Items

- We can rearrange, add or remove menu items in our menu with the Menu Editor.

1. **Inserting or Deleting Items in a Menu System :**

    To add a new menu item to a menu, to the menu system, select an item in the Menu Editor and click the Insert button. This inserts a new, empty entry in the menu just before the item you selected :
    ```
    File
    .....New
    .....Open
    .....
    Edit
    .....Cut
    .....Copy
    ....Paste
    ```
    Now just enter the new item's Caption and Name properties, and we are all set.

    To remove menu items, just select that menu or item and click the **Delete** button.

2. **Rearranging Items in a Menu System :**

    We can use the four arrow buttons in the Menu Editor to move items up and down, as well as indent or outdent.

    - **Right arrow :** Indents a menu item.
    - **Left arrow :** Outdents a menu item.
    - **Up arrow :** Moves the currently selected item up one level.
    - **Down arrow :** Moves the currently selected item down one level.

Adding A Menu Separator

- A menu separator is a horizontal rule which has one important purpose to divide menu items into groups. And using the Menu Editor, we can add separators to our menus.
- To add a menu separator for our menu select an item in the Menu Editor and Click Insert to create a new item just before the item we selected.

- To make this new item as menu separator, we just give use a hyphen (–) for its Caption property.
- We must give all menu items a name even if they can not do anything so give it a dummy **Name** property value as well, such as **mnuSeparator.**
- When we run the program, you will see the menu separators in place, as in the menu in Fig. 4.41. Now we are adding menu item separators to our menus.

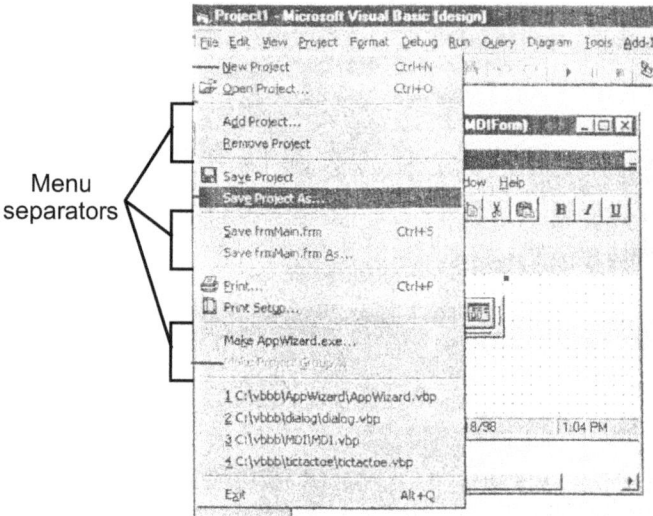

Fig. 4.41 : A Menu With Menu Separators

Creating Submenus

- What the user wants in Fig. 4.42. As we can see in Fig. 4.42, the Colors item in the Edit menu has a small arrow at the right.
- This indicates that there is a submenu attached to color menu item. Selecting the menu item opens the submenu, as also shown in Fig. 4.42.
- Submenus appear as menus attached to menus.

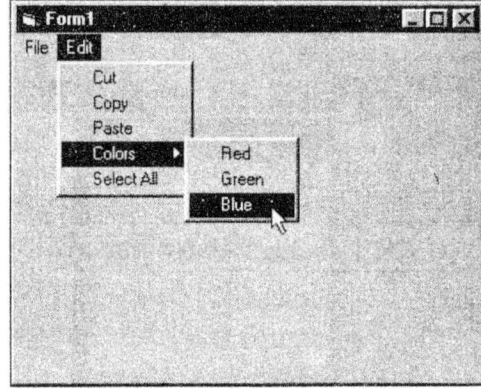

Fig. 4.42 : A Program With A Submenu

For example : Now say we started this way, with a Red, Green and Blue menu item in the Edit menu :

```
Edit
    .....Cut
    .....Copy
    .....Paste
    .....Red
    .....Green
    .....Blue
    .....Select All
```

To put those items in a submenu, we first add a name for a submenu-say, Colors :

```
Edit
    .....Cut
    .....Copy
    .....Paste
    .....Colors
    .....Red
    .....Green
    .....Blue
    .....Select All
```

All that's left is to indent the items that should go into that submenu.

```
Edit
    .....Cut
    .....Copy
    .....Paste
    .....Colors
        .....Red
        .....Green
        .....Blue
    .....Select All
```

4.6.3 Adding Shortcut and Access Keys to Menu Item

1. Adding shortcut Keys :

One of the most powerful and important aspects of menus are shortcut keys-single keys or key combinations that let the user execute a menu command immediately.

In Menu editor it is easy to give a shortcut key to menu item. Just open the Menu editor, select the item to which we want to give a shortcut key, then select the shortcut key in the Menu editor box infront of the label.

Shortcut Key

- Shortcut keys are similar to access keys.
- Shortcut keys are combination of the Control key and a function or character key.
- To assign a shortcut key to a menu command, drop down the Shortcut list in the Menu Editor are select a keystroke.
- Fig. 4.43 shows some of the possible shortcut keys we can assign to menus.

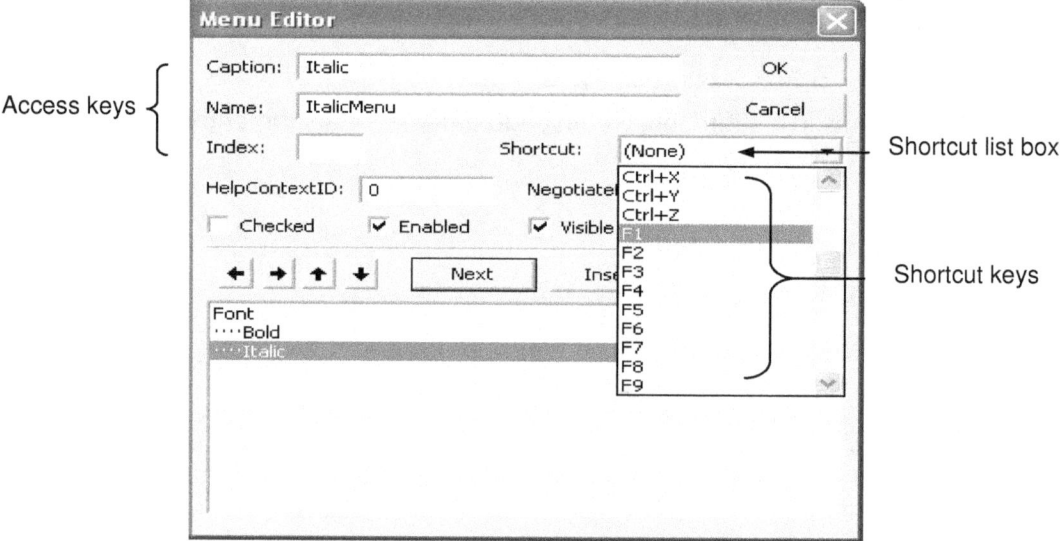

Fig. 4.43 : Setting a Shortcut Key

2. Access Keys :

In Visual Basic, Access keys allow the user to open a menu by pressing the Alt key and a letter key. To open the file menu in all Windows application, for example, we can press Alt+F. F is the file menu's access key.

Access keys are designated by designer of an application and access are marked with an underline character. The underline under the character F in the File menu denotes that F is the menu's access key and that the keystroke Alt+F opens the File command. To assign an access key to a menu command, insert the ampersand symbol (&) in front of the character we want to use as an access key in the menu's caption.

4.6.4 Adding Code to Menus

- For coding menus user will develop an application in which he/she create Color menu. Blue, Yellow, Red, Pink will be the menu items.
- User will also create Size menu in which Small and Large will be the menu items.
- **Steps are :**
  1. Start a new Standard EXE application from the File, New Project menu option.
  2. The form is designed as per the following property table.

Object	Properties	Value
Form	Name	fmcolor
	Caption	Menu Program

3. Design the menu item as per following specifications.

Caption	Name
and Colors	mnuColors
….. and Red	mnuBlue
….. and Yellow	mnuYellow
….. and Green	mnuRed
….. and Blue	mnuPink
and Size	
….. and Small	mnuSmall
….. and Large	mnuLarge

- The following code is entered in mnuBlue_Click procedure.

```
Private Sub mnuBlue_Click ()
   frmColor.Back color = vcbBlue
   mnuRed.Enabled = false
   mnuyellow.Enabled = true
   mnuGreen.Enabled = true
   mnuBlue.Enabled = true
End sub
```

So, when user selects Blue menu, Back color of form will become Blue.

Similarly, we have following code in mnuYellow_Click ( ) procedure.

```
Private Sub mnuYellow_Click ()
   From Color.Backcolor vbYellow
   mnuyellow.Enabled = False
   mnuRed.Enabled = True
   mnuGreen.Enabled = True
   mnuBlue.Enabled = True
End sub,
   Code for mnuRed_Click ()
Private submnuRed_Click ()
   frmColor.backcolor = vbRed
   mnuGreen.Enabled = false
   mnuRed.Enabled = true
```

```
       mnuyellow.Enabled = true
       mnuBlue.Enabled = true
    End sub
```

- Similarly, we have following code for mnuPink _ Click ( )

```
    Private Sub mnuPink_Click()
       frmColor.Back color = vbPink
       mnuBlue.Enabled = false
       mnuGreen.Enabled = true
       mnuRed.Enabled = true
       mnuYellow.Enabled = true
    End sub
```

- Similarly, we have mnuLarge and mnuSmall menu item in size menu. The purpose of mnuSmall is to minimize the form windows if it is in normal state.

  Hence, we have the following code in mnuSmall _ Click ( ) procedure.

```
    Private Sub mnuSmall _Click()
       frmColor.Windowstate = vbMinimized
       mnuLarge.Enabled = true
       mnuSmall.Enabled = false
    End sub
```

- So this is a way to add the code for menu items.

4.7 POP-UP MENU   (April 10, 13)

- A pop-up menu is a floating menu that is displayed over a form, independent of the menu bar.
- The items displayed on the pop-up menu depend on the location of the pointer when the right mouse button is pressed. Therefore, it is also called as context menus.
- We should use pop-up menus to provide as efficient method for accessing common, contextual commands. Displays a pop-up menu on an **MDIForm** or **Form** object at the current mouse location or at specified co-ordinates.
- In Windows XP, we activate context menus by clicking the right mouse button as shown in the following Fig. 4.44.
- A pop-up menu is a menu that is not visibly connected to the menu bar and typically, appears when the use right-clicks the mouse.
- The appearance of a particular pop-up menu depends on the location of the mouse pointer when the user right-clicks the mouse.
- We should provide a pop-up menu that gives the user the most useful commands for the current location.
- For example, if the user right-clicks in a form, we should display a pop-up menu that includes commands that are commonly applied to a form.

Fig. 4.44 : Pop-up Menu in Windows XP

- **Types of pop-up menus :** There are two types of pop-up menus we can create with Visual Basic :
    1. **System pop-up menu :** The system pop-up menu is provided automatically with certain controls. For example, the system pop-up menu for a Textbox control contains commands that apply to text editing, such as **Undo, Cut, Copy, Paste, Delete, and Select All.** All commands on the system pop-up menus are fully functional, no additional code is required.
    2. **Custom pop-up menu :** A custom pop-up menu is a menu we create that is specific to our application. We then write code to display the pop-up menu when needed.
- A pop-up menu is a menu.
- Pop-up menu displayed on the form when user right click on the form.
- Pop-up menus are also called as context menus because the items displayed on Pop-up menu depend on where the pointer is located when the right mouse button is clicked.
- Whenever, user right clicks anywhere on the form mnuColors will appear. To do this, we use mouse Down event of form.
- Enter following code in Form1_Mouse Down ( ) event procedure.

```
Private sub form_MouseDown (Button As Integer, shift as Integer,
                                   X As Sing, Y as Single)
    If Button = 2 then
       PopupMenu_mnu_Color
    End If
End Sub
```

- In the above event procedure, button variable contains the value, which indicates whether, left or right mouse button is clicked, so

    If Button = 1 it is a left button click.

If Button = 2 it is a right button click.

```
Option Explicit
Dim RunTimeMenu
  Private Sub AddCommand_Click ()
    RunTimeMenu = RunTimeMenu + 1
    If RunTimeMenu = 1 Then RunTimeOptions(0).Caption = "Run Time
    Options"
    Load RunTimeOptions (RunTime menu)
    RunTimeOptions(RunTimeMenu).Caption="Option # "&RunTimeMenu
  End sub

  Private Sub RemoveCommond_Click()
    If RunTimeMenu = 0 Then
       MsgBox "Menu is empty"
       Exit Sub
    End If
    Unload RumTimeOptions (RunTimeMenu)
    RunTimeMenu = RunTimeMenu - 1
  End Sub
```

4.7.1 Creating Pop-up Menu

- To create a pop-up menu, use the Menu Editor as you do to create any other menu. However, set the visible property to False so that the menu is not displayed automatically.
- Displays a pop-up menu on an **MDIForm** or **Form** object at the current mouse location or at specified co-ordinates. To display the pop-up menu, use the PopupMenu method.
- To call the Pop-up Menu method, use the following syntax :

  Syntax :

      object.PopupMenu menuname, flags, x, y, boldcommand

  The PopupMenu method syntax has these parts :

Part	Description
object	Optional. An object expression that evaluates to an object in the Applies To list. If *object* is omitted, the form with the focus is assumed to be *object*.
Menuname	Required. The name of the pop-up menu to be displayed. The specified menu must have at least one submenu.
Flags	Optional. A value or constant that specifies the location and behaviour of a pop-up menu, as described in Settings.

X	Optional. Specifies the x-co-ordinate where the pop-up menu is displayed. If omitted, the mouse co-ordinate is used.
Y	Optional. Specifies the y-co-ordinate where the pop-up menu is displayed. If omitted, the mouse co-ordinate is used.
boldcommand	Optional. Specifies the name of a menu control in the pop-up menu to display its caption in bold text. If omitted, no controls in the pop-up menu appear in bold.

- We typically call PopupMenu method in the MouseUp event for the object that will serve as the context for the pop-up menu.
- The secondary mouse button is either the right button for right-handed mouse, or the left button for a left-handed mouse. The MouseUp event checks the current mouse setting in the Control Panel.
- By default, an item on the pop-up menu will respond only to the left button. If we want to make it respond to either the left or right button, use the vbPopupMenuRightButtonflag.

For example :
```
frmmaster.PopupMenu   mnushortcut,   vbPopupMenuRightButton
```
Settings : The settings for *flags* are :

Constant (location)	Value	Description
vbPopupMenuLeftAlign	0	(Default) The left side of the pop-up menu is located at *x*.
vbPopupMenuCenterAlign	4	The pop-up menu is centered at *x*.
vbPopupMenuRightAlign	8	The right side of the pop-up menu is located at *x*.

Constant (behaviour)	Value	Description
vbPopupMenuLeftButton	0	(Default) An item on the pop-up menu reacts to a mouse click only when we use the left mouse button.
vbPopupMenuRightButton	2	An item on the pop-up menu reacts to a mouse click when we use either the right or the left mouse button.

Note : These constants are listed in the Visual Basic (VB) object library. We specify the unit of measure for the x and y co-ordinates using the **ScaleMode** property. The x and y co-ordinates define where the pop-up is displayed relative to the specified form. If the x and y co-ordinates aren't included, the pop-up menu is displayed at the current location of the mouse pointer.

- When we display a pop-up menu, the code following the call to the **PopupMenu** method isn't executed until the user either chooses a command from the menu (in which case the code for that command's Click event is executed before the code following the **PopupMenu** statement) or cancels the menu.
- In addition, only one pop-up menu can be displayed at a time; therefore, calls to this method are ignored if a pop-up menu is already displayed or if a pull-down menu is open.

4.7.2 Activating Pop-up Menu

- **Some Mouse events :** Understanding mouse events is the key to implementing drag and drop in our programs. There are three mouse events in Visual Basic :
- **Mouse Down :** It occurs when the user clicks any mouse button.
- **Mouse Up :** It occurs when the user releases any mouse button.
- **Mouse Move :** It occurs when the user moves the mouse.
- Each of these events takes four parameters. To code the Mouse Down event procedure, use following syntax :

Syntax :
```
Private Sub Form_MouseUp(Button As Integer, Shift As Integer, X As Single, Y As Single)
```

Parameter	Returns	Values
Button	Which mouse button was pressed.	VbLeftButtton VbRightButtton VbMiddleButtton
Shift	Which key or keys are held down	VbShiftMask=SHIFT VbCrtlMask=CRTL VbAltMask=Alt Combination can be checked by adding the values together. e.g. CTRL+SHIFT=3=1+2
X	Current X position	Not applicable.
Y	Current Y Position	Not applicable.

4.8 ADDING MENU ITEMS AT RUN-TIME

- A menu control array is a set of menu items on the same menu that share the same name and event procedures.

- A control array has at least one element and can grow to as many elements as our system resources and memory permit; its size also depends on how much memory and Windows resources each control requires.
- The maximum index we can use in a control array is 32767. Elements of the same control array have their own property settings. Common uses for control arrays include menu controls and option button groupings.
- Use a menu control array to :
    (1) Create a new menu item at run time when it must be a member of a control array. The MDI Notepad sample, for example, uses a menu control array to store a list of recently opened files.
    (2) Simplify code, because common blocks of code can be used for all menu items.
- Each menu control array element is identified by a unique index value, indicated in the Index property box on the Menu Editor.
- When a member of a control array recognizes an event, Visual Basic passes its Index property value to the event procedure as an additional argument.
- Our event procedure must include code to check the value of the Index property, so we can determine that which control we are using.

Why Use Control Arrays ?
- Adding controls with control arrays uses fewer resources than simply adding multiple controls of the same type to a form at design time.
- Control arrays are also useful if we want several controls to share code.
- For example, if three option buttons are created as a control array, the same code is executed regardless of which button was clicked.
- If we want to create a new instance of a control at run time, that control must be a member of a control array. With a control array, each new element inherits the common event procedures of the array.
- Using the control array mechanism, each new control inherits the common event procedures already written for the array.
    For example : If our form has several text boxes that each receive a date value, a control array can be set up so that all of the text boxes share the same validation code. A menu can grow at run time.
    For example : As files are opened in the SDI NotePad application, menu items are dynamically created to display the path names of the most recently opened files.
- Menu control array elements created and displayed at run time in the following Fig. 4.45.
- We must use a control array to create a control at run time. Because the mnuRecentFile menu control is assigned a value for the Index property at design time, it automatically becomes an element of a control array — even though no other elements have yet been created.

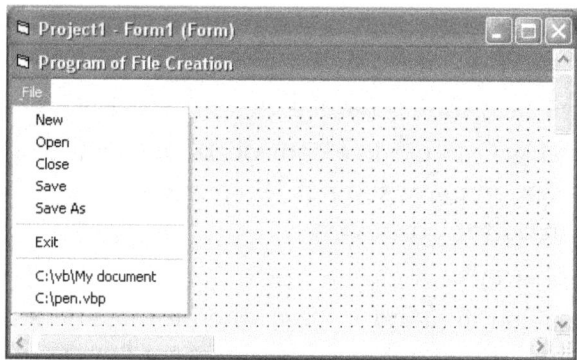

Fig. 4.45

- When we create mnuRecentFile(0), we actually create a separator bar that is invisible at run time. The first time a user saves a file at run time, the separator bar becomes visible, and the first file name is added to the menu. Each time we save a file at run time, additional menu controls are loaded into the array, making the menu grow.
- Controls created at run time can be hidden by using the Hide method or by setting the control's Visible property to False. If we want to remove a control in a control array from memory, use the Unload statement.

Modifying Menus at Run-time

- The menus we create at design time can also respond dynamically to run-time conditions.
- For example, if a menu item action becomes inappropriate at some point, we can prevent users from selecting that menu item by *disabling* it. In the MDI NotePad application, for example, if the clipboard doesn't contain any text, the Paste menu item is dimmed on the Edit menu, and users cannot select it.

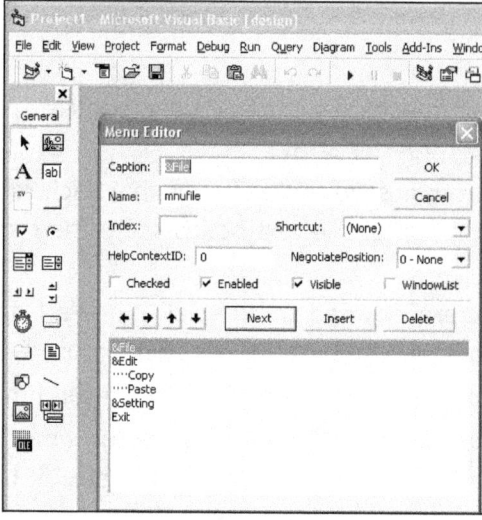

Fig. 4.46

- We can also dynamically add menu items, if we have a menu control array. we can also program our application to use a check mark to indicate which of several commands was last selected.
- For example, the Options, Toolbar menu item from the MDI NotePad application displays a check mark if the toolbar is displayed.
- Other menu control features described in this section include code that makes a menu item visible or invisible and that adds or deletes menu items.

Changing Menu Item Properties
- During Runtime programmer may change properties of menu item. According to requirement of user, programmer can change the properties of menu item by adding code.
- It is possible to enable/disable menu, visible, checked, WindowList, caption, parent, name, tag etc. property of menu item.

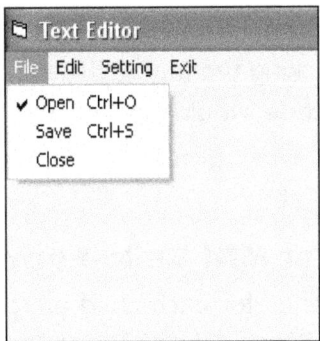

Fig. 4.47

```
Private Sub mnuopen_Click()
mnuopen.Checked = True
mnusave.Checked = False
mnuclose.Checked = False
End Sub

Private Sub mnusave_Click()
mnuopen.Checked = False
mnusave.Checked = True
mnuclose.Checked = False
End sub
```

Enabling Menu Item in response to Program State
- Menus can be Enabled/Disabled using menu item's Enabled property.
- All menu controls have an Enabled property, and when this property is set to False, the menu is disabled and does not respond to user actions. Shortcut key access is also disabled when Enabled is set to False.

- A disabled menu control appears dimmed, like the Paste menu item.

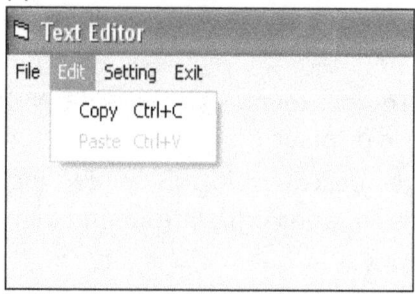

Fig. 4.48

- For example, this statement disables the Paste menu item on the Edit menu of the MDI NotePad application :

    ```
    mnuPaste.Enabled = False
    ```
- Disabling a menu title in effect disables the entire menu, because the user cannot access any menu item without first clicking the menu title.
- For example, the following code would disable the Edit menu of the MDI Notepad application :

    ```
    mnuEdit.Enabled = False
    ```

4.9 Adding Menu Items for MDI Child Form

- In an MDI application, the menus for each child are displayed on the MDI form, rather than on the child forms themselves.
- When a child form has the focus, that child's menu (if any) replaces the MDI form's menu on the menu bar.
- If there are no child forms visible or if the child with the focus does not have a menu, the MDI form's menu is displayed.
- It is common for MDI applications to use several sets of menus. When the user opens a document, the application displays the menu associated with that type of document.
- Usually, a different menu is displayed when no child forms are visible. For example, when there are no files open, Microsoft Excel displays only the File and Help menus.
- When the user opens a file, other menus are displayed (File, Edit, View, Insert, Format, Tools, Data, Window and so on).

Creating Menus for MDI Applications

- We can create menus for our Visual Basic application by adding menu controls to the MDI form and to the child forms.
- One way to manage the menus in our MDI application is to place the menu controls we want displayed all of the time, even when no child forms are visible, on the MDI form.
- When we run the application, the MDI form's menu is automatically displayed when there are no child forms visible, as shown in Fig. 4.49.

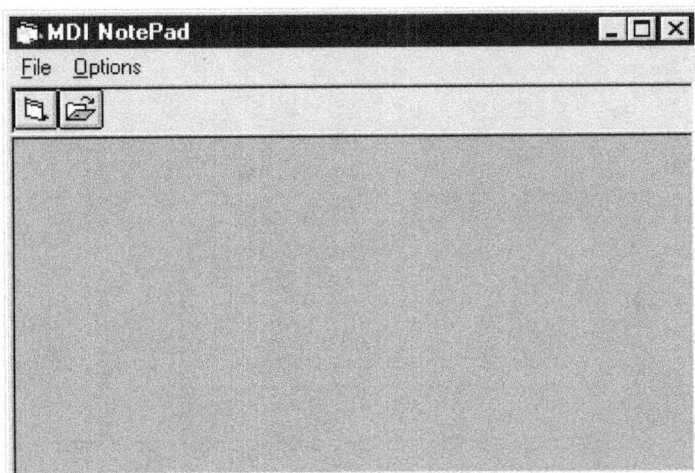

Fig. 4.49 : The MDI Form Menu is Displayed When No Child Forms Are Loaded

- Place the menu controls that apply to a child form on the child form. At run time, as long as there is at least one child form visible, these menu titles are displayed in the menu bar of the MDI form.
- Some applications support more than one type of document.

  For example : In Microsoft Access, we can open tables, queries, forms and other document types. To create an application such as this in Visual Basic, use two child forms. Design one child with menus that perform spreadsheet tasks and the other with menus that perform charting tasks. At run time, when an instance of a spreadsheet form has the focus, the spreadsheet menu is displayed and when the user selects a chart, that form's menu is displayed. If all the spreadsheets and charts are closed, the MDI form's menu is displayed.

Creating a Window Menu

- Most MDI applications (for example, Microsoft Word for Windows and Microsoft Excel) incorporate a Window menu.
- This is a special menu that displays the captions of all open child forms, as shown in Fig. 4.50.
- In addition, some applications place commands on this menu that manipulate the child windows, such as Cascade, Tile and Arrange Icons.
- Any menu control on an MDI form or MDI child form can be used to display the list of open child forms by setting the WindowList property for that menu control to True.
- At run time, Visual Basic automatically manages and displays the list of captions and displays a check mark next to the one that had the focus most recently. In addition, a separator bar is automatically placed above the list of windows.

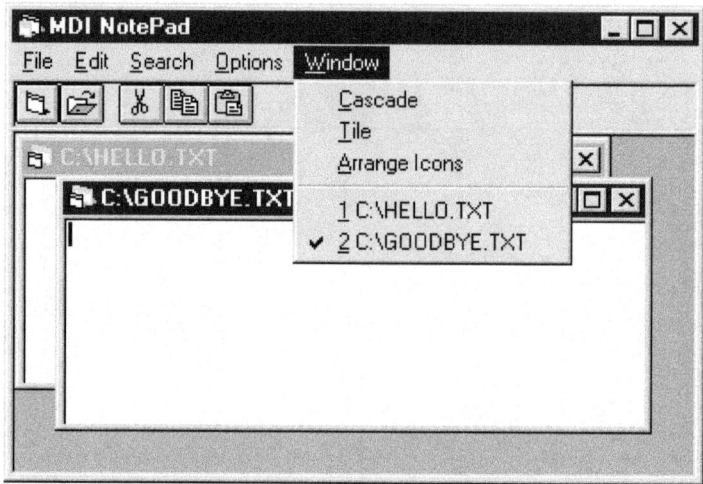

Fig. 4.50 : The Window Menu Displays The Name of Each Open Child Form

- **To set the WindowList property :**
  1. Select the form where we want the menu to appear, and from the **Tools** menu, choose **Menu Editor**.

> **Note :** The WindowList property applies only to MDI forms and MDI child forms. It has no effect on standard (non-MDI) forms.

  2. In the **Menu Editor** list box, select the menu where we want the list of open child forms to display.
  3. Select the **WindowList** check box.

     At run time, this menu displays the list of open child forms. In addition, the WindowList property for this menu control returns as True.

Arranging Child Forms

- As mentioned earlier, some applications list actions such as Tile, Cascade and Arrange Icons on a menu, along with the list of open child forms.
- Use the Arrange method to rearrange child forms in the MDI form.
- We can display child forms as cascading, as horizontally tiled or as child form icons arranged along the lower portion of the MDI form.
- The following example shows the Click event procedures for the Cascade, Title and Arrange Icons menu controls.

```
Private Sub mnuWCascade_Click()
   ' Cascade child forms.
   frmMDI.Arrange vbCascade
End Sub
```

```
Private Sub mnuWTile_Click()
    ' Tile child forms (horizontal).
    frmMDI.Arrange vbTileHorizontal
End Sub

Private Sub mnuWArrange_Click ()
    ' Arrange all child form icons.
    frmMDI.Arrange vbArrangeIcons
End Sub
```

Using Menu Item Array

- A group of controls that share a common name, type, and event procedures. Each control in an array has a unique index number that can be used to determine which control recognizes an event.
- To create a menu control array in the Menu Editor :
  1. Select the form.
  2. From the **Tools** menu, choose **Menu Editor**.

     –or–

     Click the **Menu Editor** button on the toolbar.
  3. In the **Caption** text box, type the text for the first menu title that we want to appear on the menu bar.

     The menu title text is displayed in the menu control list box.
  4. In the **Name** text box, type the name that we will use to refer to the menu control in code. Leave the **Index** box empty.
  5. At the next indentation level, create the menu item that will become the first element in the array by setting its **Caption** and **Name**.
  6. Set the **Index** for the first element in the array to 0.
  7. Create a second menu item at the same level of indentation as the first.
  8. Set the **Name** of the second element to the same as the first element and set its **Index** to 1.
  9. Repeat steps 5 – 8 for subsequent elements of the array.

> **Important :** Elements of a menu control array must be contiguous in the menu control list box and must be at the same level of indentation. When we are creating menu control arrays, be sure to include any separator bars that appear on the menu.

Practice Questions

1. What is a Menu ?
2. How to create a Menu ?
3. Describe design consideration for menu designing.
4. What is a Menu editor ?
5. How to create menu using menu editor ?
6. Explain the term shortcut keys.
7. What is a pop-up menu ? How to create it ?
8. How to adding menu items in a menu ?
9. How to activate a pop-up menu ?
10. What is meant by ActiveX controls ?
11. Why we required ActiveX controls ?
12. What is status bar ?
13. How to create a toolbar ?
14. Explain image list control in brief.
15. How to create a simple status bar ?
16. What is pannel in status bar ?
17. What is progress bar ?
18. Describe uses of toolbar control.
19. How to add images in toolbar buttons.
20. Enlist various types of common dialog boxes.
21. Describe procedure for adding separators for toolbars.
22. How to add and delete images in image list control ?

University Question & Answers

April 2010

1. Write short note on : Popup menu. **[4 M]**

Ans. Please refer to Sections 4.7.

2. Write short note on : Progress bar. **[4 M]**

Ans. Please refer to Section 4.3.

3. Write short note on : Status Bar.　　[4 M]
Ans. Please refer to Section 4.2.

October 2010

1. Write a menu driven program in VB for :
   i) Area of circle,
   ii) Area of rectangle.　　[4 M]
Ans. Please refer to Sections 4.6.1.

2. How do you create menus in visual basic ?　　[4 M]
Ans. Please refer to Sections 4.6.

3. Write short notes on status bar.　　[4 M]
Ans. Please refer to Section 4.2.

April 2011

1. Write a menu driven program in VB for :
   i) Area of triangle,
   ii) Area of rectangle.　　[4 M]
Ans. Please refer to Sections 4.6.1.

October 2011

1. Write short note on : Menus in visual basic.　　[4 M]
Ans. Please refer to Sections 4.6.

2. Write short note on Toolbar.　　[4 M]
Ans. Please refer to Section 4.4.

April 2012

1. What is a menu ? How to create menus using menu editor ?　　[4 M]
Ans. Please refer to Sections 4.6 and 4.6.2.

2. Write short note on : Progress bar.　　[4 M]
Ans. Please refer to Section 4.3.

October 2012

1. How to create a Menu? Explain with an example.　　[4 M]
Ans. Please refer to Sections 4.6.2.

2. Write short note on Status Bar.　　[4 M]
Ans. Please refer to Sections 4.2.

April 2013

1. Write short notes :
   i) Popus Menu
Ans. Please refer to Sections 4.7.
   ii) Progress Bar [4 M]
Ans. Please refer to Sections 4.3.

October 2013

1. Explain different types of dialog boxes. [4 M]
Ans. Please refer to Sections 4.5.2.
2. How will you create a new menu in Menu Editor. [4 M]
Ans. Please refer to Section 4.6.

❖ ❖ ❖

Chapter 5...

Working with Database

Contents ...

This chapter gives concepts of Working with Database in Visual Basic such as:

5.1 INTRODUCTION
    5.1.1 Concepts of Database
    5.1.2 Accessing Data using Visual basic

5.2 DATA CONTROL
    5.2.1 Studying the Properties and Methods of Data Control
    5.2.2 Connectivity with MS-Access
    5.2.3 Operations of Database through Coding

5.3 ADO DATA CONTROL
    5.3.1 Advantages of ADODC over DC(data control)
    5.3.2 Studying the Properties and Methods of ADODC
    5.3.3 Connectivity with MS-Access
    5.3.4 Connectivity with Oracle
    5.3.5 Report Generation

5.4 DEVELOPING ADO APPLICATION THROUGH ADODC AND CODING

5.5 REPORT GENERATION
    * Practice Questions
    * University Question & Answers

5.1 INTRODUCTION

- Visual Basic was designed to allow you to create database applications for the windows environment quickly and easily.
- If you have an existing database that you want to access, Visual Basic makes it easy for you to write a complete data management application with almost no programming.
- You just need to drop a few controls on a form and set the properties. In fact, Visual Basic makes it so easy that it can even create the data forms for you.
- The component that makes all these capabilities possible is the data control, which is used to access the database along with the data-bound controls that display the data.
- With these controls, you can create a wide range of applications, from simple to complex.

5.1.1 Concepts of Database

- A collection of information, tables, and other objects organized and presented to serve a specific purpose, such as facilitate searching, sorting, and recombining data. Database are stored in files.

    1. **Database File :** A file in which databases are stored. One database can be stored in several files.

    2. **Database Language :** The language used for accessing, querying, updating, and managing data in relational database systems. SQL is a widely used database language. With SQL, you can retrieve data from a database, create databases and database objects, add data, modify existing data, and perform other complex functions. Many of these capabilities are implemented by using one of three types of SQL statements: Data Definition Language (DDL), Data Manipulation Language (DML), and Data Control Language (DCL).

    3. **Database Management System (DBMS) :** A repository for the collection of computerized data files that enables users to perform a variety of operations on those files, including retrieving, appending, editing, updating, and generating reports.

    4. **Database Name :** A name that must correspond to the rules for identifiers and can have up to 30 characters (for example, sales or payroll98).

    5. **Database Object :** One of the components of a database: a table, index, trigger, view, key, constraint, default, rule, user-defined data type, or stored procedure.

    6. **Online Analytical Processing (OLAP) :** A technology that uses multidimensional structures to provide rapid access to data for analysis. The source data for OLAP is commonly stored in data warehouses in a relational database.

    7. **Online Transaction Processing (OLTP) :** A database management system representing the state of a particular business function at a specific point in time. An online transaction processing (OLTP) database is typically characterized by having large numbers of concurrent users actively adding and modifying data.

    8. **Open Database Connectivity (ODBC) :** A database-material Application Programming Interface (API) aligned with the American National Standards Institute (ANSI) and International Organization for Standardization (ISO) standards for a database Call Level Interface (CLI). ODBC supports access to any database for which an ODBC driver is available.

    9. **Record :** A group of related fields (columns) of information treated as a unit. A record is more commonly called a row in an SQL database.

10. **Recordset :** The ADO object used to contain a result set. It also exhibits cursor behavior depending on the recordset properties set by an application. ADO recordsets are mapped to OLE DB rowsets.

11. **Table :** An object in a database that stores data as a collection of rows and columns. The database management system (DBMS) hides low-level details and frees the programmer to concentrate on managing information, rather than on the specifics of manipulating files or maintaining links among them.

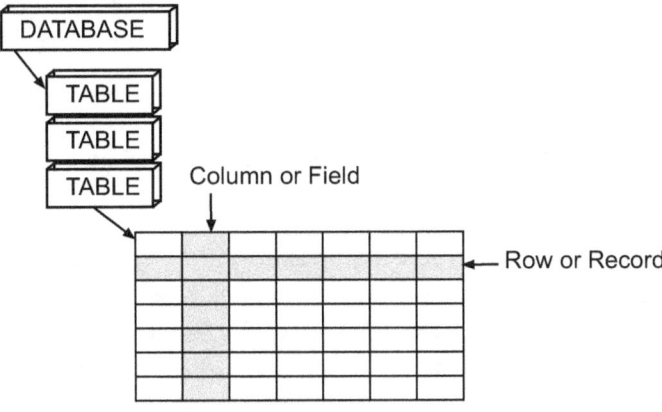

Fig. 5.1 : Table

- Visual Basic 6.0 provides a wealth of tools for creating and accessing databases on both individual machines and networks.
- The two major tools of visual basic Database are :
    1. Data Control (DC), and
    2. Data Access Object (DAO).
    1. **Data Control:** It gives user access to databases without any programming. User can set a few properties of the control and use regular controls such as textboxes to display the values of the fields in the database. Data control is the no-code approach to database programming, which is implemented quite nicely in Visual Basic.
    2. **Data Access Object :** It is a structure of objects for accessing databases through your code. All the functionality of the Data control is also available to your code, through the Data Access Object (DAO).

5.1.2 Accessing Data using Visual basic

- Fig. 5.2 shows a roadmap of data access technologies found in Visual Basic.
- The Fig. 5.2 features "hot" zones, which you can click to find out more information about any particular set of data, access tools or technologies.

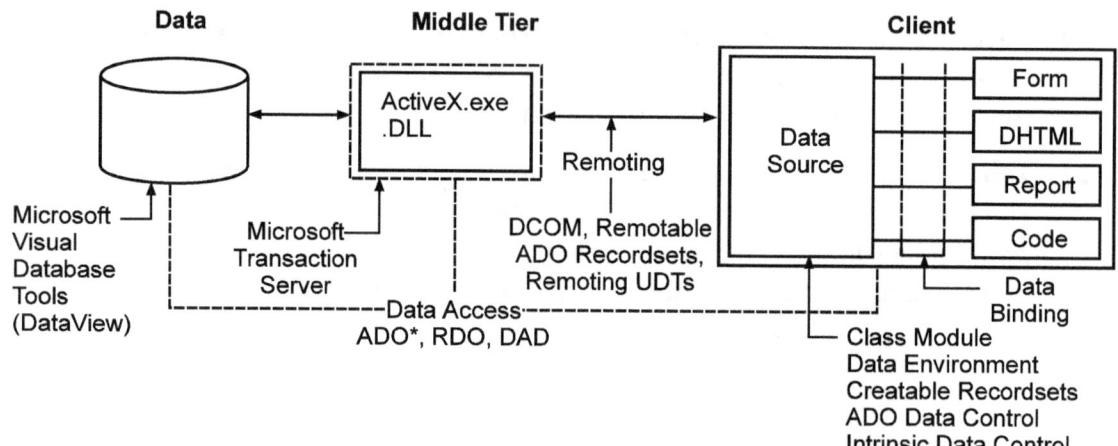

Fig. 5.2: Data Access Technologies found in VB 6.0

1. **Microsoft Visual Data Tools :**

   Using Visual Basic 6.0 you can create components that encapsulate every step in a data access system. Beginning with the data source, Microsoft Visual Data Tools (accessible through the Data View window) give you the ability to view and manipulate tables, views, stored procedures, and database schemas on SQL Server and Oracle systems.

2. **Middle Tier Components and Microsoft Transaction Server :**

   The power of Visual Basic is also leveraged to create the middle tier components in your application, as you make your own ActiveX DLLs and EXEs. Visual Basic now includes enhancements that tailor applications to work with Microsoft Transaction Server.

3. **Data Sources and Data Controls:**

   On the client side, several new data sources are available, including the Data Environment, a graphical designer that allows you to quickly create ADO Connections and Commands to access your data. The Data Environment designer provides a dynamic programmatic interface to the data access objects in your project. In addition, the Data Environment provides advanced data shaping services — the ability to create hierarchies of related data, aggregates, and automatic groupings, all without code.

   The new ADO Data control is similar to the intrinsic data control and Remote Data control, except that it uses ADO to access data. You can now use an ADO Recordset as a data source for your controls and objects in Visual Basic.

   In Visual Basic you can now create your own data sources either as user controls or classes, to encapsulate business rules or proprietary data structures. The class module now features the DataSourceBehavior property and the GetDataMember event, which allow you to configure a class as a data source.

4. **Dynamic Data Binding:**

   The ability to dynamically bind a data source to a data consumer is now possible in Visual Basic. At run time, you can now set the DataSource property of a data consumer (such as the DataGrid control) to a data source (such as the ADO Data control). This capability, unavailable in previous versions of Visual Basic, allows you to create applications, which can access a multitude of data sources.

5. **Presenting Data to the End User:**

   Visual Basic offers a variety of rich ways to present data to your end users. ADO/OLE DB-based versions of all the data bound controls are included in Visual Basic :
   - The DataList and DataCombo controls are the ADO/OLE DB equivalents of DBList and DBCombo controls.
   - The DataGrid is the successor to DBGrid.
   - The Chart control is now data bound.
   - A new version of the FlexGrid control, called the Hierarchical FlexGrid, supports the hierarchical abilities of the Data Environment.
   - The new DataRepeater control functions as a scrolling container of data bound user controls where each control views a single record.

   The Data Report is a new ActiveX designer that creates reports from any data source, including the Data Environment. With the Data Report designer, formatted reports can be viewed online, printed, or exported to text or HTML pages.

6. **Data Formatting and Data Validation :**

   The new DataFormat object allows you to display data with custom formatting, but write it back to the database in the native format. For example, you can now display dates in the format appropriate to a country, while the actual data is stored in a date format. Data is formatted coming out of the source, and unformatted going back in. You can also do custom formatting and perform additional checks using the Format and Unformat events.

   Data validation is also enhanced using the CausesValidation property with the Validate event. By setting the CausesValidation property to True, the Validate event for the previous control in the tab order will occur. Thus, by programming the Validate event, you can prevent a control from losing focus until the information it contains has been validated.

7. **Language Features :**

   New data-related enhancements to the Visual Basic language include the ability to pass User-defined Types (UDTs) and arrays across processes. You can now define a UDT and pass it as a parameter to another process, such as an ActiveX EXE or DLL.

8. **DHTML and Data Access :**

   Using Visual Basic, you can create complete web applications for data access. All of the data tools and technologies can also be used in DHTML pages, and on web server (IIS) applications.

5.2 DATA CONTROL (April 11)

- The data control is used to create simple database applications without writing any code.
- It can also be used to create more full-featured applications that give you a high degree of control over your data.
- The data-bound list, data-bound combo, data-bound grid, and Microsoft Flex grid controls are all capable of managing sets of records when bound to a data control.
- All of these controls permit several records to be displayed or manipulated at once.
- The intrinsic picture, label, text box, check box, image, OLE container, list box and combo box controls are also data-aware and can be bound to a single field of a Recordset managed by the data control.
- Additional data-aware controls like the **Masked edit** and **Rich text box** controls are available in the Professional and enterprise editions and from third-party vendors.
- The data-bound list box, combo box, and grid controls are used with the data control to display information from a database.
- You can use the data control to create applications that display, edit and update information from many types of existing database, including Microsoft Access, dBase, Microsoft FoxPro and paradox etc.
- You can also use it to access Microsoft Excel and standard ASCII text files as if they were true databases. In addition, the data control allows you to access and manipulate remote Open Database Connectivity (ODBC) database such as Microsoft SQL Server and oracle.
- The data control implements data access by using the Microsoft Jet database engine that power Microsoft Access.
- The technology gives you seamless access to many standard database formats and allows you to create data-aware applications without writing any code.
- You can use the data control to create simple database applications without writing any code at all. You can also use it together with visual Basic code to create full-featured applications that gives you a high degree of programming control over the behavior of your application's a data.

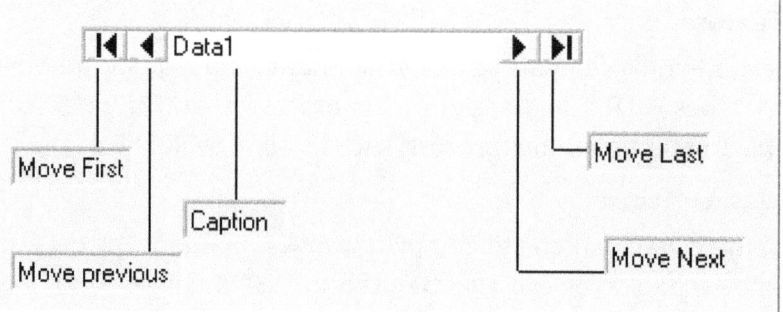

Fig. 5.3 : Data control tool

- The data control can perform the following tasks without the use of code :
    1. Connect to local or remote database.
    2. Open a specified database table or define a set of records based on a Structured Query Language (SQL) query of the tables in that database.
    3. Pass data fields to bound controls, where you can display or change the values.
    4. Add new records or update a database based on any changes you make to data displayed in the bound controls.
    5. Trap errors that occurs as data is accessed.
    6. Close the database.

5.2.1 Studying the Properties and Methods of Data Control

- To create a database application, you add the data control to your forms just as you would any other Visual Basic control.
- You can have as many data controls on your form as you need. As a rule, you will use one data control for each database table that you need to manipulate.
- Data control's properties define the connection between a Visual Basic application and the Database. Each data control will always access a single record at a time.
- You can bind other Visual Basic controls, (Data aware) to the data control. Controls bound to a data control automatically display data from a specified fields for current record.
- Changes are automatically saved in the database when the control moves to a new record. You can use validate, Reposition, error events and data changed properties to fine tune your application.
- **How to create a simple database application using Data Control ?**
    Use following steps to create simple database using Data Control :
    1. Add the data control to a form
       Set its properties to indicate the database and table from which you want to get information.
    2, Add bound controls (such as a text boxes, list boxes, and other controls that you bind to the data control)
    3. Set the properties of the bound controls to indicate the data source and data field to be displayed.
- When you run the application, these bound controls automatically display fields from the current record in the database.

5.2.1.1 Properties of Data Control

1. Database Property

Returns a reference to a Data control's underlying Database object.

Syntax

```
object.Database
Set databaseobject = object.Database
```
(Professional and Enterprise Editions only).

The Database property syntax has these parts :

Part	Description
databaseobject	An object expression that evaluates to an valid Database object created by the Data control.
object	An object expression that evaluates to an object in the Applies To list.

2. **Recordset Property :**

   Returns or sets a Recordset object defined by a Data control's properties or by an existing Recordset object.

   Syntax :

   ```
   Set object.Recordset [= value ]
   ```

   The Recordset property syntax has these parts :

Part	Description
Object	An object expression that evaluates to an object in the Applies To list.
Value	An object variable containing a **Recordset** object.

3. **Setting Data-Related Properties of the Data Control :**

   The following data-related properties can be set at design time. The list suggests a logical order for setting the properties :

   (i) **Connect** : The Connect property specifies the type of database to open. It can include arguments such as user ID and password. For example, Access, dBaseIII, dBaseV, paradox, text etc.

   (ii) **Database Name** : The Database Name specifies the type of database to open. It can include arguments such as Name of the database or the directory of the database (for external database).

   (iii) **RecordSource** : The RecordSource property specifies the source of the records accessible through bound controls on your form. You can specify
   - Database table name
   - Sql query string
   - QueryDef name

Options :

Options specifies the characteristics of the recordset created by Data Control.

Constant	Description
vbDataDenyWrite	Other users cannot change records in recordset.
vbDatadenyRead	Other users cannot read records in recordset
vbdataReadOnly	No user can change records in recordset.
vbDataAppendOnly	New records can be added to the recordset, but existing records cannot be read.
vbDataInconsistent	Updates can apply to all fields of the recordset.
vbDataConsistent	Updates apply only to those fields that will not affect other records in the recordset.
vbDataSQLPassThrough	Sends an SQL statement to an ODBC database.

(iv) Exclusive : The Exclusive property determines whether or not you have exclusive use of the database. If you set the Exclusive property to True, and then successfully open the database, no other application will be able to open the database until you close it.

(v) ReadOnly : The ReadOnly property determines whether or not you can update the database. If you do not plan to update the database, it is more efficient to set the ReadOnly property to True.

(vi) RecordsetType : The RecordsetType property determines if the recordset is a table, dynaset, or snapshot. The choice affects what recordset properties are available. For example, snapshot-type recordsets are more limited than dynaset recordsets.

RecordsetType settings :

Constant	Value	Description
vbRSTypeTable	0	Table-type recordset
vbRStypeDynaset	1	Dynaset-type recordset
vbRSTypeSnapShot	2	Snapshot-type recordset

- **Table Type Recordset :** A set of records that represents a single database table. Changes can be made to the recordset.
- **Dynaset Type Recordset :** A dynamic set of records that represents a database table or result of a query. It can contain fields from one or more tables. Changes can be made to the recordset.
- **SnapShot Type recordset :** It is a static copy of records. It can contain fields from one or more database tables. It cannot be updated. It is used to find data or generate reports.

(vii) DefaultType : The DefaultType property specifies whether JET or ODBCDirect workspaces are used.

(viii) DefaultCursorType : The DefaultCursorType property determines the location of the cursor. You can allow the ODBC driver to determine the cursor location, or specify server or ODBC cursors. The DefaultCursorType property is valid only when using ODBCDirect workspaces.

(ix) Exclusive : Determines if the data is for a single- or multi-user environment.

(x) Options : The property determines the characteristics of the recordset. For example, in a multi-user environment, you can set the Options property to deny changes made by others.

(xi) BOFAction, EOFAction : These two properties determine what will happen when the control is at the beginning and end of the cursor. Choices include staying at the beginning or end, moving to the first or last record, or adding a new record (at the end only).

5.2.1.2 Methods of Data Control

- The following are the methods of Data Control :

1. **Refresh :** The Refresh method refreshes the Recordset object. If you change the RecordSource property at run time, you must call the Refresh method to refresh the recordset.

   The following code shows how to use the Refresh method :
   ```
   Data1.RecordSource="Select * from employee where emp_id=" & txtemp_id Data1.Refresh
   ```
   The Refresh method rebuilds the recordset for the data control. If already open then closes and reopens with new properties taking into effect. In the recordsetcreated sets the current record pointer to the first record.

2. **Updaterecord :** The Updaterecord method saves current record to the database except no event (validate) occurs. It is typically used inside validate event.

3. **Updatecontrol :** use Updatecontrol method if the changes made to the bound controls are to be cancelled. Reads current record from the buffer again and updates bound controls to original values.

4. **CancelUpdate :** To cancel an AddNew or Edit method and refresh the bound controls with data from the recordset, you use the CancelUpdate method.

   For example, if a user has modified the fields on a form, but has yet updated them, the CancelUpdate method will referesh the fields with the original data from the recordset.

   If a user select an Add button on a form, and then decides not to add the record, the CancelUpdate method will cancel the operation and display the current record.

5.2.2 Connectivity with MS-Access

- The following example gives you a brief overview of How to connect Visual Basic Form or application with Ms-Access database.
- The example uses the **Biblio.mdb** sample database supplied with Visual Basic.

1. Open **New project**. When you open a project you get blank **Form.** Then change properties of Form as follows :

Property Name	Description
Name	frmDatacontrol
Caption	Example of Data Control

Then add following tools to form to display data on them.

Tool Name	Property	Description
Label1	Name	Title :-
Label2	Name	ISBN :-
Label3	Name	Year :-
Text1	Name	txttile
	Text	(empty)
	DataSource	Data1
Text2	Name	txisbn
	Text	(empty)
	DataSource	Data1
Text3	Name	txtyr
	Text	(empty)
	DataSource	Data1
Data1(Data Control)	Name	Data1
	Connect	Access
	DatabaseName	C:\Program Files\Microsoft Visual Studio\VB98\BIBLIO.MDB
	RecordSource	Titles

- Your Form look like in the following way :

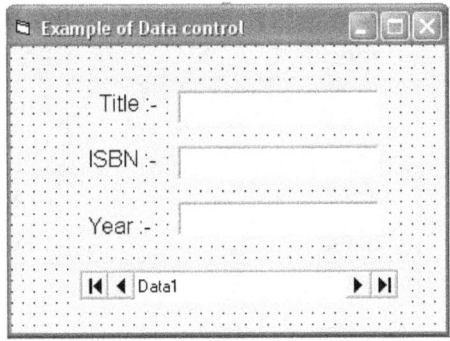

Fig. 5.4

2. Now run the application. You can use the four arrow buttons on the **Data Control** to move to the beginning of the data, to the end of the data, or from record to record through the data.
- You can modify the information in the database by changing the value displayed in any of the bound controls. When you click a button on the data control to move to a new record. Visual Basic automatically saves any changes you have made to the data.

5.2.3 Operations of Database through Coding

- You can perform different operations on database.
- The following example help you to explain operations on database.
  1. You can create **New Project.**
  2. In form you can create following controls given in the table.

Tool Name	Property	Description
Label1	Name	PPO_No :-
Label2	Name	Pensioner's Name :-
Text1	Name Text DataSource	txtppono (empty) Data1
Text2	Name Text DataSource	txtname (empty) Data1
Data1(Data Control)	Name Connect DatabaseName RecordSource	Data1 Access e:\bran0609 jan0609
Command1	Name Caption	Cmdadd &Add
Command2	Name Caption	Cmdprevious Previous
Command3	Name Caption	Cmdnext Next
Command4	Name Caption	Cmdselect select
Command5	Name Caption	Cmdexit &Exit

3. Your form looks like :

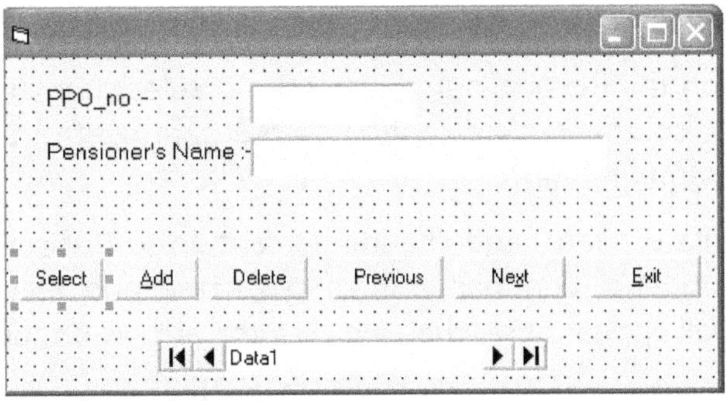

Fig. 5.5

4. Write the following code on each command button by double clicking on the command button.

```
Private Sub cmdadd_Click()
Data1.Recordset.AddNew
End Sub
Private Sub cmddelete_Click()
Data1.Recordset.Delete
End Sub
Private Sub cmdexit_Click()
End
End Sub
Private Sub cmdnext_Click()
Data1.Recordset.MoveNext
    End Sub
Private Sub cmdprevious_Click()
Data1.Recordset.MovePrevious
End Sub
Private Sub cmdselect_Click()
Data1.RecordSource = "select * from jan0609"
Data1.Refresh
End Sub
```

5. Run the program by pressing **F5**.

- Visual basic allows us to manage databases created with different database programs such as MS Access, Dbase, Paradox and etc. In the following example, we will create a simple database application which enable one to browse customers' names.

- To create this application, insert the data control into the new form. Place the data control somewhere at the bottom of the form. Name the data control as data_navigator.

- To be able to use the data control, we need to connect it to any database.

- To connect the data control to this database, double-click the DatabaseName property in the properties window and select the above file, i.e. NWIND.MDB.

- Next, double-click on the RecordSource property to select the customers table from the database. You can also change the caption of the data control to anything but we use "Click to browse Customers" here.

- After that, we will place a label and change its caption to Customer Name. Last but not least, insert another label and name it as cus_name and leave the label empty as customers' names will appear here when we click the arrows on the data control.

- We need to bind this label to the data control for the application to work. To do this, open the label's DataSource and select data_navigator that will appear automatically.

- One more thing that we need to do is to bind the label to the correct field so that data in this field will appear on this label. To do this, open the DataField property and select ContactName.

- Now, press F5 and run the program. You should be able to browse all the customers' names by clicking the arrows on the data control.

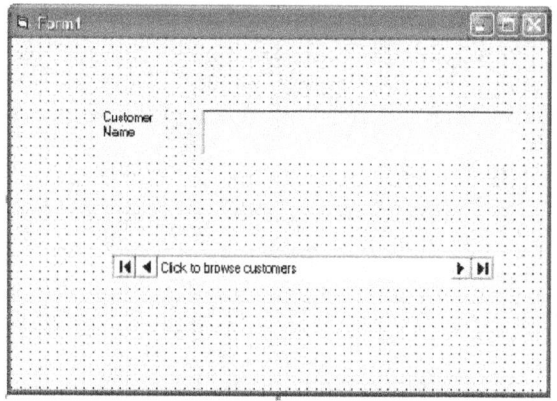

Fig. 5.6 : Design interface

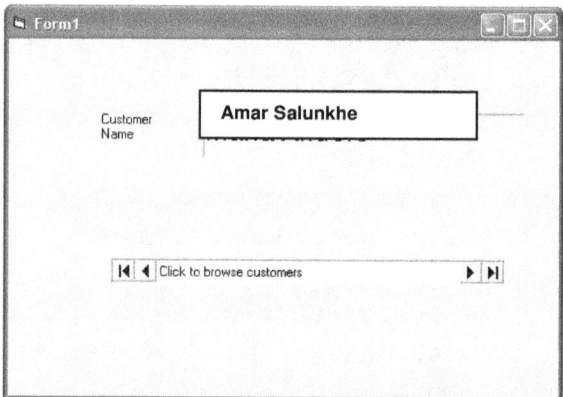

Fig. 5.7 : Runtime interface

5.3 ADO DATA CONTROL (Oct. 10, 12; April 10, 13)

- ADO is Microsoft's strategic application-level programming interface to data and information. It provides an easy-to-use application-level interface to OLE DB, which provides the underlying access to data.

- ADO is implemented with a minimal number of layers between the front end and data source to provide a high performance interface.

- ADO supports a variety of development needs, including the creation of front-end database client applications.

Understanding OLEDB

- ADO provides its functionality through OLE DB an open standard designed to allow access to all kinds of a data.
- Conceptually, OLEDB has three components :
  1. **Data providers :** A data provider is any OLE DB provider that owns data and exposes its data in a tabular form. Examples of data providers include : relational DBMS, spreadsheets, file systems and e-mail also.
  2. **Data consumers :** Data consumers are applications that use data exposed by data providers. In other words any application that uses ADO is an OLE DB consumer.
  3. **Service components :** Although data providers can provide some database functionality, OLE DB service components perform data processing and transport functionality between data consumers and data providers. In this scenario, neither the front-end application nor the back-end database is responsible for providing its own database functionality. Instead, service components provide functionality that any application can use when accessing data.

5.3.1 Advantages of ADODC over DC (Data Control) (April 14)

- ActiveX Data Objects (ADO) provides quick, high-performance access to all types of data and information.
- The ADO Data control uses Microsoft **ActiveX Data Objects (ADO)** to quickly create connections between data-bound controls and data providers. Data-bound controls are any controls that feature a **DataSource** property.
- Data providers can be any source written to the OLE DB specification. You can also easily create your own data provider using Visual Basic's class module.
- Although you can use the ActiveX Data Objects directly in your applications, the ADO Data control has the advantage of being a graphic control, (with Back and Forward buttons) and an easy-to-use interface that allows you to create database applications with a minimum of code.
- You can incorporate data-access features into your Visual basic program by using the following techniques :
  - **ADO Data control :** The ADO Data control provides data access functionality with a limited amount of code. In this course, the discussion of data access focuses on using the ADO Data control.
  - **ActiveX Data Objects (ADO) :** ActiveX Data objects(ADO) provides a complete programming interface that gives you access to all types of data.
  - **Data Form Wizard :** The Data From Wizard is used in conjunction with the ADO Data Control and is designed to automatically generate Visual Basic forms. These forms contain individual bound controls and procedures used to manage information derived from database tables and queries. You can use the Data Form wizard to create either single query forms to manage the data from a single table or simple

query or Master/Detail type forms used to a mange more complex on-to-many data relationships.

- **ADO Data environment Designer :** The Data environment designer provides an interactive, design-time environment for creating ADO objects. These can be used as a data source for data-aqarw objects on a form or report, or accessed programmatically as methods and properties.
- **Query Designer :** Using the Query Designer, you can create queries that modify a database by updating, adding, or deleting rows, or by copying rows. You can also create special-purpose queries, such as parameter queries in which search values are provided when the query is executed. If you are familiar with SQL, you can also enter SQL statements directly or edit the SQL statements created by the Query Designer.
- **Third-Party Controls :** Various third party developers offer database connectivity options.

Fig. 5.8 : ADO Data Control

- It look like Data Control. Previous versions of Visual Basic featured the intrinsic Data control and the Remote Data control (RDC) for data access.
- Both controls are still included with Visual Basic for backward compatibility. However, because of the flexibility of ADO, it's recommended that new database applications be created using the ADO Data Control.

Uses of ADO Controls

1) Connect to a local or remote database.
2) Open a specified database table or define a set of records based on a Structured Query Language (SQL) query or stored procedure or view of the tables in that database.
3) Pass data field values to data-bound controls, where you can display or change the values.
4) Add new records or update a database based on any changes you make to data displayed in the bound controls.

- To create a client, or front-end database application, add the ADO Data control to your forms just as you would any other Visual Basic control. You can have as many ADO Data controls on your form as you need.
- Be aware, however, that the control is a comparatively "expensive" method of creating connections, using at least two connections for the first control, and one more for each subsequent control.

Implementing the ADO Data Control

- When you use ADO Data Control, you connect to a database and specify a record source within the database. The associated records becomes available as a recordset.

- To return a set of records by using the ADO Data control, you must set the **ConnectionString** and **RecodSource** properties of the control.
- You can set these properties at design time through the properties window or at run time, typically in the **Form_Load** event.

1. Creating a Front-end Database Application with Minimal Code :

It's possible to create a database application using a minimum of code by setting a few properties at design time. If you are using an OLE DB data source, the Microsoft Data Link Name (.UDL) must be created on your machine.

Example : To create a simple front-end database application.

1. Draw an ADO Data Control on a form. (The icon's ToolTip is "ADODC.")

    If the control is not available in the Toolbox, press CTRL+T to display the **Components** dialog box. In the **Components** dialog, click **Microsoft ADO Data Control 6.0**.

2. On the Toolbox, click the **ADO Data Control** to select it. Then press F4 to display the **Properties** window.

3. In the **Properties** window, click **ConnectionString** to display the **ConnectionString** dialog box.

4. If you have created a Microsoft Data Link file (.UDL), select **Use OLE DB File** and click **Browse** to find the file on the computer. If you use a DSN, click **Use ODBC Data Source Name** and select a DSN from the box, or click **New** to create one. If you wish to use create a connection string, select **Use ConnectionString**, and then click **Build**, and use the **Data Link Properties** dialog box to create a connection string. After creating the connection string, click **OK**. The **ConnectionString** property will be filled with a string like :

    ```
    driver={SQL Server};server=bigsmile;uid=sa;pwd=pwd;database=pubs
    ```

5. In the **Properties** window, set the **RecordSource** property to a SQL statement. For example,

    ```
    SELECT * FROM Titles WHERE AuthorID = 72
    ```

    You should always include a WHERE clause when accessing a table. Failing to do so will lock the entire table, which would be a major hindrance to other users.

6. Draw a **TextBox** control on the form to display the database information.

7. In the **Properties** window, set the **DataSource** property for Text1 to the name of the ADO Data control (ADODC1). This binds the text box to the ADO Data control.

8. In the **Properties** window, click **DataField** and a list of available fields will drop down. Click the name of the field you want to display.

9. Repeat steps 6, 7, and 8 for each additional field you want to access.

10. Press F5 to run the application. You can use the four arrow buttons on the ADO Data control to move to the beginning of the data, to the end of the data, or from record to record through the data.

- It is also possible to set the ConnectionString, Source, DataSource, and DataField Programmatically. Example is given below :
- The code below shows how to set these four properties programmatically. Note that setting the DataSource property requires the Set statement.

```
Private Sub Form_Load()
With  ADODC1  .ConnectionString  =  "driver={SQL  Server};"  &  _
  "server=bigsmile;uid=sa;pwd=pwd;database=pubs"   .RecordSource  =
  "Select * From Titles Where AuthorID = 72"
  End With
  Set Text1.DataSource = ADODC1
  Text1.DataField = "Title"
End Sub
```

5.3.2 Studying the Properties and Methods of ADODC

5.3.2.1 Menu Design Considerations

- Most common properties of ADODC control are :
  1. **ConnectionString :** The ConnectionString property of the ADO Data control contains the information used to establish a connection to a data source. This property can be set at design time using the properties window. The Fig. 5.9 shows the three ConnectionString options when setting the value through the properties window.

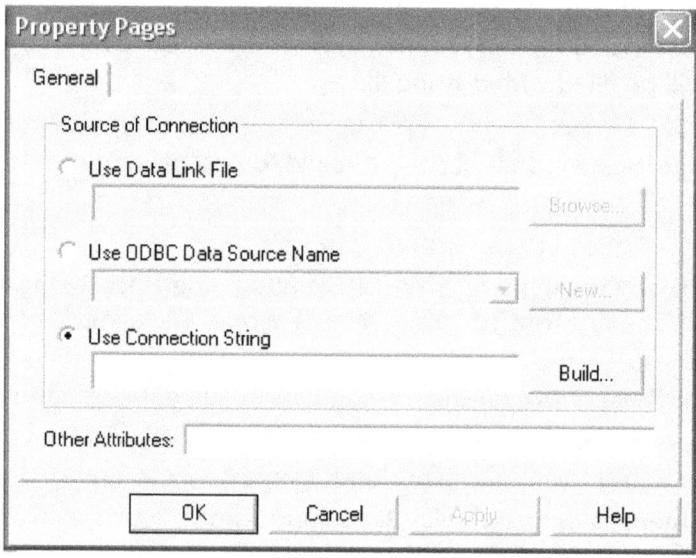

Fig. 5.9

When you set the ConnectionString value through the properties window, you have three connection options, as described in the following table.

Option	Definition
Use Data Link file	Specifies that you are using a custom connection string that connect to the data source. When this is selected, you can click **Browse** to access the **Organize Data sources** dialog box, from which you can select your Data Link file.
Use ODBC Data Source Name	Specifies that a system-defined data source name (DSN) is used for the connection string. You can access a list of all system-defined DSNs set through the ODBC option in Windows Control Panel. You can click **New** to access the **Create New Data Source** wizard dialog box to add to or modify DSNs on the system.
Use Connection String	Specifies that you are using a connection string to access data. You can click **Build** to access the **Data Link Properties** dialog box. Use this dialog box to specify the connection, authentication and advanced information required to access data using an OLEDB provider.

2. **RecordSource :** The RecordSource property can be either an individual table in the database, a stored query, or a query string that uses the Structured Query Language (SQL). The RecordSource property can be set at design run time. The following illustration shows the dialog box used to set the RecordSource property at design time.

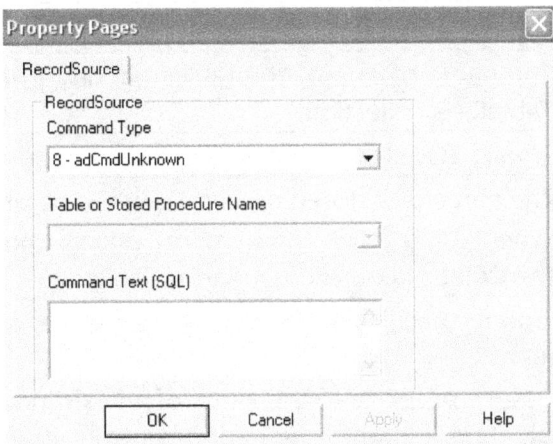

Fig. 5.10

In the RecordSource setting dialog box, you set the command type parameter which tells ADO which type of command object to use. The following table explains the different command type options.

Value	Description
adCmdUnknown	The type of command in the CommandText property is not known. This is the default value.
adCmdText	Evalutes CommandText as a textual definition of a command or stored procedure call.
adCmdTable	Evaluates CommandText as a table name whose columns are all returned by an internally generated SQL query.
adCmdStoredProc	Evaluates CommandText as a stored procedure name.

If you select either adCmdTable or adCmdStoredProc, you set table or stored procedure name in the **Table or Stored Procedure Name** drop-down list box below the command type drop-down list box. You can set the **RecordSource** property to a string values at a run time, as shown in the following example code :

```
adcEmployees.RecordSource="Employees"
```

Syntax :

```
object.RecordSource [= value ]
```

The RecordSource property syntax has these parts :

Part	Description
object	An object expression that evaluates to an object in the Applies To Data control
value	A string expression specifying a name, as described in Settings.

Settings : The settings for value are :

Setting	Description
A table name	The name of one of the tables defined in the Database object's TableDefs collection.
An SQL query	A valid SQL string using syntax appropriate for the data source.
stored procedure	The name of a stored procedure in the database. When using DAO, the name of one of the QueryDef objects in the Database object's QueryDefs collection.

The RecordSource property specifies the source of the records accessible through bound controls on your form.

If you set the RecordSource property to the name of an existing table in the database, all of the fields in that table are visible to the bound controls attached to the Data control. For table-type recordsets (RecordsetType = vbRSTypeTable), the order of the records retrieved is set by the Index object that you select using the Index property of the Recordset. For dynaset-type and snapshot-type Recordset objects, you can order the records by using a SQL statement with an Order By clause in the RecordSource property of the Data control. Otherwise, the data is returned in no particular order.

If you set the RecordSource property to the name of an existing QueryDef in the database, all fields returned by the QueryDef are visible to the bound controls attached to the Data control. The order of the records retrieved is set by the QueryDef object's query. For example, the QueryDef may include an ORDER BY clause to change the order of the records returned by the Recordset created by the Data control or a WHERE clause to filter the records. If the QueryDef does not specify an order, the data is returned in no particular order.

Note : At design-time, the QueryDef objects displayed in the Properties window for the RecordSource property are filtered out to display only QueryDef objects that are usable with the Data control. QueryDef objects which have parameters, and QueryDef objects which have the following types are not displayed : dbQAction, dbQCrosstab, dbQSQLPassThrough and dbQSetOperation.

If you set the RecordSource property to an SQL statement that returns records, all fields returned by the SQL query are visible to the bound controls attached to the Data control. This statement may include an ORDER BY clause to change the order of the records returned by the Recordset created by the Data control or a WHERE clause to filter the records. If the database you specify in the Database and Connect property is not a Microsoft Jet engine database, and if the dbSQLPassThrough option is set in the Options property, your SQL query must use the syntax required by that database engine.

Note : Whenever your QueryDef or SQL statement returns a value from an expression, the field name of the expression is created automatically by the Microsoft Jet database engine. Generally, the name is Expr1 followed by a three-character number beginning with 000. For example, the first expression would be named : Expr1000.

In most cases you will want to alias expressions so you know the name of the column to bind to the bound control. After changing the value of the RecordSource property at run time, you must use the Refresh method to enable the change and rebuild the Recordset.

At run time, if the Recordset specifies an invalid Table name, QueryDef name, or contains invalid SQL syntax, a trappable error will result. If this error occurs during the initial Form_Load procedure, the error is not trappable.

Note : Make sure each bound control has a valid setting for its DataField property. If you change the setting of a Data control's RecordSource property and then use Refresh, the Recordset identifies the new object. This may invalidate the DataField settings of bound controls and cause a trappable error.

3. BOFAction and EOFAction : Returns or sets a value indicating what action the Data control takes when the BOF or EOF properties are True.

   Syntax :
   ```
   object.BOFAction [= integer]
   object.EOFAction [= integer]
   ```
   The BOFAction and EOFAction property syntax's have these parts :

Part	Description
object	An object expression that evaluates to an object in the Applies To data control.
integer	An integer value that specifies an action, as described in Settings.

Settings : For the **BOFAction** property, the settings for integer are :

Setting	Value	Description
vbBOFActionMoveFirst	0	MoveFirst (Default) : Keeps the first record as the current record.
vbBOFActionBOF	1	**BOF** : Moving past the beginning of a Recordset triggers the Data control Validate event on the first record, followed by a Reposition event on the invalid (BOF) record. At this point, the Move Previous button on the Data control is disabled.

For the EOFAction property, the settings for integer are :

Setting	Value	Description
vbEOFActionMoveLast	0	**MoveLast** (Default) : Keeps the last record as the current record.
vbEOFActionEOF	1	**EOF** : Moving past the end of a Recordset triggers the Data control's Validation event on the last record, followed by a Reposition event on the invalid (EOF) record. At this point, the MoveNext button on the Data control is disabled.
vbEOFActionAddNew	2	**AddNew** : Moving past the last record triggers the Data control's Validation event to occur on the current record, followed by an automatic AddNew, followed by a Reposition event on the new record.

These constants are listed in the Visual Basic (VB) object library in the Object Browser.

If you set the EOFAction property to vbEOFActionAddNew, once the user moves the current record pointer to EOF using the Data control, the current record is positioned to a new record in the copy buffer. At this point you can edit the newly added record. If you make changes to the new record and the user subsequently moves the current record pointer using the Data control, the record is automatically appended to the Recordset. If you do not make changes to this new record, and reposition the current record to another record, the new record is discarded. If you use the Data control to position to another record while positioned over this new record, another new record is created.

When you use code to manipulate Recordsets created with the Data control, the EOFAction property has no effect it only takes effect when manipulating the Data control with the mouse.

In situations where the Data control Recordset is returned with no records, or after the last record has been deleted, using the vbEOFActionAddNew option for the EOFAction property greatly simplifies your code because a new record is always editable as the current record. If this option is not enabled, you are likely to trigger a "No current record" error.

4. **Mode :** It indicates the available permissions for modifying data in a Connection.

   Settings and Return Values : Sets or returns one of the following ConnectModeEnum values.

Constant	Description
adModeUnknown	Default. Indicates that the permissions have not yet been set or cannot be determined.
adModeRead	Indicates read-only permissions.
adModeWrite	Indicates write-only permissions.
adModeReadWrite	Indicates read/write permissions.
adModeShareDenyRead	Prevents others from opening connection with read permissions.
adModeShareDenyWrite	Prevents others from opening connection with write permissions.
adModeShareExclusive	Prevents others from opening connection.
adModeShareDenyNone	Prevents others from opening connection with any permissions.

Use the Mode property to set or return the access permissions in use by the provider on the current connection. You can set the Mode property only when the Connection object is closed.

Remote Data Service Usage : When used on a client-side Connection object, the Mode property can only be set to adModeUnknown.

5.3.2.2 Methods of ADODC

- Different methods of ADODC are given below :
  1. **Refresh :** Updates the objects in a collection to reflect objects available from and specific to the provider.

  Syntax :
  ```
  collection.Refresh
  ```

- The Refresh method accomplishes different tasks depending on the collection from which you call it.
- If you use the Refresh method to obtain parameter information from the provider and it returns one or more variable-length data type Parameter objects, ADO may allocate memory for the parameters based on their maximum potential size, which will cause an error during execution. You should explicitly set the Size property for these parameters before calling the Execute method to prevent errors.
- Using the Refresh method on the Fields collection has no visible effect. To retrieve changes from the underlying database structure, you must use either the Requery method or if the Recordset object does not support bookmarks, the MoveFirst method.
- Using the Refresh method on a Properties collection of some objects populates the collection with the dynamic properties the provider exposes. These properties provide information about functionality specific to the provider beyond the built-in properties ADO supports.

2. **Drag :** Begins, ends, or cancels a drag operation of any control except the Line, Menu, Shape, Timer, or CommonDialog controls. Does not support named arguments.

   Syntax :
   ```
   object.Drag action
   ```
   The Drag method syntax has these parts :

Part	Description
object	Required. An object expression that evaluates to an object in the data control. If object is omitted, the object whose event procedure contains the Drag method is assumed.
action	Optional. A constant or value that specifies the action to perform, as described in Settings. If action is omitted, the default is to begin dragging the object.

   Settings : The settings for action are :

Constant	Value	Description
vbCancel	0	Cancels drag operation
vbBeginDrag	1	Begins dragging object
vbEndDrag	2	Ends dragging and drop object

- Using the Drag method to control a drag-and-drop operation is required only when the DragMode property of the object is set to Manual (0). However, you can use Drag on an object whose DragMode property is set to Automatic (1 or vbAutomatic).
- If you want the mouse pointer to change shape while the object is being dragged, use either the DragIcon or MousePointer property. The MousePointer property is only used if no DragIcon is specified.

- The Drag method generally acts synchronously, meaning that subsequent statements are not executed until the drag action is complete. It can, however, act asynchronously if the DragMode property for the control is set to Manual (0 or vbManual).

3. **Move : Moves an MDIForm, Form, or control.**

   Syntax :
   ```
   object.Move left, top, width, height
   ```
   The Move method syntax has these parts :

Part	Description
object	Optional. An object expression that evaluates to an object in the data control. If object is omitted, the form with the focus is assumed to be object.
left	Required. Single-precision value indicating the horizontal coordinate (x-axis) for the left edge of object.
top	Optional. Single-precision value indicating the vertical coordinate (y-axis) for the top edge of object.
width	Optional. Single-precision value indicating the new width of object.
height	Optional. Single-precision value indicating the new height of object.

- Only the left argument is required. However, to specify any other arguments, you must specify all arguments that appear in the syntax before the argument you want to specify. For example, you cannot specify width without specifying left and top. Any trailing arguments that are unspecified remain unchanged.
- For forms and controls in a Frame control, the coordinate system is always in twips. Moving a form on the screen or moving a control in a Frame is always relative to the origin (0,0), which is the upper-left corner. When moving a control on a Form object or in a PictureBox (or an MDI child form on an MDIForm object), the coordinate system of the container object is used. The coordinate system or unit of measure is set with the ScaleMode property at design time. You can change the coordinate system at run time with the Scale method.

4. **Setfocus :** Moves the focus to the specified control or form.

   Syntax :
   ```
   object.SetFocus
   ```

- The object placeholder represents an object expression that evaluates to an object in the data control. The object must be a Form object, MDIForm object or control that can receive the focus. After invoking the SetFocus method any user input is directed to the specified form or control. You can only move the focus to a visible form or control. Because a form and controls on a form are not visible until the form's Load event has finished, you cannot use the SetFocus method to move the focus to the form being loaded in its own Load event unless you first use the Show method to show the form before the Form_Load event procedure is finished.

- You also cannot move the focus to a form or control if the Enabled property is set to False. If the Enabled property has been set to False at design time, you must first set it to True before it can receive the focus using the SetFocus method.

5. **ZOrder :** It places a specified MDIForm, Form, or control at the front or back of the z-order within its graphical level.

   Syntax :

   ```
   object.ZOrder position
   ```

   The ZOrder method syntax has these parts :

Part	Description
Object	Optional. An object expression that evaluates to an object in the data control. If object is omitted, the form with the focus is assumed to be object.
Position	Optional. Integer indicating the position of object relative to other instances of the same object. If position is 0 or omitted, object is positioned at the front of the z-order. If position is 1, object is positioned at the back of the z-order.

- The ZOrder of objects can be set at design time by choosing the Bring To Front or Send To Back menu command from the Edit menu. Within an MDIForm object, ZOrder sends MDI child forms to either the front or the back of the MDI client area, depending on the value of position. For an MDIForm or Form object, ZOrder sends the form to either the front or the back of the screen, depending on the value of position. As a result, forms can be displayed in front of or behind other running applications.

- Three graphical layers are associated with forms and containers. The back layer is the drawing space where the results of the graphics methods are displayed. Next is the middle layer where graphical objects and Label controls are displayed. The front layer is where all nongraphical controls like CommandButton, CheckBox, or ListBox are displayed. Anything contained in a layer closer to the front covers anything contained in the layer s behind it. ZOrder arranges objects only within the layer where the object is displayed.

5.3.3 Connectivity with MS-Access

- Use following procedure to connect from with MS-Access database.
    1. Open New Project.
    2. Add ADODC data control in the form.
    3. Change the ConnectionString property of ADODC as :
    - When you click on ConnectionString property you see Property Page dialog box. You click on Build button on this dialog box. You see Data Link Properties dialog box.

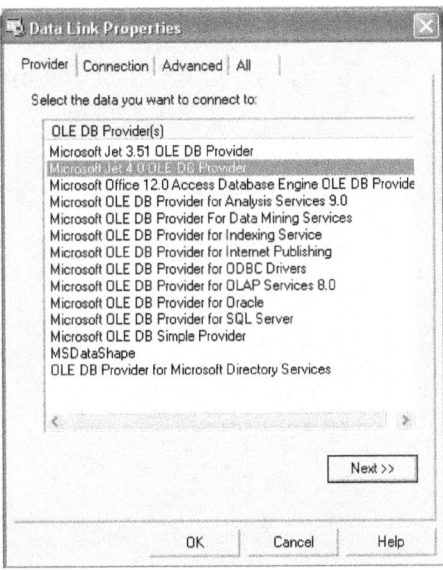

Fig. 5.11

- In this dialog box, in Provider tab you select Microsoft Jet 4.0 OLE DB provider, and click on Next button.
- Then you go to Connection tab. You click on button ... and select the MS-Access database. If your database have password and you also want use password procedure for database, then enter User name and password as clicking on Allow saving password.

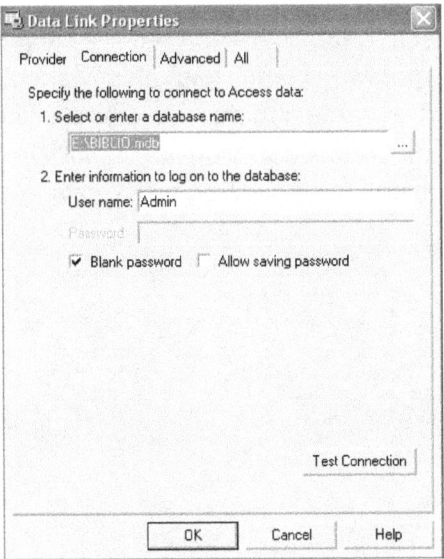

Fig. 5.12

- After this click on Test Connection button. It will check whether your database is connected correctly or not. It show dialog box having message as "Test Connection succeeded".

5.3.4 Connectivity with Oracle

Use following procedure to connect from with Oracle database.
1. Open New Project.
2. Add ADODC data control in the form.
3. Change the ConnectionString property of ADODC as :
- When you click on ConnectionString property you see Property Page dialog box. You click on Build button on this dialog box.

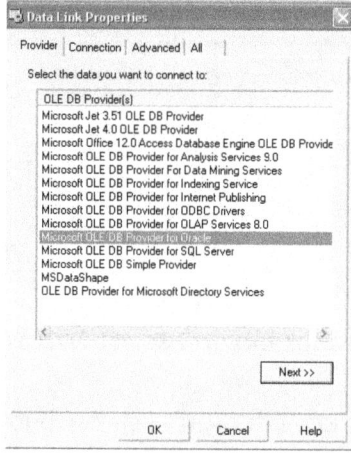

Fig. 5.13

- In this dialog box, in Provider tab you select Microsoft OLE DB provider For Oracle and click on Next button.
- Then you go to Connection tab. Here you enter a server name for Oracle database. If your database have password and you also want use password procedure for database, then enter User name and password as clicking on Allow saving password.
- After this click on Test Connection button. It will check whether your database is connected correctly or not. It show dialog box having message as "Test Connection succeeded".

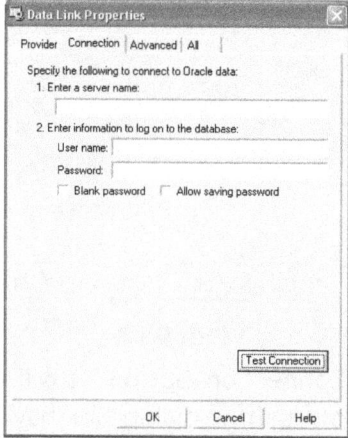

Fig. 5.14

- The following example will illustrate how to build a relatively powerful database application using ADO data control. First of all, name the new form as frmBookTitle and change its caption to Book Titles-ADO Application. Secondly, insert the ADO data control and name it as adoBooks and change its caption to book. Next, insert the necessary labels, text boxes and command buttons. The runtime interface of this program is shown in the diagram below, it allows adding and deletion as well as updating and browsing of data.

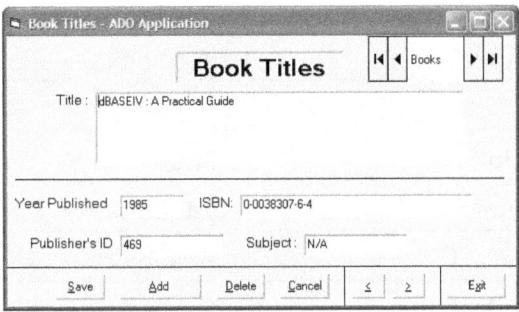

Fig. 5.15

The properties of all the controls are listed as follow :

Form Name	frmBookTitle
Form Caption	Book Titles -ADOApplication
ADO Name	adoBooks
Label1 Name	lblApp
Label1 Caption	Book Titles
Label 2 Name	lblTitle
Label2 Caption	Title :
Label3 Name	lblYear
Label3 Caption	Year Published:
Label4 Name	lblISBN
Label4 Caption	ISBN:
Labe5 Name	lblPubID
Label5 Caption	Publisher's ID:
Label6 Name	lblSubject
Label6 Caption	Subject :
TextBox1 Name	txtitle
TextBox1 DataField	Title

TextBox1 DataSource	adoBooks
TextBox2 Name	txtPub
TextBox2 DataField	Year Published
TextBox2 DataSource	adoBooks
TextBox3 Name	txtISBN
TextBox3 DataField	ISBN
TextBox3 DataSource	adoBooks
TextBox4 Name	txtPubID
TextBox4 DataField	PubID
TextBox4 DataSource	adoBooks
TextBox5 Name	txtSubject
TextBox5 DataField	Subject
TextBox5 DataSource	adoBooks
Command Button1 Name	cmdSave
Command Button1 Caption	&Save
Command Button2 Name	cmdAdd
Command Button2 Caption	&Add
Command Button3 Name	cmdDelete
Command Button3 Caption	&Delete
Command Button4 Name	cmdCancel
Command Button4 Caption	&Cancel
Command Button5 Name	cmdPrev
Command Button5 Caption	&<
Command Button6 Name	cmdNext
Command Button6 Caption	&>
Command Button7 Name	cmdExit
Command Button7 Caption	E&xit

- To be able to access and manage a database, you need to connect the ADO data control to a database file. We are going to use **BIBLIO.MDB** that comes with VB6. To connect ADO to this database file, follow the steps below :
  1. Click on the ADO control on the form and open up the properties window.
  2. Click on the ConnectionString property, the following dialog box will appear.

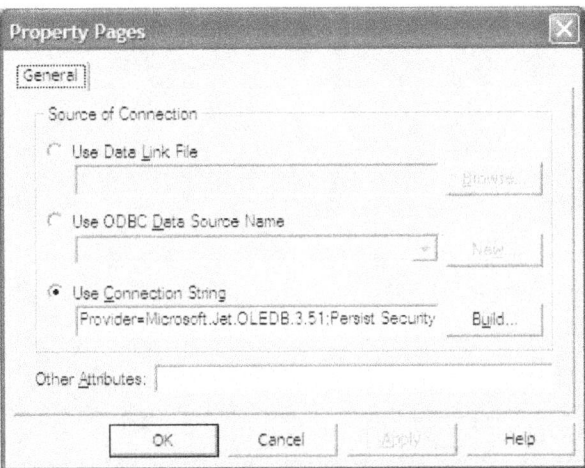

Fig. 5.16

- When the dialog box appear, select the Use Connection String's Option. Next, click build and at the Data Link dialog box, double-Click the option labeled Microsoft Jet 3.51 OLE DB provider.

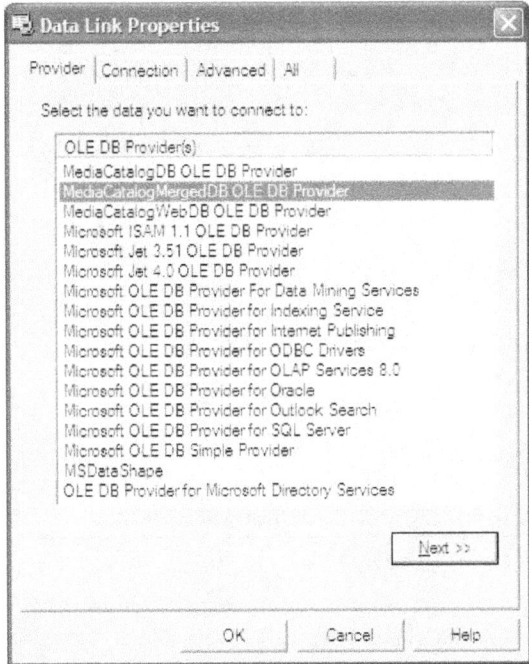

Fig. 5.17

- After that, click the Next button to select the file BIBLO.MDB. You can click on Text Connection to ensure proper connection of the database file. Click OK to finish the connection.
- Finally, click on the RecordSource property and set the command type to adCmd Table and Table name to Titles. Now you are ready to use the database file.

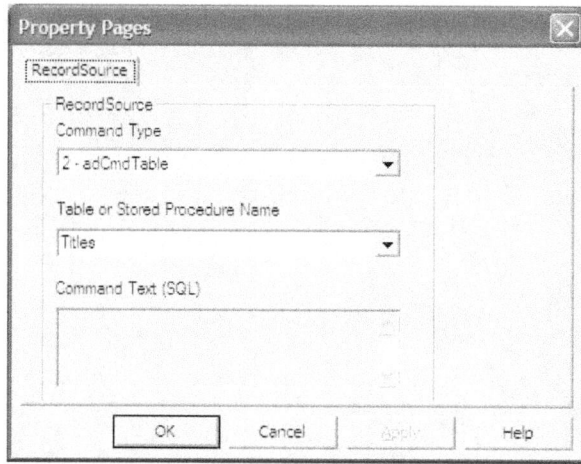

Fig. 5.18

- Now, you need to write code for all the command buttons. After which, you can make the ADO control invisible.
- For the Save button, the program codes are as follow :

```
Private Sub cmdSave_Click()
adoBooks.Recordset.Fields("Title") = txtTitle.Text
adoBooks.Recordset.Fields("Year Published") = txtPub.Text
adoBooks.Recordset.Fields("ISBN") = txtISBN.Text
adoBooks.Recordset.Fields("PubID") = txtPubID.Text
adoBooks.Recordset.Fields("Subject") = txtSubject.Text
adoBooks.Recordset.Update
End Sub
```

For the **Add** button, the program codes are as follow :

```
Private Sub cmdAdd_Click()
adoBooks.Recordset.AddNew
End Sub
```

- For the **Delete** button, the program codes are as follow :

```
Private Sub cmdDelete_Click()
Confirm = MsgBox("Are you sure you want to delete this record?", vbYesNo, "Deletion Confirmation")
If Confirm = vbYes Then
adoBooks.Recordset.Delete
MsgBox "Record Deleted!", , "Message"
Else
MsgBox "Record Not Deleted!", , "Message"
End If
End Sub
```

- For the **Cancel** button, the program codes are as follow :

```
Private Sub cmdCancel_Click()
txtTitle.Text = ""
txtPub.Text = ""
txtPubID.Text = ""
txtISBN.Text = ""
txtSubject.Text = ""
End Sub
```

- For the Previous (<) button, the program codes are

```
Private Sub cmdPrev_Click()
If Not adoBooks.Recordset.BOF Then
adoBooks.Recordset.MovePrevious
If adoBooks.Recordset.BOF Then
adoBooks.Recordset.MoveNext
End If
End If
End Sub
```

- For the Next(>) button, the program codes are

```
Private Sub cmdNext_Click()
If Not adoBooks.Recordset.EOF Then
adoBooks.Recordset.MoveNext
If adoBooks.Recordset.EOF Then
adoBooks.Recordset.MovePrevious
End If
End If
   End Sub
```

- In this sample, you will create a ADO database application to manage your home library. First of all, create a database in MS : Access and name home_Library. In this database, create a table with the following field names :

    Title :

    Author :

    Publisher :

    Year :

    Category :

    and save the table as booktitle.mdb

    Design the Interface as follow :

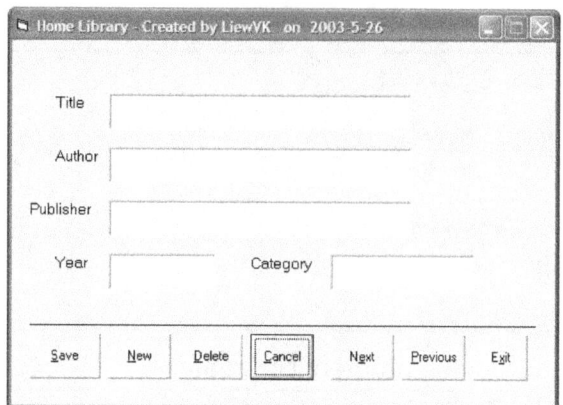

Fig. 5.19

Code as follows :

```
Private Sub cmdCancel_Click()
txtTitle.Text = ""
txtAuthor.Text = ""
txtPublisher.Text = ""
txtYear.Text = ""
txtCategory.Text = ""
End Sub
Private Sub cmdDelete_Click()
Confirm = MsgBox("Are you sure you want to delete this record?", vbYesNo, "Deletion Confirmation")
If Confirm = vbYes Then
adoLibrary.Recordset.Delete
MsgBox "Record Deleted!", , "Message"
Else
MsgBox "Record Not Deleted!", , "Message"
End If
End Sub
Private Sub cmdExit_Click()
End
End Sub
Private Sub cmdNew_Click()
adoLibrary.Recordset.AddNew
End Sub
Private Sub cmdNext_Click()
If Not adoLibrary.Recordset.EOF Then
adoLibrary.Recordset.MoveNext
If adoLibrary.Recordset.EOF Then
adoLibrary.Recordset.MovePrevious
End If
End If
```

```
End Sub
Private Sub cmdPrevious_Click()
If Not adoLibrary.Recordset.BOF Then
adoLibrary.Recordset.MovePrevious
If adoLibrary.Recordset.BOF Then
adoLibrary.Recordset.MoveNext
End If
End If
End Sub
Private Sub cmdSave_Click()
adoLibrary.Recordset.Fields("Title") = txtTitle.Text
adoLibrary.Recordset.Fields("Author") = txtAuthor.Text
adoLibrary.Recordset.Update
End Sub
```

5.3.5 Report Generation

- There is another way to generate report. For this you can use following steps.
1. You can add Add Data Environment from Project menu. (Refer Fig. 5.20).

Fig. 5.20

2. You change property as :

Property name	Value
Name	**Connection1** as **cn**
Name	**Dataenvironment1** as **de**

- You can right click on cn, select Properties... . You get Data Link Property window. Select Microsoft Jet 4.0 OLE DB provider, and click on Next button.
- Then you go to Connection tab. You click on button ... and select the MS-Access database. If your database have password and you also want use password procedure for database, then enter User name and password as clicking on Allow saving password.

3. Click on Test button. This will help you to validate whether the database is connected properly or not. If it is succeeded then your database is connected properly.
4. You can right click on cn, select Add Command. It add command1 under the connection cn.
5. You can right click on command1, select Properties.... Change Command Name as cmdtitle.

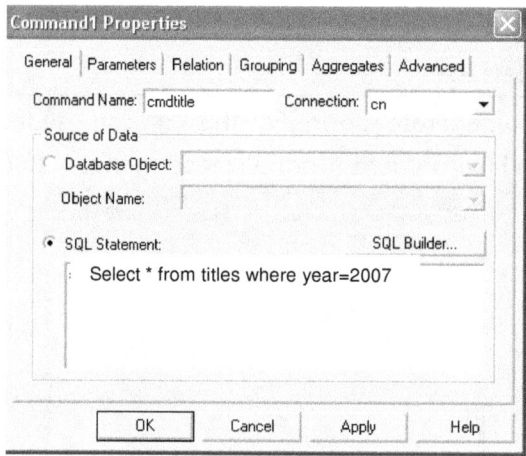

Fig. 5.21

6. Click on SQL Statement. Write SQL query and click on Ok or Apply button.
7. Add Add Data Report from Project menu. You see following data report.

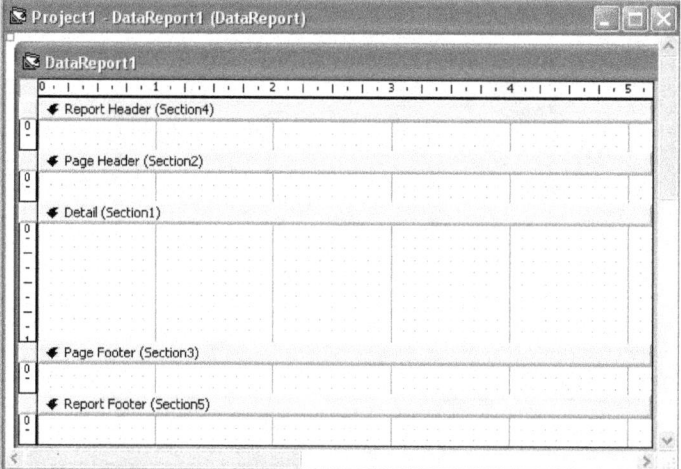

Fig. 5.22

7. Change the following property of DataReport1 as :

Property Name	Value
Name	drtitle
Caption	Report of Book's title after 1994
DataSource	de
DataMember	cmdtitle
WindowStatus	vbMaximized

8. Then double click on de and drtitle from Project browser. Double click on + sign of cmdtitle, you see fields of Titles table.

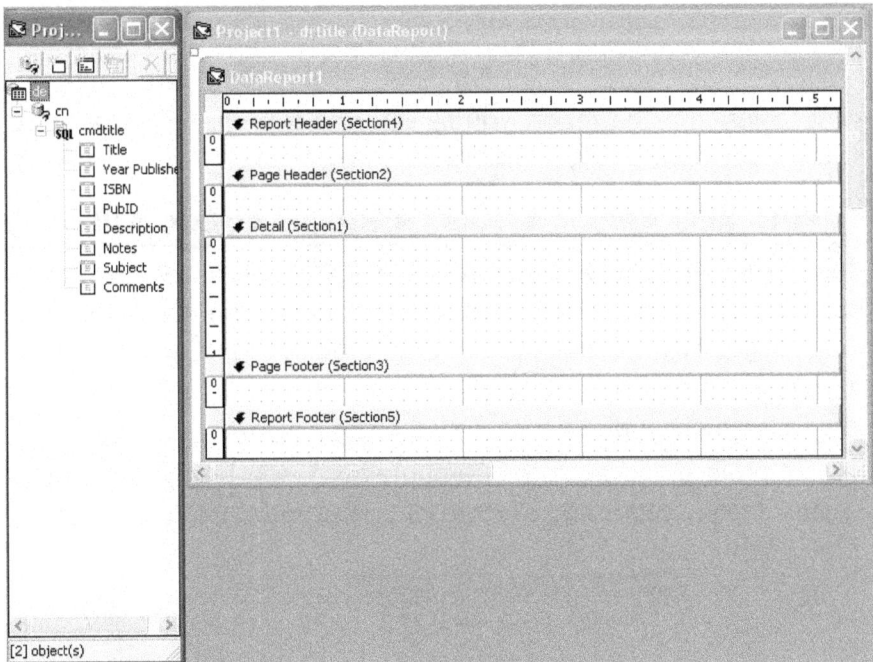

Fig. 5.23

9. You add label to Report Header section, change caption as Book List After 2005. Then drag Title, Description, Subject fields to Detail section. You move Title:, Description :, Subject: to Page Header section and keep Title[cmdtitle], Description[cmdtitle] and subject[cmdtitle] as in Detail section.

10. Then add **sum** tool from tool box in **Report Footer.** Change its property as :

Property name	Value
Datamember	Cmdtitle
Datafield	title

11. Your report looks like :

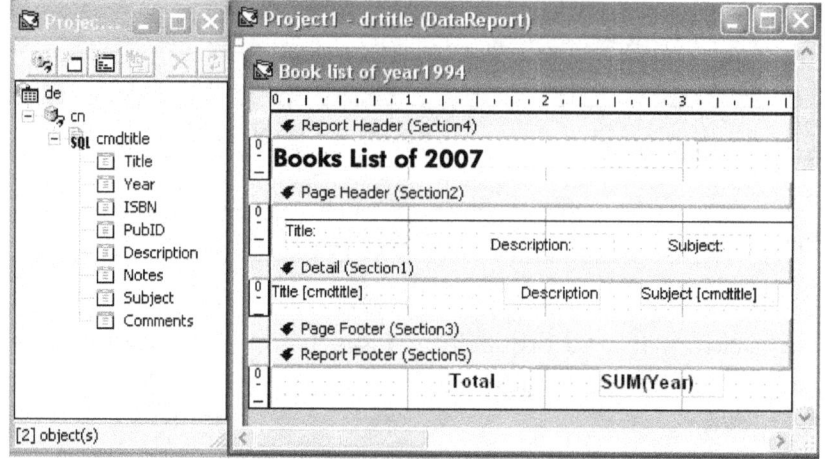

Fig. 5.24

12. If you want to just run the report you select Project menu, go to Project Properties... option. Change the Startup Object as drtitle. Run the report by pressing F5.

5.4 DEVELOPING ADO APPLICATION THROUGH ADODC AND CODING

- For developing the ADODC application use ADODC control on the form and set the ConnectionString property of that control to connect the database. We are already learning how to get ADODC data control in the toolbar. Then you just drag the ADODC control on the form. You just use it for database connection.
- To build the first sample application, follow the steps below :

  Start a new VB project, and from the Components dialog box (invoked from the Project → Components menu), select Microsoft ADO Data Control 6.0 (SPx) as shown below and click OK.

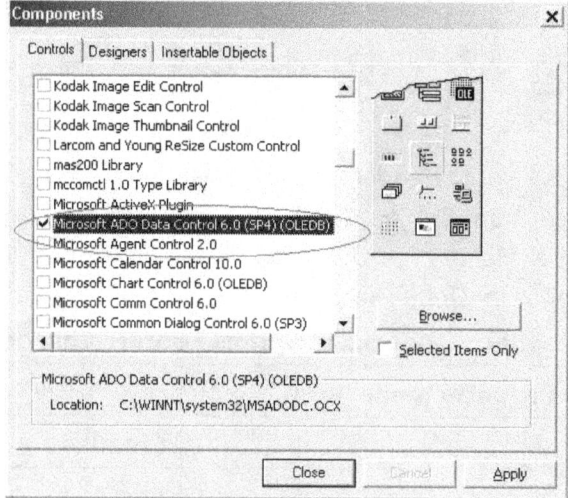

Fig. 5.25

The ADO Data Control should appear in your toolbox as shown below :

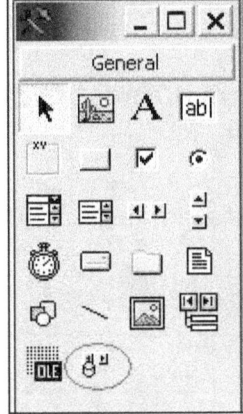

Fig. 5.26

- Put an ADO Data Control on your form, and set the properties as follows :

Property	Value
Name	adoBiblio
DataSourceName	Biblio
SQL	select * from authors

- Now put three text boxes on the form, and set their Name, DataSource, and DataField properties as follows:

Name	DataSource	DataField
txtAuthor	adoBiblio	Author
txtAuID	adoBiblio	Au_ID
txtYearBorn	adoBiblio	Year Born

- Save and run the program. Notice how it works just like the other data control.
- Now change the SQL property of the data control to select * from authors order by author and run the program again. Notice the difference.
- Change the SQL property back to what it was and add three command buttons to the form, and set their Name and Caption properties as follows :

Name	Caption
cmdNameOrder	Order by Name
cmdYearOrder	Order by Year
cmdIDOrder	Order by ID

- Put the following code in the **cmdNameOrder_Click** event:

```
adoBiblio.SQL = "select * from authors order by author"
adoBiblio.Refresh
```

Put the following code in the **cmdYearOrder_Click** event:
```
adoBiblio.SQL = "select * from authors order by [year born]"
adoBiblio.Refresh
```
- Put the following code in the **cmdIDOrder_Click** event :
```
adoBiblio.SQL = "select * from authors order by au_id"
adoBiblio.Refresh
```
- Save and run the program and see what happens when you click the buttons.

Output :

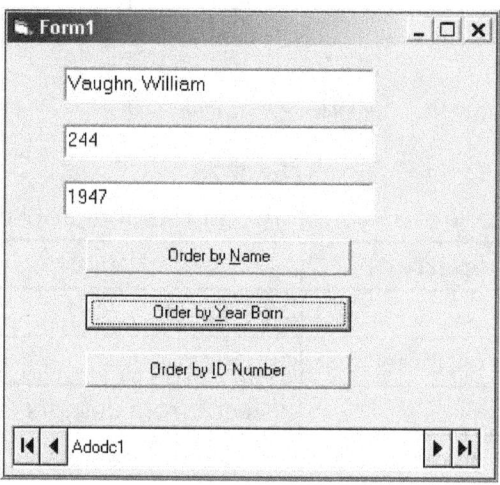

Fig. 5.27

5.5 REPORT GENERATION (Oct. 12, April 13)

- There are two ways to generate report. They are :
  1. Using crystal report
  2. Using Data Environment

1. **Using crystal report :** 'Crystal Reports' is a popular third party package that is included with Visual Basic, which allows you to create reports for your application. The package consists of a designer - where you can design and test the reports, Crystal Reports API calls and Crystal Reports control. Fig. 5.28 shows crystal report control tool.

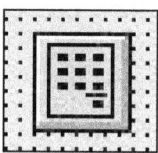

Fig. 5.28 : Crystal report control tool

- When you have designed your report, the saved file should have an extension .rpt. You can use this report with the Crystal Report control to display or print your report in a VB application.

- You will have to add the Crystal Report control to the toolbox, this is done by going to the Project menu and selecting Components, then looking down the list for the control and clicking on it.
  To use the control add it to a form and set the following properties :
  - **ReportFileName :** The path and the filename of the **.rpt** file you have created
  - **DataFiles(0) :** The path and the filename of the database that you want it to use. If this is left blank it will use the one in the report.
  - **SelectionFormula :** The formula to select the subset of data that you want.
  - **Destination :** 0 to Preview, 1 to Print
- To display the report use the **.printreport** method i.e. **CrystalReport1 .PrintReport**.

How to Print a Crystal Report from a VB Program

- First, you must add the Crystal Report control to your VB toolbox. To do so, go to Project ↵ Components and check Crystal Report Control 4.6 from the Components dialog box, as shown in Fig. 5.29.

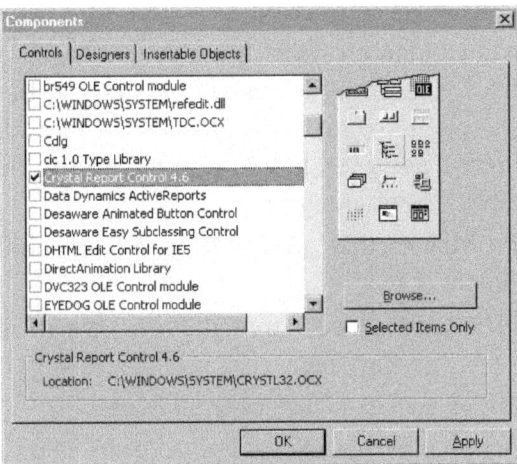

Fig. 5.29

- The Crystal Reports control will then appear in the VB toolbox.

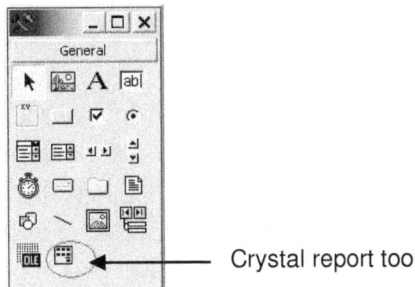

Crystal report tool

Fig. 5.30

2. **Using Data Environment :** The Data Environment designer provides an interactive, environment for creating programmatic data access. At design time, you set property values for Connection and Command objects, write code to respond to ActiveX Data Object (ADO) events, execute commands, and create aggregates and hierarchies. You can also drag Data Environment objects onto forms or reports to create data-bound controls. With the Data Environment designer, you can accomplish the following tasks :
   - Add a Data Environment designer to a Visual Basic project.
   - Create Connection objects.
   - Create Command objects based on stored procedures, tables, views, synonyms and SQL statements.
   - Create hierarchies of commands based on a grouping of Command objects or by relating one or more Command objects together.
   - Write and run code for Connection and Recordset objects.
   - Drag fields within a Command object from the Data Environment designer onto a Visual Basic form or the Data Report designer.

- **Differences Between the UserConnection and Data Environment Designers :**
   The Data Environment designer provides a means to easily access data in your Visual Basic project. In previous releases, you used the ActiveX UserConnection designer to create Remote Data Objects (RDO) at. Now, you can create ADO objects at design time using the Data Environment designer. In addition to supporting all of the functionality of the, the Data Environment designer supports :
   - Multiple Connection objects that allow you to access multiple data sources within a single Data Environment.
   - Connection and Command objects that you can organize by either connection or object.
   - OLE DB data sources, as well as ODBC data sources.
   - Drag-and-drop functionality that allows you to drag fields and tables from your Data Environment designer onto a form or the Data Report ActiveX designer. Data-bound controls are automatically created on the form. You can also specify the default control type that is created.
   - Execution of commands included in your Data Environment as programmatic methods.
   - Programmatic access to a Data Environment that is bound to controls on a form without a variable reference, such as moving to a new record.
   - The ability to relate Command objects to create a relation hierarchy, or to group Command objects to create a grouped hierarchy.
   - The ability to create aggregates that automatically calculate values within any Command hierarchy.

- The ability to manually bind data-aware controls to Field objects within a Command object.
- The Data Environment extensibility object model, which allows you to create add-ins. These add-ins can programmatically manipulate any DataEnvironment object within a Visual Basic project.

UserConnection Designer vs. Data Environment Designer

Functionality	UserConnection designer	Data Environment designer
Data Access exposed using...	Remote Data Objects (RDO).	ActiveX Data Objects (ADO).
Objects exposed include...	Only one RDO connection with multiple queries.	Multiple ADO Connection and Command objects within one DataEnvironment object.
Events exposed include...	Only events from the UserConnection object.	All ADO events for the Connection and Command object.
Direct data binding...	Cannot be used as a direct data source.	Can be directly bound to controls on a form.
Programmatic access exposes...	Queries as methods from the UserConnection object with one ResultSet property.	Command objects as methods from the DataEnvironment object, with one RecordSet property per Command object.
Design environment provides...	A basic view that only displays the list of queries in the UserConnection.	Two views of objects that list Connection and Command objects, as well as the Field objects returned from each Command object.

- **Working with Data environment in Visual Basic :** At, you can use the Data Environment designer to create a DataEnvironment object.
- The DataEnvironment object can include Connection and Command objects, hierarchies (relationships between Command objects), groupings, and aggregates.
- Before designing your DataEnvironment object, you should determine what information you want to present, identify the databases that contain the information, and determine your objective, (for example, creating a or Hierarchical FlexGrid control).
- To add a Data Environment designer object to a new Visual Basic project :
  1. From the **New** tab of the **New Project** dialog box, choose **Standard EXE** project and then click **Open**.
  2. From the **Project** menu, choose **Add Data Environment**.

The Data Environment designer is added to your Visual Basic project, the Data Environment designer window appears, and a Connection object is added to your Data Environment.

Once you have added a Data Environment designer to your project, you can create a Connection. Once a Connection is created, you can add Commands to it.

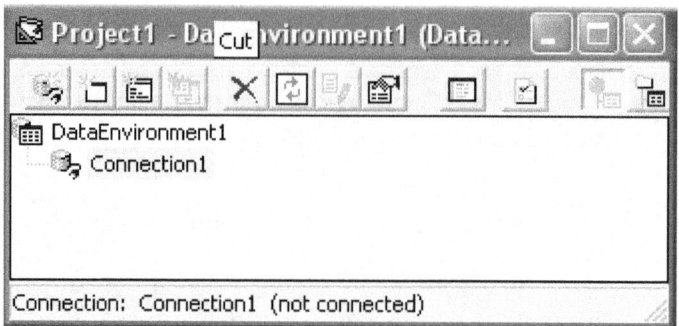

Fig. 5.31

3. To access data using your Data Environment, you must create a Connection object. Therefore, every Data Environment should include at least one Connection object. A Connection object represents a connection to a remote database that is used as a data source.

- Upon adding a Data Environment to your Visual Basic project, the Data Environment designer automatically includes a new connection, called **Connection1**. At design time, the Data Environment opens the connection and obtains metadata from the connection, including database object names, table structures, and procedure parameters.

Note : If Show properties immediately after object creation is selected in the Options dialog box, the Data Link Properties dialog box will appear when you add a Data Environment to your project. This option is not selected by default.

Creating a Connection Object

- The **Add Connection** function is available at all times and is independent of the existence of other objects.
- To create a database connection :
  o Click **Add Connection** on the Data Environment designer toolbar.

    –or–

    Right-click your Data Environment designer and select Add Connection from the shortcut menu.

    Once, you have added a Connection, the Data Environment is updated to show the new Connection object. The default name for this object is "Connection," followed by a number, such as Connection1.

    Use the following procedure to specify Connection object properties.

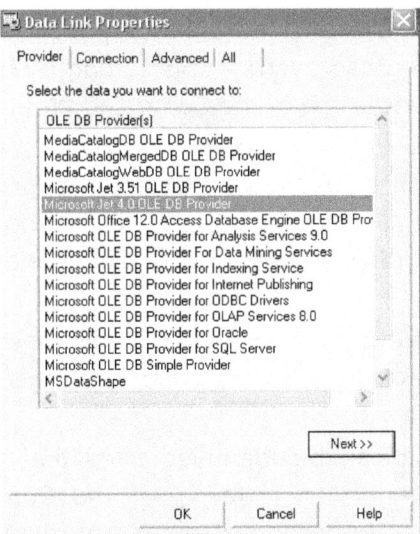

Fig. 5.32

- To set the Connection Name and Data Source :
  1. In the Visual Basic Properties window, change the default Name to a more meaningful name for your data source database. For example, you may wish to change Connection1 to "Northwind" if the data source is the Northwind database.
  2. Right-click the Connection object and choose Properties to access the Data Link Properties dialog box.
  3. From the Data Link Properties dialog box, specify the connection information on the Provider and Connection tabs. This is typically a database that contains data or stored procedures. You may select only one source for each Connection object. If you want to connect database to Access, then you select Microsoft Jet 4.0 OLE DB Provider.

Note : Regardless of the selected data source type, the Data Environment accesses all data via ADO and OLE DB interfaces.

  4. Click **OK** to apply the properties and close the dialog box.
  5. Command objects define specific detailed information about what data is retrieved from a database connection. Command objects can be based on either a database object (such as a table, view, stored procedure or synonym) or a Structured Query Language (SQL) query. You can also create relationships between Command objects to retrieve a set of related data in the form of a hierarchy.

Note : To be valid, a Command object must be associated with a Connection object.

- If a Command object returns data, it is "recordset returning," and the results can be accessed using a Recordset object available from the DataEnvironment object. However, if a Command object does not return data (for example, stored procedures or SQL text that performs an update), it is "non-recordset returning".

- The Data Environment Designer automatically identifies whether the Command is recordset returning. You can override this setting by using the Recordset Returning check box on the Advanced tab of the Command Properties dialog box.
- At, how you access the Command object depends on whether the Command object is recordset returning. If the Command object is recordset returning, you can access the Command object as either a property or method from the DataEnvironment object. If it is non-recordset returning, your Command object is only accessible as a method.
- The Add Command function is available at all times and is independent of the existence of other objects. However, a Command object that is not associated with a Connection object is invalid.
- If a Connection object can be identified from the current focus during the add process, the ActiveConnection property of the Command object is set to that Connection object. If a Connection object is not identified, the Command object is invalid until you associate it with a connection.

To Add a Command object

- Click Add Command in the Data Environment designer toolbar.

–OR–

Right-click a Connection object, or your Data Environment designer, and choose Add Command from the shortcut menu.

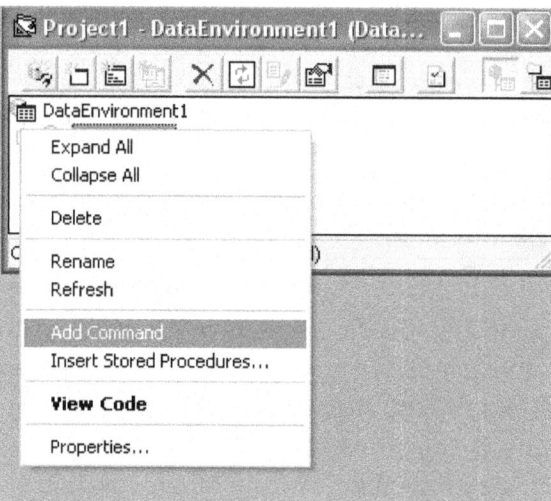

Fig. 5.33

Once a Command object is added, the Data Environment's outline view shows the new Command object. The default name for this object is "Command," followed by a number, such as Command1.

Use the following procedure to specify Command object properties.

- **To specify Command object properties :**
  1. Right-click the Connection object and choose **Properties** to access the **Command Properties** dialog box.
  2. Click the **General** tab, and set the following :

Item	Purpose
Command Name	Change the default **Command Name** to a more meaningful name for your database object. For example, you may wish to change Command1 to "Customers" if the Command object is based on a table called "customers."
Connection	If the Command object was created from a Connection object's shortcut menu, the Connection name is automatically set. However, you can change this connection. **Note :** To be valid, each Command object must be associated with a Connection object.
Database Object	Select the type of database object from the drop-down list. This can be a stored procedure, synonym, table, or view.
Object Name	Select an object name from the drop-down list. The listed objects are from the connection and match the selected **Database Object** type.
– or –	
SQL Statement	If this is selected as your data source, type an SQL query that is valid for your database in the **SQL Statement** box. - OR - To build the query, click **SQL Builder** to launch the .

  3. If the Command object is based on a parameterized query or a stored procedure, it may have a parameters collection. To set the, click the **Parameters** tab in the **Command Properties** dialog box.
  4. Use the **Relation**, **Grouping**, and **Aggregates** tabs to define relationships and shape the data included in the Recordset. Click the **Advanced** tab in the **Command Properties** dialog box to set the properties that change how the data is retrieved or manipulated at. On this tab, set the that provide your Data Environment control over the Command object properties and its resulting Recordset object.
  5. Click **OK** to apply the properties to the new Command object and close the dialog box.

If a recordset-returning Command object was successfully created, you can click the expand (+) from the Data Environment designer's outline view to see a list of fields. If no fields are shown, the cause could be an empty Recordset, an invalid Command object, or an invalid connection. If you are sure you have a valid connection, right-click the DataEnvironment icon, and make sure the **Show Fields** menu command is checked.

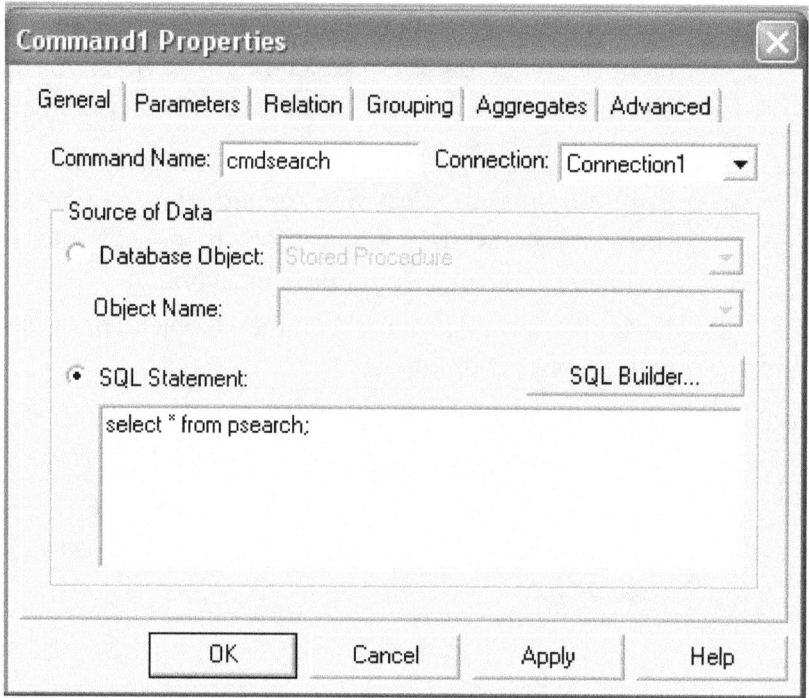

Fig. 5.34

- **Customizing the Parameter Objects of a Command Object :**

    If a Command object is based on a parameterized query or a stored procedure with parameters, the Command object has a Parameters collection. You may want to customize the Parameter objects contained in the collection by changing the data type or making the name more descriptive.

- **Changing the Properties of Associated Parameter Objects :**

    The following procedure describes how you can change the properties of Parameter objects that are associated with a Command object.

- To change a Command object's associated Parameter object properties :
    1. Right-click the Command object that you wish to customize and then select **Properties** from the shortcut menu.
    2. From the **Parameters** tab, select a Parameter object from the **Parameter** list box, and then set the following properties :

Item	Purpose
Name	Provide a unique, meaningful name for the selected Parameter object.
Direction	Specify whether this is an input or output parameter, or both, or if the parameter is the return value from the procedure.
DataType	Specify the data type to which the Parameter object is converted.
Precision	Specify the maximum size, in bytes.
Scale	Specify the maximum number of digits to the right of the decimal point.
Size	Specify the maximum size, in bytes.
Host Data Type	Specify the data type used when this Parameter object is referenced by the host application. Changing this setting affects the used in building the type library information for the host.
Required	Specify whether the parameter value is required when the Command object is executed. **Note :** If a required parameter is not set when the Command object is executed, the command will fail.
Value	Specify the default value that is used at run time (unless a value is provided programmatically), and if necessary, at design time, if the Command object must be executed to obtain the field information.

3. Click **OK** to apply the parameter properties to the selected Command object and exit the dialog box.

- **Dragging From a Data View to Your Data Environment :**

   You can automatically create Command objects by dragging from the Data View window to your Data Environment designer. This is an easy and efficient way to create Command objects from tables, views, or stored procedures that are listed in your Data View. If the connection associated with the Command object being dropped does not already exist in the Data Environment, a Connection object is automatically created.

- **Creating Multiple Command Objects from Stored Procedures :**

   You can create multiple Command objects in your Data Environment designer from stored procedures using the Insert Stored Procedures dialog box.

- To insert multiple stored procedures :
   1. Click **Insert Stored Procedures** in the Data Environment designer toolbar.

-or-

Right-click a DataEnvironment or Connection object and choose **Insert Stored Procedures** from the shortcut menu.

2. In the **Insert Stored Procedures** dialog box, move one or more stored procedures from the **Available** list to the **Add** list using the arrows.

   Use > to move the stored procedures to the **Add** list one at a time, or use >> to move all stored procedures at once. Use < to remove the stored procedures from the **Add** list one at a time or use << to remove all stored procedures at once.

3. Once, the stored procedures are in the **Add** list, click **Insert** to add them to your Data Environment. A new Command object is created for each stored procedure.

   Note : The name of the Command object defaults to the name of the stored procedure.

4. Click **Close** to exit the dialog box.

Practice Questions

1. What is meant by database ?
2. Define the following terms :
   (i) DBMS
   (ii) Record
   (iii) Record set
3. How to access data in Visual basic ?
4. What is data control ?
5. Enlist various properties of Data control.
6. Describe different methods of Data control.
5. What is ADO ? How to use it ?
8. State advantages of ADODC over DC.
9. How to create report ?
10. Enlist various properties of ADODC.
11. With suitable example describe database connectivity with MS-Access.
12. Enlist various methods of ADODC.
13. How to connect a database with oracle VB.
14. Explain crystal report.
15. Compare ADO and ADODC.
16. Explain operations of database through coding.

Programming in Visual Basic (BCA : IV) — 5.51 — Working with Database

University Question & Answers

April 2010

1. Compare ADO and ADODC Controls. [4 M]

Ans. Please refer to Section 5.3.

2. Write a program to accept details of teachers from user and store those details into the database (Don't use standard control). Teachers having fields Tno, Tname, Salary, Dateofjoining. [8 M]

Ans. Please refer to Section 5.2.3.

October 2010

1. Explain briefly ADO Data Control.

Ans. Please refer to Section 5.3.

2. Write short note on : Data Report.

Ans. Please refer to Section 5.5.

April 2011

1. Explain steps to connect MS0Access database using ADO control. [4 M]

Ans. Please refer to Section 5.3.3.

2. Write a program in VB to accept product details and store it into the database and display amount. The database fields are Itemno, Itemname, Rate, Quanity. [4 M]

Ans. Please refer to Section

3. Write short note on : Data Control. [4 M]

Ans. Please refer to Section 5.2.

October 2011

1. Write a program to accept the details of students from user and store that details along with total and percentage into the database. (Don't use standard control). Student, having fields stud_rollno, stud_name, stud_mark1, stud_mark2, stud_mark3. [8 M]

Ans. Please refer to Section 5.2.3

April 2012

1. Compare ADO and ADODC controls. [4 M]

Ans. Please refer to Section 5.3.

2. Write a program to accept the details of customer from user and store that details into the database. (Don't use standard control). Customer having fields custid, custname, custaddress. [8 M]

Ans. Please refer to Section 5.2.3.

October 2012

1. Explain ADOO Data Control. [4 M]
Ans. Please refer to Section 5.3.
2. Short note : Data reports. [4 M]
Ans. Please refer to Section 5.5.

April 2013

1. Explain briefly ADO Control. [4 M]
Ans. Please refer to Section 5.3.
2. Short note : Data reports. [4 M]
Ans. Please refer to Section 5.5.

April 2014

1. Explain ADODC? Write the advantages of ADODC over Data control. [4 M]
Ans. Please refer to Section 5.4.

❖❖❖

www.ingramcontent.com/pod-product-compliance
Lightning Source LLC
Chambersburg PA
CBHW080740230426
43665CB00020B/2813